Every Life a Story

Every Life a Story

Natalie Jacobson Reporting

By Natalie Jacobson

Peter E. Randall Publisher
Portsmouth, New Hampshire
2022

ISBN: 978-1-942155-45-4
ebook ISBN: 978-1-942155-46-1
Library of Congress Control Number: 2022902246

Published by
Peter E. Randall Publisher
5 Greenleaf Woods Drive, Suite 102
Portsmouth, NH 03801
www.perpublisher.com

Book design: Tim Holtz
Cover photo: Reproduced by permission of WCVB Channel 5 Boston.

Printed in the United States of America

Grateful acknowledgment is made to the following for permission to quote copyrighted materials:

Excerpt from "Freedom of the Press," https://www.aclu.org/issues/free-speech/freedom-press, copyright 2022 American Civil Liberties Union.

Excerpt from "I Want a Wife" by Judy Brady, originally published in Ms. December 20–27, 1971, reprinted by permission of Maia D. Syfers.

Excerpts from WCVB broadcasts reprinted by permission of WCVB Channel 5 Boston. All rights reserved.

Unless otherwise noted, all photos courtesy of Natalie Jacobson.

For

Lindsay Dawn

Olivia and James

Your love is the gift of my life.

Acknowledgments

First and foremost, thank you to WCVB-TV and the extraordinarily dedicated and talented people who worked there throughout my thirty-five years at the station (1972–2007). We were a family that argued, cried, and laughed, and together we defined teamwork. Believing nothing was impossible, we scaled the heights of information and entertainment as no television station in the country did before. Be proud of yourselves.

Thank you, Chet Curtis, my best friend, my co-anchor, my husband. For over two decades we lived as one, and while nothing lasts forever, I treasure what we had.

Thank you, Rob Cocuzzo, for our Sunday review sessions in 2020 when I was first writing this book. Your encouragement was critical to my completing that first draft. You kept saying it was interesting! You gave me courage.

Thank you, Dick Flavin, for reading my early drafts. Your knowledge of baseball and Tip O'Neill made those chapters sharper. Your sense as both a reader and writer were a constant guide.

Thank you, Alexis Rizzuto, for your attention to detail and flow. As my editor, you asked questions when something needed clarifying. You gave me the incentive to find a word, a phrase, an example, and as a result, you made the book better for the reader.

Thank you, Deidre Randall, for agreeing to publish my book. None of the agents who work with the major publishing houses was interested and self-publishing was a daunting thought. But you guided me through the process from copyediting to distribution, to design, to finally a book! *Every Life a Story* would still be sitting in my computer were it not for you.

And finally, and most importantly, thank you to my mother and father, who by example taught me to appreciate all life has to offer, to be kind to people, to believe anything is possible if you work hard, to believe in God, and always to hold country and family dear.

Contents

Hello

Recently, I hailed a cab at Boston's Logan Airport. The cabbie came over to put my bag in his trunk, then looked at me in disbelief.

"Natalie?"

"Yes."

"Oh my God. I cannot believe I have you in my cab. I think of you always. Remember me? I took you to the opening of the Seaport Hotel. And I told you I was Russian and you told me about your family. How is your father? I remember we talked about him and your family coming from Serbia. And your daughter. How is your daughter?"

Aaron had so many questions. He didn't wait for answers.

"Where have you been? Are you living here in Boston?"

He told me about Putin and now, when he goes home to Russia, he says he is afraid even to speak to his friends. He said he is very sad.

As he dropped me off, he said, "I'm so happy to see you, Natalie."

He took my hand.

"When I came from Russia, you were my introduction to America. I watched you every night. You were my friend. Since I don't see you anymore, I have been worried. Now, thanks to tonight, I won't worry anymore. But my," he paused looking for a word, "I miss you. It's not the same anymore."

I was overwhelmed, and as I reflected on his passion, I felt anxious. He was telling me he felt abandoned. I had abandoned him.

After forty years in broadcast television, I said goodbye in 2007, and to this day I miss the people with whom I worked and the many thousands of people I never met but with whom I felt a kinship.

I experienced a lifetime connection that has nothing to do with celebrity and everything to do with soul.

In March of 2020, the Covid-19 pandemic found me in a condo I rented for a few months in Florida. In what seemed a nanosecond, we went from a normal life with the economy growing and unemployment at an all-time low to a frightening lockdown. Schools closed. Businesses closed. People were out of work. Men and women were dying in nursing homes, alone. Hospitals were desperate for ventilators and masks and gowns. Suddenly we were living in the eye of an invisible storm. What just happened?

COVID-19, Sars CoV-2, happened. The virus took the world by surprise. It seemed to creep in and then explode.

The Trump Administration fast-tracked the development and approval of a vaccine. Operation Warp Speed knocked years off the normal time to introduce a new vaccine, and, by the time the Biden Administration took over in January of 2021, the country was lining up to get the Pfizer, Moderna, or Johnson & Johnson vaccines. Availability has increased, as have the logistics of getting "shots in arms." Surprisingly, many people are refusing the vaccine, which adds another dimension to a virus with which we likely will have to learn to live.

In the middle of a crisis, it can be helpful to look for a silver lining. Amid the fear, the quarantine isolated us and gave us time, time with loved ones, time to think about our lives, our values.

All alone, with nothing to do, I decided to use my time to write this book, which I was sure I would get to "someday." Someday had arrived.

When I began working in local television in Boston in 1969, news was in its infancy, maybe early adolescence. It was a learning experience, personally and collectively. During my early years, I quickly saw the importance of the connection between people's lives and the news they watched and read.

Beginning in the 70s, and before cable and the internet, the vast majority of Americans said they got most of their news from television. One could not overestimate television's influence and, therefore, responsibility.

We took that responsibility very seriously. The medium was young. We were young. There were few rules, few mentors, which left a lot of room for innovation, experimentation, and soul-searching.

Those of us who worked for WCVB-TV in Boston had a unique environment. We were locally owned by a group of successful Boston men who wanted to create the greatest local station in the history of television. They wanted a station connected to the community, a station which produced innovative new programming to benefit its viewers, a station that honored the medium and the people of New England. Boston Broadcasters Inc. (BBI) fought hard and long to gain the license to accomplish that mission. They won the license and quickly surpassed even their most optimistic promises, creating some sixty hours of new local programming a week and making a ton of money in the process. The *New York Times* in 1981 allowed that WCVB-TV was perhaps "America's best television station."

For people like me, BBI offered an opportunity to take risks, to try new ideas, and to live to try again if they failed. I cannot imagine a more energetic, optimistic environment where everyone had a voice. Our founding general manager, Robert Bennett, believed we were all on one team and that team would be the best.

Honest, factual information is a critical component of a free society, of a democracy, of our republic. We will not survive without it. At WCVB-TV, we proved by honoring the truth and by respecting the people to whom and about whom we report that journalism is also good business.

EVERY LIFE A STORY. This book is as much your story as it is mine. News as we knew it was about you. We reporters were there to give you information, every day, information that was accurate, information to help you make informed decisions. We invited you to be part of it, and you were. It all seemed so natural and important to get it right.

I was twenty-eight years old when we went on the air as WCVB-TV on March 19, 1972, and for the next thirty-five years, I went to bed thinking (most nights anyway) *hurry and fall asleep so I can wake up to begin a new day in this extraordinary arena called TV news.*

CHAPTER 1

John Silber

In 1990, Dr. John Silber, president of Boston University, lost a significant lead over former prosecutor William Weld in their race for governor of the Commonwealth of Massachusetts. It was a stunning defeat. From Texas (Silber's former home) to Boston, fingers pointed to an interview I did with Silber as the reason he lost. Some voters felt he attacked me, and others were turned away by his angry demeanor.

Dr. John Silber: "I think the Natalie Jacobson interview was costly. I don't think I blew that. I think she entered my house under false pretenses."

Chris Reidy, the *Boston Globe*: "Never mind Silber's comments on day care. The image of an angry man at home seemed to be his undoing."

November 6, 1990. NewsCenter 5 Studio.

Director: "Stand by in five. Music. Roll the video."

"And now WCVB-TV, Boston NewsCenter 5 at 6 with Natalie Jacobson and Chet Curtis."

"Fade. Take Camera 1."

Natalie: "Good evening. The most expensive gubernatorial campaign in Bay State history is drawing to a close. Polls remain open until 8 PM. It is likely to be a long night, and if exit polling is accurate, we may well be witness to a stunning turn-around in the contentious race for the corner office.

"Vying for the open seat left by Michael Dukakis is former US attorney and federal prosecutor, William Weld, and Boston University president, Dr. John Silber."

Chet: "Each man stunned the pundits by clobbering his primary opponents. High taxes, a disappearing 'Massachusetts Miracle,' crime and drugs, drove record numbers of people to the polls in the primary and again today in the final election."

It was a "throw the bums out" kind of a year. The climate in Massachusetts was as angry as I had ever seen it. Political advisor Ann Lewis was quoted as saying the spirit of revolution was so intense, she expected to see crowds surging through the streets "with Dukakis's head on a pike."

After three terms as governor, Michael Dukakis lost his bid for the presidency to George H. W. Bush in a crushing forty-to-ten-state loss and decided to retire from politics.

The Massachusetts Miracle he had touted was tanking. Dukakis's taxes were hitting home. The Citizens for Limited Taxation had a petition on the ballot to roll back taxes and fees to their 1988 positions.

In the fight to take the open seat, John Silber dominated the narrative. He called it the way he saw it, refused to "speak plastic," as he put it. And he made it clear, he was running against the press.

Silber's penchant for what the *Boston Herald* called "Silber Shockers" dominated the headlines: "When you've lived a good life and you're ripe, it's time to go." "Why should I give a speech on crime control to a bunch of drug addicts in Roxbury?" "Why has Massachusetts suddenly become so popular for people accustomed to living in a tropical climate? There has to be a welfare magnet going on here."

Curtis Wilke of the *Boston Globe* wrote, "For months Silber commanded a following of angry alienated voters and articulated their anxieties better than any other political figure in Massachusetts' year of rage." He was up eight points in the polls two weeks before the election. But then something began to change. Polls indicated his lead was evaporating.

Boston Herald columnist Marjorie Egan, a Silber voter, wrote she started to understand what had happened and felt it herself: "The nastiness, the unrelenting coldness, began to wear me down."

And that election night at one o'clock in the morning, John Silber made his concession speech.

Massachusetts, as blue a state as there is, elected its first Republican governor since Francis "Frank" Sargent (1969–1975). The man Silber called an "orange-headed wasp" and "back-stabbing son of a bitch," William Weld, would take up residence in the corner office.

The overwhelming opinion by pundits, columnists, and the candidate himself put the blame for the loss on his interview with me:

> *The election was not about the CLT* [Citizens for Limited Taxation] *petition, voter anger or John Silber…When Silber shocked good old Nat, the Commonwealth rose up in horror and gave him the ballot box boot.*
>
> —*The Boston Phoenix*

The year 1990 was the first of my "At Home" interviews. Many would follow, but none would compare with the reaction to this one. After covering countless elections, I sensed that many, if not most people, did not base their votes on a particular issue. Certainly, some people were issue activists and others would vote their party no matter what. But I heard many people say, "I like that guy. I'm going to vote for him. No particular reason. I just like him," or not.

The media did a good job of explaining the candidates' positions. But if I was right and many voted their gut, then maybe we journalists had a responsibility to give voters a better sense of who these candidates were as people.

How to do that?

We all know candidates will tell you what you want to hear, John Silber excepted. But before they were running for office, who were they? What did they value? How did they raise their children? What was their inner compass? What do they worry about? What makes them laugh, or conversely, what keeps them up at night? What do they demand from their friends, families, and co-workers? In short, what defines their character?

My superiors at WCVB-TV Boston thought this was a good idea. It is much more difficult to learn about the character of a person than about his or her positions on issues. The preparation took weeks, months. I called scores of people, friends and foes, old classmates, and colleagues who could help me get to know the person better. I read books and papers they had written.

Then, I wondered, how to do the interview? Where would the candidate be most like himself?

At home.

We decided to meet both candidates, John Silber and Bill Weld, in their homes with their families present. I urged them to try and assimilate something normal, like having dinner as a family or playing with the kids, whatever they usually did when they were together.

As scheduled as these candidates were, time was the most prized commodity. I held my breath when I explained the only way to achieve my goal of allowing voters to get to know them as people was to spend time together, time, as in several hours. Both men agreed.

I had met Dr. Silber and covered him many times from the time he came to Boston in 1971 from Texas to take charge of Boston University. I came to know him as a man of high intelligence, deeply held opinions on everything, little patience, and a quick temper. He was one of those people so sure he is right, he can't believe you don't get it.

For example, we had a spirited discussion one day about American education vs. Germany's, which he felt was superior. As I understood him to explain it, German children were tracked around the age of eight, when educators would decide who was college material and who was not. The two groups would be offered different paths toward graduation. I argued it was unfair to make such a judgment at such an early age. And what recourse did a kid have if the superiors were wrong?

Not long afterward, much to my surprise, Dr. Silber invited me and Chet Curtis, my former/late husband and co-anchor to lunch in his office. A highly persuasive man, Silber spent most of the time trying to convince us of the value of tracking kids early. Well, he didn't succeed, but it clearly mattered to him that we be persuaded.

Fired from his position as dean of the College of Arts and Sciences at the University of Texas in Austin, Silber made news in Boston right from the start, publicly criticizing just about everything about Boston University. BU was seen as a commuter school in the shadows of Harvard and Boston College. If the trustees were looking for a person to recreate and grow the school, they found him. Acerbic, combative, intemperate, intelligent with an extraordinary capacity for knowledge, he was a man with a vision for the university and nothing would stop him. No faculty strikes, no lawsuits, would deter his mission. In his three decades at Boston University, Silber brought BU to prominence, attracting top students and faculty. He took a failing school and brought it to unprecedented heights. Few among the faculty or student body liked him. That mattered not a whit to Dr. John Silber.

In 1989, having transformed Boston University, Silber decided to fix what he saw as wrong with Massachusetts. He would run for governor.

My camera crew and I arrived at the Silber home in Boston late Sunday afternoon on October 14, 1990. Silber's wife, children, grandson, and several staff members were there. The family was preparing dinner in the kitchen and setting the table in the dining room, which gave me an opportunity to get pictures and speak with each of them on camera.

Silber with his young grandson on his lap took to the piano, a sweet scene. Suddenly one of his daughters came into the living room and said, "Dad you have a phone call." I jumped up and offered to turn off his mike so he could have some privacy. He demurred and said, "No, come with me. You might find this interesting."

No one said who was on the phone, so clearly he was expecting the call. My antennas were up.

We watched and listened to him say, "Ah ha, OK, that's great," or something to that affect. He hung up and I waited. Finally, he said, "That was Henry Kissinger on the phone. He's coming to Boston on Thursday to endorse me."

I laughed and said, "What's the joke?"

He looked incredulous. "What do you mean what's the joke?"

"Well, everyone knows you and Henry Kissinger are not at the top of each other's dance card. You sparred publicly when you were both on President Reagan's National Bipartisan Commission on Central America."

"Well, he's coming here Thursday."

I made a mental note to confirm this when I got to the station the next day.

Silber's position on women in the workplace had been a hot topic during the campaign. As he walked around the dinner table filling everyone's wine glass, he launched into his opinions on working mothers. He had eight children: two sons, six daughters. Some of his daughters had careers, one chose to be a stay-at-home mom. Sitting at the table with his daughters present offered an opportunity to allow him to clarify his thoughts. He said that he agreed the women's movement had helped his daughters as "they would have had a more difficult time living the kind of lives they had." But "there is no question we have a generation of neglected children by women who have thought that a third-rate daycare center was as good as a first-rate home."

I noted that many working mothers had no choice but to work. He responded, "I'm not talking about them. Look if this is another one of these Silber Shockers then the hell with this damn program. I'm talking about the woman who is married to a lawyer who is making $75,000 a year and the wife who has to have her career and has to have her baby. We see child neglect over and over again."

Because the daycare issue was so important to voters, I decided to air that exchange, essentially in its entirety. I thought it important to allow him to speak to voters directly, unedited. And when the interview first aired, it was the working mother's issue that dominated the news media.

After dinner, Dr. and Mrs. Silber and I moved to the living room for a more formal interview. I brought up the "Silber Shockers" and the polarity of opinions about him during the campaign. This was his opportunity to tell the voters how he saw himself. I asked him to describe himself by citing his strengths and weaknesses. He listed his strengths. I then asked, "And your weaknesses?"

He exploded: "You find a weakness. I don't have to go around telling you what's wrong with me."

Natalie: "Is this an unfair question?"

Silber: "Perhaps you have no faults."

Natalie: "I have plenty of faults."

Silber: "Well I'm not interested in your faults."

Natalie: "Neither is anyone else. You are the candidate. I wish you weren't so defensive. I'm just trying to get you to give voters an insight into how you view yourself."

I knew Silber was a volatile man, easily angered, but I was surprised at his reaction to a simple question, "What are your strengths and weaknesses?" Mrs. Silber looked faint and now I and everyone else was uncomfortable. Somehow, we got through that and finished the interview. My photographers packed up our gear and took it out to the car. I stood at the front door saying good-bye.

We had a friendly exchange. He asked about Chet and our daughter. I dared to ask if he was feeling all right. "I know campaigns are draining, are you getting enough sleep? You seem very uptight."

His response stunned me.

Raising his right arm, truncated from birth above the elbow, he gestured and strained, "It's the medii, the medii, the medii!"

The media was the issue.

I felt grateful my cameras did not capture that because it would have given me a dilemma. Do I air that tirade? Is it relevant? Does it speak to his character, which is what this whole piece is about?

And what about Kissinger?

The next day, I dialed New York directory assistance, 555-1212, and asked for Henry A. Kissinger. New York City was a good guess, I thought, maybe Washington. I'm a local reporter and not likely to have Kissinger in my Rolodex.

A woman answered, "Dr. Kissinger's office."

I identified myself, told of the phone call in Silber's home the night before, and said I was calling to confirm Dr. Kissinger would be coming to Boston on Thursday to endorse Dr. Silber in his bid for governor. The woman burst out laughing. She put me on hold, returned and asked me to repeat that. I did and asked if Dr. Kissinger was in. She said he was and put me on hold again.

When she returned, she said, "Dr. Kissinger did not call Dr. Silber yesterday and has no plans to endorse Dr. Silber for governor."

Well, I can't say I was surprised, but why did Silber pretend? Did he really think I would report that without checking? It was all very troubling.

I spent hours, days, reviewing the tapes, editing. It had to be accurate, an honest presentation of the man. Having known Silber for some years, I knew the hair trigger anger of the man expressed during this interview was not a case of his having a bad day. It was who he was. Had I not had that history with him, I likely would have questioned those outbursts.

As a local reporter, I did not cover William Weld in Washington, where he served as US assistant attorney general for the Criminal Division of the Justice Department, but I knew him from his previous five years as US attorney in Massachusetts. He oversaw the prosecution of the highly publicized extortion case against State Representative Vincent Piro. Piro was defended by noted defense attorney Robert Popeo, who argued that Piro had no predisposition to commit a crime. Instead, he argued, the government created the crime through its scheme of entrapment. Putting the FBI on trial worked. In a big loss for Weld, the jury acquitted Piro.

Weld was among six key players in the US Department of Justice who suddenly quit in 1986 over legal and leadership issues they had with then Attorney General Edwin Meese. Meese was under criminal investigation regarding separate dealings with the Wedtech Corporation and the Bechtel Corporation. Weld and the others asked President Reagan to fire him. He refused and they resigned. Meese said he was shocked.

Weld, easily bored, returned to Massachusetts and decided to run for governor.

I would come to learn that the two men, both intelligent, learned, determined, and confident, were opposite personalities. If Silber was scrappy, Weld held the demeanor of the patrician he is. Where Silber was the son of a German immigrant, Weld was a Brahmin, part of the New England upper class. Weld's wife, Susan, spoke twelve languages. Educated at Harvard and Oxford, Weld was trained in the law. Silber in philosophy. Weld spoke deliberatively and often seemed guarded. At times, he seemed lost in thought. During one of our sessions at his home, we were seated before a warm fireplace and when I asked a question, he didn't respond. I was puzzled as some time passed. I asked if he was all right. He said his mind tended to wander when he stared into the fire.

I found Weld as calm as Silber was not. Weld expressed a kind of inevitability about life. How badly did he want to win this election? As I remember it, he didn't express a lot of enthusiasm. But he told me years later he very much wanted to win.

Weld had his five school-age children sit around the breakfast table. He was making "daddy's eggs." He hammed it up, pouring orange juice in the egg batter, as the kids rolled their eyes. I asked if he had ever made them before.

Later, when the Welds and I sat in the living room for a more formal talk, I asked him the same question that riled Silber. "What are your strengths and your weaknesses?"

With a wry smile, Weld began by ticking off his weaknesses. "I'm lazy. If I can get someone else to do something, I will. My lieutenant governor will be very busy." I began to understand his sense of humor.

So, my first attempt at giving voters more information about the character of the candidates, certainly contrasted two very different personalities.

The reaction to Silber's outburst upended his campaign, and he lost by 4 percentage points.

It bothered me that my interview with him apparently decided an election. I replayed it and all the field tapes. Had I been fair? Honest? I believe I had.

I was happy that I had decided not to report the Kissinger story or the "medii" outburst. Something at the time within me said, no, let this go. I can't explain it any better than that. It just didn't seem the right thing to do.

When it became obvious that Silber was losing his lead, and that the anger he displayed in his home was hurting him, he went on television and radio and told newspaper reporters that I had attacked his cubs and he, as papa bear, had to protect them.

After the election he called me and asked me to join him on his radio show at BU to talk about what was going on in Serbia and Croatia. He knew my grandparents had emigrated from Serbia. I declined, saying I was sure he knew more than I did. But he called again. I think he wanted to embarrass me. I declined again.

Years later, Henry Kissinger, referring to his time with Silber on the Latin American Commission, said, "My only question was if I killed him, would it be considered murder or justifiable homicide? He is very fierce in his convictions. He takes no prisoners. I swore I'd kill him and then as the weeks went by, I grew extremely fond of him."

And following Silber's passing in 2012, one of Silber's famed faculty recruits, German concentration camp survivor, Elie Wiesel, speculated that Silber was now "giving his advice to God."

CHAPTER ❷

Growing Up

There is no way this Serbian kid from the city of Chicago could have imagined I would be interviewing prospective governors. What fortune-teller might have looked into her ball and seen me in the hallowed halls of Congress watching members of the House of Representatives impeach a president? Where on those streetcars I rode through the city of Chicago did I look to be in Rome for the installation of a Cardinal?

When you live in a small world where no one dreams of much past today, when you grow up during a time when there is no television or internet to show you life outside your neighborhood, dreams are limited. I wish I could tell you that it was reading a book about Amelia Earhart that led me to earn a pilot's license. I have no recollection of seeing a map of the world and thinking someday I might live in Bangkok, Thailand.

I do remember standing at the kitchen sink, on a chair, helping my mother stir blueberries into a batter of pancakes. But nowhere in that bowl did Julia Child reach up to hand me her Peugeot pepper mill. When dinner was an ethnic cornmeal dish, how could I dream someday I would be invited to a dinner with Les Amis D'Scoffier Society?

When only boys could play baseball, what girl could imagine that she'd ever find herself standing side by side with Ted Williams, or throwing out the first pitch at Fenway Park?

When I started kindergarten, speaking a mixture of Serbian and English, how might I have dreamed the president of CBS would offer me a job on national television? I had never yet seen a television.

I was born Natalie Salatich in 1943 at Cook County Hospital in Chicago, Illinois. My parents are Dawn Trbovich and Bill Salatich, first-generation Americans of Serbian descent.

All four of my grandparents came to this country from Serbia, as did everyone I knew of their generation. They had escaped the horrors that were to follow.

Their stories of WWII are heart-breaking. My father's mother told us harrowing tales of the Croatian Ustashe (*Ustaše*), who partnered with the Nazis to kill Serbs, Jews, and Romani (the "Gypsies"). She said the Ustashe would ride on horseback into the Serbian villages and gather families to an open field, forcing the males, fathers and sons, to dig their own graves as the wives and mothers watched. The Ustashe would shoot the boys first so the fathers could endure the agony, then shoot the fathers and force the women to throw dirt on their dead children and husbands. The women from one of the families were my grandmother's sisters.

When my grandmother's first husband (my father's dad) died of lung disease, likely from working the copper mines in Minnesota, she married Tripo Susich. To me they were Baba (grandmother) and Jedo (grandfather) Susich. Tripo told us he began his journey to America when his parents hid him in an empty oil drum and loaded it on a boat heading across the Adriatic to Italy. From there he said he boarded a train to France, where he managed to get on a ship to the United States.

Barely out of their teens, none of my grandparents ever saw their parents again.

Like so many immigrants of the time, each traveled alone in steerage for months with little food but plenty of rats. In New York, they were given new names which immigration officials could better pronounce. If they were lucky, a distant relative might meet them and bring them to their home.

There was no welfare or other public assistance back then, so they found work where they could on railroads, farms, or in the mines. They counted on their Christian faith and their fellow Serbs for support.

It was hard to imagine how difficult life was for them: no money, no access to health insurance, non-English speaking. Yet, I do not remember any of them ever complaining. They made do. And they were grateful to be in the United States and so proud to become American citizens.

When my father tried to help his Serbian family in Serbia, he learned the Tito regime, in control of Yugoslavia at the time, would keep close watch on those receiving help from the US. He said if Tito's soldiers saw a man suddenly had six sheep when last week he had two, they would confiscate the sheep and anything else—money, clothing, appliances. I remember seeing my Baba crying at not being able to help her family.

There is no question that listening to their stories made me realize how lucky we were to be born in the United States.

My mother and father benefited from the sacrifices of their parents. First-generation Americans, my parents went to public school, married young, at nineteen and twenty-one, and had four children, I being the first. Jean followed three-and-a-half years later, Billy eight years after me, and sixteen years later, Sandra.

With two babies at home, there was no one to take me to Cook County Hospital where I went weekly for multiple allergy shots to help with my hay fever. While my mother later shuddered at the thought, she sent me to the hospital across the city by myself. I was eight. Changing three streetcars was not a problem. I guess crime was not what it is today, and no one worried about me being kidnapped. I do remember a man in a white coat, perhaps a doctor, asking me where my mother was. I told him I was not allowed to talk to strangers and ran to the next streetcar.

How ironic a near-lethal blow would come from that hospital. I later learned that one of those allergy shots had been injected with a dirty needle which gave me hepatitis. It was Christmas time, and I was back in City Hospital in a children's ward near death.

My poor parents. Before hay fever and hepatitis, as a toddler, I had an emergency appendectomy. Apparently, I was born with my appendix wrapped around my intestines, so breakfast was the only meal I seemed to digest easily. I was told my mother's mother, Baba Trbovich, would carry me around singing to me, trying to get me to eat.

Then my parents had to live through my little sister Jean's issues with asthma. I remember ambulances coming in the middle of the night for her. I was so upset, my parents took me to see her at Cook County Hospital. The image of her in an oxygen tent was frightening. A few years later while in the hospital for one of my checkups, Jean and I ate a candy bar, a Chunky. Almost immediately she had trouble breathing and we were surrounded by white coats and a flurry of activity. It turned out she was and is allergic to nuts.

Then child number three provided even more drama and worry for my parents. Baby Billy kept slapping at his ears. Mom took him to our family doctor, who saw nothing troublesome. No one knows a child better than the mother and Mom knew something was wrong. She took us all (no baby sitters) to doctor after doctor. I can still remember the scene. Jean and I stood in a corner. With Billy on the examining table, this doctor said to Mom, "We have to lance his ears right now or the fluid will burst and he could be deaf for life." Oh my God.

Thanks to Mom's persistence and that doctor, my brother's hearing was saved.

After the army, Dad drove a taxicab for a while and later ran a bowling alley in Chicago when I was a young child. Mom said she tried to juggle my sleeping hours so I would have some time to see my father. I've decided to attribute my inability to sleep well to that erratic schedule.

One day, some years later, my mother saw an ad in the *Chicago Tribune* for a salesman's position with the Gillette Safety Razor Company and suggested my dad give it a try. A few days later, she asked if he got an interview. He said he called but the position had been filled. Ah, never try and fool Mama. She told him she had called for him and he had an appointment at 8 AM the next day.

I might not have believed that story if my own father hadn't told it many years later. My mother never mentioned it. She was an unassuming woman and didn't seem the type to take that initiative for him. She likely was driven in part by the desire for her husband to have a day job. Plus, she knew he was a salesman at heart.

He did get the job and loved it. No one could possibly have guessed that years later Dad would become the president of Gillette North America. Only in America.

We lived in various flats in Chicago until settling into an apartment above Baba and Jedo Susich. It was a second-floor walk-up near the railroad tracks. We had very little in the way of material things. I guess we were poor, but we didn't know we were poor because we didn't know anyone who had much more than we did.

We did not have a television, so radio shows like *Ma Perkins* and Sergeant Joe Friday on *Dragnet* provided entertainment, together with a goldfish bowl and the Sears catalog.

The Sears catalog was three-inches thick, filled with hundreds of pages of stuff we had never seen before: dolls, bicycles, and books. Each Christmas, we were allowed to choose one "big gift," like a doll, and two small ones. My sister Jean and I would spend forever poring through the choices. Think of it as the precursor to online shopping.

One favorite game was 7-Up, played with a pink rubber ball bounced against the brick building. One Christmas, Santa brought roller skates, the kind you strap on to your shoes and tighten with a metal key. The many cracks in the sidewalks made for a run on BAND-AIDs. Once a year, our neighbors allowed us to climb a ladder and pick their cherries, which were sour, but the picking was fun.

Doing laundry once a week was a major event. Mom, Jean, and I trudged down to the basement, which I remember as a creepy place, dark and full of cobwebs. Off in the corner hung slabs of lamb or pork. Jedo used to salt and hang the meat to cure, much the way prosciutto is still made in parts of Italy and elsewhere.

Like most washers of the time, ours had a tub with an agitator for washing. Then you had to empty the tub and with a hose pour in fresh water to rinse. From there you put the clothes, one at a time, between a set of rollers to wring out the water. It was a long process.

One day while helping mom pull the wet sheets through rollers, Jean got her fingers caught in the middle. I remember a lot of screaming and panic, but mom managed to separate the rollers. Jean and her hand survived intact.

We would hang the clothes on the lines in the little yard. It seemed often as not, it would rain before the clothes were dry and we would run down the back steps to unpin everything only to have to hang it all again after the rain.

Save for the Dorsey family's three girls across the alley, there were no other children in the neighborhood. Most residents were "old" people, like my grandparents. How relative age can seem.

Twice a year our cousins, Ron and Don Salatich, visited from Indianapolis. Starved for kids to play with, Jean and I would sit on the sidewalk for hours waiting for their arrival. Visits to their little house in Indy were magical, especially with all of us kids on army cots in the basement telling ghost stories. Not so much fun, was having to weed Auntie Millie's strawberry garden.

Today people often talk of poverty limiting good nutrition. I think we ate pretty well on a very low budget. I remember eggs or hot oatmeal for breakfast. Lunch was a peanut butter sandwich with crisp iceberg lettuce, still my favorite, or something that might have been left over from supper. Supper was soup, or chicken or hotdogs and macaroni and cheese, meatloaf, *pura* (a Serbian dish of cornmeal, water, and cheese), stuffed cabbage, liver and onions, or round steak smothered in onions and ketchup. You had to slice it very thin to be able to chew it. Lamb stews were the best, inexpensive cuts of meat, which when braised for hours were delicious. Even canned vegetables tasted good in that natural juice. Once my grandmother made baccala, a salt cod, that you could smell walking up the street. I never could get that down.

Canned vegetables and fruits accompanied most meals along with a glass of milk. I don't remember having dessert.

We did not have money for extras like potato chips or French fries. There was no McDonalds or other fast-food place. There was one chain in the area, Chicken in the Rough, featuring fried chicken served in a shallow plastic basket with honey. That was a fun treat and once in a while we had an ice cream cone.

I'll never forget the first time I ate fresh asparagus. I couldn't believe it was the same thing that was in a can that made me regurgitate. I think Birds Eye frozen foods were just making their way to mass production.

We didn't have a car or bikes, so we got plenty of exercise because we walked everywhere: to the grocer, the butcher, and to the streetcars.

We went to school about a twenty-minute walk away, crossing major, busy Chicago streets where cars competed with the streetcars. Brentano Elementary School seemed huge to me, and intimidating.

Since we lived above my grandparents who didn't speak English easily, we spoke Serbian at home. Later, my mother told me I came home from kindergarten crying most days because kids made fun of me. She said that by Thanksgiving I spoke fluent English. Total immersion worked and of course it helped that my parents were bilingual.

Serbian traditions were an integral part of our childhood. People of the Christian Eastern Orthodox faith celebrated Christmas and Easter according to the old Julian calendar, which differs in the number of days in a year from the Gregorian Calendar which the world uses today. As a result, Christmas falls on January 7 on today's calendar. We celebrated Christmas on December 25, and Santa came then, but Serbian Christmas was primarily a celebration of the birth of Christ. Some orthodox churches moved the holiday to the Gregorian calendar.

According to Serbian tradition, male friends of the family competed to be the first to arrive after midnight on Christmas day bringing an apple with a coin imbedded, signifying wishes for good health and wealth. We reciprocated by throwing rice on our *polaznik*. The house was filled with Serbian music and the smell of food in the oven. We waited for the priest to stop at our home before we could break the traditional Christmas three-day fast. In the old country, they roasted a whole pig, but with smaller families, Mom made a small pork roast. Together with Dad and any other men in the family, the priest rotated Mom's specially created bread, braided on top, breaking it and pouring wine in the name of the Father, Son and Holy Ghost. Mom put one good luck coin in the bread dough, which made for a bit of competition. Women did not participate in the ritual of the blessing bread. Among Serbian families, the house might stand on the woman, *"kuća stoji na ženi,"* but the man is the king.

Every Sunday we attended our church, the Serbian Eastern Orthodox Church on Schiller Street in Chicago. Dressed in our best clothing, including white gloves, we went to Sunday school in the basement of the church while the adults were inside the cathedral, standing, as there were no pews. Or, as we later saw, many of the men were outside on the steps smoking and laughing. On some Sundays, after what seemed like an interminable service, a meal was served in the basement of the church, the food prepared by the wives, including my mother.

For my parents, church was their social life, and ours. They both sang in the church choir, some eighty-people strong! The church dances, known as *kolos*, were the most fun. Kolos are fast-paced Serbian circle dances where anyone can join, including little kids. I always tried to link hands with someone who knew the steps in simple form as I found that magic "hop" impossible. My mother and three of my aunts, Beatrice, Millie, and Helen, were the best dancers of them all. We all loved these affairs in the basement of the church as it was such a happy time, filled with the loud tambura music and raucous laughter. Serbian songs, all tales of love and of Serbian pride, were the only music we knew.

My other grandparents, my mother's folks, Stevo and Cveta Trbovich, were also from Serbia and lived on the south side of Chicago, then an enclave of European immigrants. Fun in the summer there was waiting for one of the older kids to open up the fire hydrants, filling the street with enough water to create a wading pool. That was fantastic because Chicago was brutally hot in August. I'm sure the streets were not any cleaner than today, but I don't remember anyone worried about that. We were more concerned about the cops and fire department arriving. The gangs of today and the murders did not exist.

This Southside neighborhood was a buzz of activity, very different from where we lived on the north side. Kids were everywhere, a variety store sold ice cream, ten cents a cone. My Uncle Laddie and Aunt Della ran a butcher shop on the first floor of my Baba's building, which was always busy, and on occasion they let me work the register.

My grandfather, Jedo Trbovich, had a little workshop in the back of the building. He was a gifted carpenter and made me a red rocking chair which my brother had for his four children and now I have for my grandchildren.

Baba grew herbs and garlic, onions, and potatoes in a tiny, rocky garden. It is hard to imagine anything could grow in that barren patch. Not many feet away was the fence to the alley. Buildings were separated by alleys lined with garbage cans and the biggest rats I'd ever seen. Jedo told me to make a lot of noise when I took out the garbage so the rats would run away. That was also true of the flat we lived in on the north side of the city.

But the very best part of staying with Baba Trbovich was when I had a cold. Baba would make me soup loaded with garlic, often called the Serbian flower. There was no central heat in the building, so she warmed several bricks in the wood stove and wrapped them in soft cotton rags. She always gave me her bed, which I felt bad about, but she would have it no other way. She filled the bed with the hot bricks and would rub my back and tummy with Vicks VapoRub, then tuck me in under a heavy down comforter which she had made.

I remember one time when Mom came to get me, I fibbed and said I still didn't feel good so that I could continue to be so pampered. As I recall, Mom didn't buy it, most likely because it was not easy to have to take the streetcars back home and then back again to get me.

I don't remember when we got a car, but once a year my parents borrowed a car and drove eight hours on two-lane roads to a place called Glen Lake near Traverse City in northern Michigan.

They rented a tiny two-room cabin right on the lake! I returned to Glen Lake years later to look for that cottage. I found it and tears came easily. It was being used as a storage shed. I also saw that now the lake has nice homes surrounding it, but back then there wasn't much there except the extraordinary beauty of a huge lake which was so clean we bathed in it. There was no running water in our cottage, so we learned to man the pump, which for us kids was a game. The outhouses were another issue. Huge merry widow spiders considered those toilets theirs.

There was a mountain. It really was a hill, but to us children it seemed like a mountain. It was made of sand and called Sleeping Bear. We ran up and rolled down a hundred times and had the time of our lives. I still remember my baby brother rolling down the hill as though he were a ball and laughing at the bottom for the sheer joy of it.

An older kid up the lake had a small sailboat, maybe a Sunfish. He taught me to sail, and eager to show off my new skill, I asked my father to come for a ride. I explained that when I yelled "tack," he had to duck so I could swing the boom across. That went well for a while, but soon his 6-foot-5 frame had had it and he directed me to just go straight. "But we'll end up in the rocks, we can't go straight." I didn't win many arguments with my father and that day was no exception. So, we ended up in the rocks, hurt the boat and trudged miles back to the cabin.

That nightmare aside, Glen Lake was what we dreamed about fifty-one weeks a year. And looking back now, I have to marvel at my parents to make such an effort for us. No matter how poor we were, we would have one week of vacation each year. And we had the 16 mm film to keep the memories fresh. Dad loved to ham it up and did his version of "Look Sharp, Feel Sharp, Be Sharp" Gillette Safety Razor commercials. And I love the scene with my adorable baby brother Billy trying to chomp on a cigar, and my little sister Jean posing for the camera with her precious smile. Sandra had not yet been born.

Aside from Glen Lake, we traveled on some weekends to Battle Creek, Michigan. Many Serbian families had settled in the area, including my grandmother's sister and brother. Baba Susich's brother Pete and his wife Sava lived on a small farm in the little town of Athens. They had cows, chickens and raised corn for animal feed. They did not have indoor plumbing. We eventually got used to the outhouse, no merry widows! Many years later when Dad made enough money, he helped pay for an indoor bathroom and one year bought Sava a stove. Pete by then had died. Pete and Baba Susich's sister Rista also had a farm a few miles away. She too had cows, chickens, and hay.

Teta is Serbian for aunt, and of all my relatives of that generation, Teta Rista was my hero. While still in Serbia, Rista's parents had promised her to a Serbian man she did not know. After arriving at Staten Island, she hid at the train station in New York City, afraid this man might come for her. As the week passed, a Serbian woman approached her in the bathroom. She was a family friend and had heard Rista was coming. My aunt reluctantly but gratefully accompanied her.

Somehow, Rista escaped that prearranged altar and after a time, she met a Serbian man, married and had two sons. Rista's husband died, likely from the same lung disease contracted in the copper mines of Minnesota that killed my grandfather.

Teta eventually remarried and moved to Battle Creek, Michigan. I remember her sending me to the barn to get eggs. The hens were not eager to relinquish them, so I returned to the house and told Teta that there were no eggs. A strong woman with a stronger tongue, Teta dragged me to the hen house. She thrust my little hand beneath a pecking hen, again and again, until the basket was full.

There was nothing that woman couldn't do. She would harvest the hay and the corn, milk the cows, bake bread every day, and feed the DP's as they were called. DP's were displaced persons, in this case,

Serbian immigrants with no place to go. With Teta, there was always a bed and a warm meal.

And no one could tell a better story, albeit laced with language that would never make broadcast television. And if one had to alter the facts a bit to make it more interesting...

If ever a girl of the 1940s had a mentor who, by example, would teach her that a woman could do anything, survive anything, create anything, it was I. Teta Rista was my first and lasting hero. Considering all the obstacles this girl would face, I was lucky to have her in my early life. Years later, my sister Jean said, "You are a modern day Teta Rista." I wonder if she realized she gave me the ultimate compliment.

One of Teta Rista's sons, Mickey, was the character of all time. Like his mother, he had no filter. He would say anything, made everyone laugh, and would give you his last dime. He knew every Serbian song ever written and would regale us with stories and music. All the Serbian men I knew learned to play some kind of stringed instrument, including my dad, who played a tambura. Following the war, Mickey got a job as a streetcar conductor in Chicago, the only mode of transportation for us at the time. My sister Jean and I would be so excited if we landed on his car, as he always gave us a fistful of transfer tickets to take home to play with. Mickey never talked about the war, as was true of so many men who fought in WWII.

Among his many talents, Mickey could cook and was the number one chef when it came to the Serbian tradition of roasting whole lambs on a spit above a wood fire. He taught us all how to prepare the lamb, filling its cavity with a hundred garlic cloves and lemons and then sewing it up so it wouldn't flop as it went around on the spit. We all had to take turns manning the spit, which was really boring, dousing the lamb with water and lemon. I dared to tackle this task just a few years ago for friends at my home in Nantucket. Thankfully an island friend pitched in and had an electric spit. Now that is progress. Somehow though, it was never as good. The whole process was missing Mickey's laughter and profanity-laced stories.

Along with my father's new job at Gillette came moving, several times, to Boston, back to Chicago, back to Boston.

The first move in 1954 brought us our first house in Needham, Massachusetts, a suburb outside Boston. That we could afford it was a stroke of luck, or maybe divine intervention. Dad was sent to Las Vegas on business while we were still living in Chicago. He parlayed $10 at a craps table into $1,700, which made for a 10 percent down payment on a tiny house. How proud he was as he spread the money, as one would a deck of cards, on the kitchen table in our flat in Chicago. We could afford a house! We were out of the city, now in a neighborhood with kids and a walk to school that didn't require crossing busy intersections.

It all seemed wonderful until a week after we moved in, when Hurricane Carol hit and water filled our basement up to the first floor. Mom, trying to be organized and excited to create our first home, had the movers put most of what little we owned in the basement. All was ruined, including the furnace and the washing machine. I still feel the pain of watching my mother crying. One week later, another hurricane, Edna, barreled into New England. This time the wind came from the opposite direction and righted whatever trees the first one had uprooted, including a beautiful tree with orange berries on our front lawn.

It seemed to be a miracle and maybe a sign that all would be all right.

A year later, the polio epidemic struck and one family in the neighborhood had malaria. I remember it as a frightening time when forces outside anyone's control could wreak such havoc on innocent people. How similar was that helpless feeling to today and COVID-19. Decades later, I would come to know a man who had been affected by that polio epidemic. My dearest friend, Robert Patrick Fitzgerald, as kind and thoughtful a man as I would ever know, who never complained, but accepted the crippling affect polio had, limiting his ability to speak.

We were only in Needham two years when my father was promoted and sent back to Chicago.

This time we lived in Park Ridge, Illinois, in a rented house. I attended eighth grade and had just begun high school at Maine Township High. I loved it. My best friend, Diane Ricketts, lived right next door. Diane and I met again fifty years later, and she reminded me of the messages we sent to each other on a clothesline strung between our bedroom windows. No text messaging then. Our neighborhood was filled with kids and being in high school was a big deal. No more grammar school.

But that high was short lived, as by the fall of my freshman year, Dad was transferred again, to Gillette's parent company, again in Boston.

This time we lived in Wellesley Massachusetts. I was miserable. I loved my friends in Park Ridge. Not only that, but Wellesley could have been another planet.

First, I was no longer in high school. Ninth grade was part of Wellesley Middle School. Also, at Maine Township High, we hung out in groups and walked everywhere together. In Wellesley it was dates, and my parents didn't let me date until my junior year. The girls at Wellesley wore make up and nylons and flats and everyone had a camel hair coat. At Maine High, we wore simple pleated skirts, crew necks, knee socks and loafers, and whatever jacket was around.

God bless Mom. We used to take the MBTA downtown to Filene's Basement in Boston, especially for the two big sales each year. We would get there two hours before they opened and stand in the freezing February cold. Then we would run to the section where we were hoping to find what we needed. It was crazy. I watched a woman grab all the dresses on the size 8 rack and then sort through them, undressing and trying each one on. I said to her, "That's kind of piggish of you to take all the dresses." She replied, "Honey, when you've been shopping here as long as I have, you will learn this is the way to do it." The next time we went, I grabbed all the dresses. A girl said to me, "Isn't that a little piggish," and I replied…

We did get a wool coat that looked like camel hair, sort of. Filene's Basement was one of a kind and a gift to people on a tight budget. A few years later at graduation, I was given $25 to buy an outfit. Back at Filene's Basement, we found a beautiful gown from a boutique in California for $15. I spent $5 to have it altered which left me $5 for shoes dyed to match. Mom pitched in a few more dollars for the shoes.

In addition to feeling like the ugly duckling, I went from being an A/B student to feeling like the dumbest kid in the class. In just about every subject, French, math, and science, the Wellesley school curriculum was far ahead of Maine High. They were actually speaking French and reading literature in the language! In science, having missed several months of physics, I didn't think I could ever catch up.

For the first time in my life, I was down. Big time. I looked like the poor stepchild, couldn't keep up in class, had no social life since everyone else it seemed had a boyfriend.

Feeling badly for me, and trying to do the right thing, my parents, at my father's boss's urging, sent me to Beaver Country Day School. And that was another solar system.

Back then girls had coming out parties, cotillions. I had never heard of the ritual. They were formal and a very big deal and all the girls had dates. No one ever invited me to one of their parties. And when Beaver had a school dance, the girls all knew the boys from whatever school was invited. I knew no one and as I recall never danced.

Thankfully it was not my nature to sulk. And I got lucky. A wonderful teacher who led the drama program took a liking to me. She took the midwestern twang out of my speech and considering the career I ended up in, what a blessing.

She also chose me for a lead role in a musical, even though I don't have much of a singing voice. I actually managed the music fairly well except for high C. No worries. My hero said when you get to that part, make sure you are above my piano, open your mouth and pantomime my voice. Amazing.

I also befriended three girls from France. They wanted to learn better English and I better French, so we hung out and helped each other.

Longing for friends, I begged my parents to let me go to Wellesley High School. They relented and I spent two years in one school. I tried out for the cheerleading squad. Of course, that's where all the popular girls were. I didn't make it. So, I tried out for varsity basketball, made it, played well, and had fun. It was a lot less pressure. On the basketball squad, it was all about athletic competition. I was a forward and back then in girls' basketball, forwards could only play half court. The defense could run full court. I managed to nail down a shot from the side of the basket with some consistency. Now that felt good.

Since I wasn't allowed to date yet, and when I was, it seemed everyone was taken, I convinced my parents to allow parties in our basement. No booze of course, but the guys didn't seem to mind, and they came. I had a lot of girlfriends and stay in touch with some of them to this day.

Very few kids smoked then, and no one I knew had ever heard of drugs. I think life was easier than for kids now.

A big joy for our family at this time was the birth of my sister, Sandra, born on the Fourth of July! I was sixteen a month after she was born. She was adorable, blonde with big blue eyes. Jean, Billy, and I were enthralled. We couldn't call my brother Baby Billy anymore. We had a new baby.

When my friends were applying to colleges, I asked my father what we could afford for my education. He said he saw no need for a girl to go to college. My mother could teach me all I needed to know.

"But Dad, girls go to college now and get jobs. They don't just get married after high school like you and Mom did."

He was not to be moved. It wasn't that he was mean. He was from another culture. In the Serbian world he knew, the man is the breadwinner, the woman the primary one to raise the children, clean the home, and cook the food.

Dad's relationship with my brother Billy highlighted the difference that Dad felt about girls and boys. For example, he taught Billy to play golf at an early age but never included me or Jean. I asked him many years later why he didn't teach Jean and me to play golf and he answered, "I don't know." It's just the way it was.

My father is testament to the opportunity offered in our country. Imagine going from peddling razorblades in Chicago to becoming the president of Gillette North America. In 1975, he was honored with the Horatio Alger Award and sitting in the crowd in NYC, I cried for him, feeling huge pride. My mind reflected on the nights we children would go into our parents' bedroom to say goodnight and find Dad reading the dictionary.

"Dad, there are more interesting books."

"No, I had no schooling, and I now work with college educated men. I need to catch up."

I didn't know it then, but I realize now, primarily I have my father to thank for my can-do attitude. He did not have a college education. He had no contacts, but he had drive. He would talk about what a great country this was. Work hard, keep trying. No one owes you anything. You need to earn it. When I had to jump my "women need not apply" hurdles, I see now why I was not disheartened. By example, my father had shown me that anything is possible if you work hard enough.

I also came to understand that my father might not have climbed that steep mountain to business success were it not for my mother who always encouraged him personally and also gave him the space and peace to pursue his goals. She ran the household, raised the children, kept our Serbian traditions alive with family and food and faith.

To this day, I think of my mother as the smartest person I know, not book smart, life smart. By her example I learned that caring about others brings you joy. Some years after she died, a deli owner wrote me a letter. "I didn't know your mother very well, but she was such a happy person, always interested to know how I was. When she left my store, I would find myself smiling. Whatever might have been bothering me before she arrived, seemed to disappear." That was her gift. She loved people. She genuinely cared about everyone. When we drove down the street and a funeral procession passed, she would cross herself and say a prayer. When she saw someone without sight walking with a red tipped cane, or someone in a wheelchair missing a limb, she would say with the affection of intimacy, "May God bless him."

While I love my mother and loved to cook with her and set a pretty table, I wanted my father's life, not hers. In fact, I wanted both, which would cause a major dilemma in years to come.

As luck would have it, in the spring of my senior year, our family drove out to Chicago from Wellesley for a family event. We were visiting my godparents. In the Serbian world, the godfather is a very important person. He vows at the baptism before God to raise his godchild should anything happen to the parents. He also promises to remain a teacher in the child's life, both religiously and otherwise. It obviously is a big promise, one not taken lightly. The godfather is revered by the family and is treated with great respect.

On this trip to Chicago, my godfather, *Kum* ("Koom") in Serbian, asked my dad, "Where is Natalie going to school?" I just happened into the room as this conversation began and ducked back out but remained within earshot.

"Are you sending Diane to school?" Kum had a daughter my age.

"Yes, of course, Willie. Girls go to school now." My father was incredulous but respected our Kum.

On the tortuous, sixteen-hour, two-lane ride back to Boston, my father said, "Maybe we should revisit this college discussion." I of course was very angry with him. "Thanks, but you are too late. Rejections and acceptances have already gone out. I plan to leave home, get a job, and put myself through school someday." I didn't need his help.

Well, a sixteen-hour ride is plenty of time to cool down. So, here was the offer: I could apply to school so long as it was within an hour of our home and the tuition was within a certain range. The second part was reasonable but not so much the first. On the other hand, it beat trying to get a job and save enough money for school. I applied to the University of Massachusetts, the University of Connecticut, and the University of New Hampshire, which were in the price range, as I recall, but not the distance. But then Harvard, Boston College, Boston University were not in the cards.

UNH by chance had an opening. Someone didn't accept their invitation. Lucky me.

Sometimes after the darkest night, the sun comes up. Nice.

CHAPTER 3

UNH

The University of New Hampshire, autumn 1961. You could hear the big clock atop Thompson Hall. The campus trees were just beginning to turn, kids and their parents were unloading, and it smelled like New Hampshire: clean, fresh, woodsy. Here I was, finally, a coed with four exciting years ahead of me.

I signed up for Freshmen Camp which preceded the start of class by two weeks. This was a great chance to learn about the school and, most importantly, to meet other incoming freshmen. We got to know each other in crowded bunk rooms, mess halls, swimming meets, hikes, and long talks by an outdoor fire. We had the advantage of entering UNH knowing a couple hundred kids. For the first time in my life, I was not an outsider.

I could not have been more excited. This was a whole new world. I was out of my parents' control, almost. I was assigned to Hitchcock Hall, first floor. I shared a room. My roommate and I each had a bed, half a closet, half a dresser. It was a palace. The dorms were single sex back then. If you brought your dad in, you had to shout, "Man on the Floor!"

To get from Hitchcock Hall to class or the dining room called the Commons, we walked on paths cut through the forest. It was beautiful, like a scene out of Currier and Ives. A narrow wooden bridge took you over a bubbling brook. It actually did bubble. Climbing a small hill brought you to Thompson Hall and the main street of the campus. UNH was bucolic, far from industry or a big city. The campus bordered the rural town of Durham, which had a gas station, a small grocer, a gift store, Town and Campus, a movie theater, a coffee shop, the post office, and a church. The town was dry.

Registration for classes was chaotic as I remember it. First come first served. I was an English Literature major and yet could not get into an American literature class. Crazy. Few electives were available to a freshman and to my chagrin, they were mostly subjects I already had in high school. I skipped my Algebra II class most days because I already knew the material. Going into finals, my professor informed me I was failing the class. How could that be? I had an A+ on both of the previous exams. "You didn't come to class. If you want to pass, you need to get a 95 or above on the final and I'll give you a D." A D?! No amount of explanation or protest would change his mind. I was pretty sure I could meet his mark, but I wanted an A.

Lesson Number One: Professors have egos. Do not insult by skipping class.

We stood in line seemingly forever at the Commons for food, which was pretty dreadful, but there was no alternative. We usually had no idea what we were eating, as whatever it was had a heavy ladle of gravy covering it. We called it "mystery meat." The Commons was the place to meet our fellow freshmen, so while the food wasn't great, the socializing was.

We spent much of our time at the Dimond Library, which was fairly new. Hard to imagine now, but there were no computers, no Google. Everyone was familiar with the Dewey Decimal categorizing system. All note taking was done in long hand.

Long-form papers often had to be typed and the sharing of typewriters was often a problem. But, when everyone is in the same boat, somehow things work.

UNH had an active Greek life community. I joined Alpha Chi Omega and loved the camaraderie of sisterhood. I lived in Hitchcock Hall freshman and sophomore years, as there was not enough room in our sorority house to accommodate underclassmen. We were allowed to eat at the house and of course attend sister meetings. The house itself was an old Cape, with creaking stairs and small rooms. Maybe the most coveted room was in the basement, affectionately dubbed the Six Pack. Six girls were packed into six bunks. The space was tight, but they had the benefit of being secluded and only they know what went on. We were so innocent back then; the worst thing probably was smuggling a boyfriend in with a real six pack, pun intended.

I made lifelong friends at UNH. Kay Lawrence, also an AXO, and I were best friends and remain so today. We were each other's maid of honor. We have lived a lot of life supporting one another through trials of careers, marriage, divorce, children, and health. I am blessed to have her in my life.

We had curfews: 9 PM for freshmen, 10 for sophomores and 11 for upper classmen. Can you imagine? You signed in upon entering the dorm. At ten minutes before the deadline, the front door area was crowded with couples saying goodnight, with long smooches and hugs.

I came to be among those couples, as I met and eventually fell in love with a tall, dark-haired, handsome Bill Jacobson, one year my senior. Jake, as he was known, was my first serious relationship with a man, as I had dated little in high school. He was from Manchester, New Hampshire, and proud of it. He was a member of ATO, a fraternity filled with fun-loving guys. Back then UNH allowed fraternities to have kegs of beer at weekend parties. Since both the town of Durham and the University were dry and few people had a car to drive off campus, our social life was limited to the grounds and those parties were a highlight.

At Winter Carnival in February, ice sculptures were the feature of the weekend, along with what you might expect in the way of partying. Every fraternity and sorority put the artists to work designing and the rest of us worker bees kept chiseling. Sam Cady of ATO seemed to guide his fraternity to the blue ribbon most years. Where we at AXO might have a great ice-sculpted tree, Sam would create an entire forest. He went on to be a terrific artist.

My sophomore year I was selected to be a member of the Sophomore Sphinx. We were a small group of maybe thirty kids whose mission was to welcome freshmen and guide them through orientation. We wore grey skirts or pants and blue blazers, so we would be recognizable around campus. I loved all of it, meeting the new class, cheerleading the joys of being a Wildcat, and helping the new students solve their problems.

One day the word went out that a small group of kids from Central or South America was on campus. Did anyone speak Spanish? I did thanks to one of the greatest teachers I had at Wellesley High School, Carlos Vacca. I spent the next day or two showing off my school. I couldn't wait to tell Señor Vacca about my experience and thank him for teaching us all conversational Spanish. Looking back to WHS, I realize how many talented teachers we had. I remember a Mrs. Heffernan who would put a word on the blackboard and ask us to write a paragraph using that word in the active voice. Then we each read our paragraph aloud and we analyzed it. It was in that class where I began to learn how to write and better understand the nuance of the English language.

I joined the UNH Pep Kittens, the cheerleading squad for the junior team. The university rules called for a parent to give permission for a student to leave the campus. My father refused, so I did not travel with the team for away games. Our squad leader was not happy, as missing one person messed up the routines. As a junior, I was on the varsity squad and either my father relented, or the rules were different for upperclassmen. In any case, I traveled with the team, and what a great opportunity that was to learn about the other colleges in New England. Colby College in Maine stands out in my memory. My younger sister's daughters, Lily and Eleanor, are students there now, and my friend, noted presidential historian Doris Kearns Goodwin, graduated from Colby before going to Harvard and later teaching there. My brother Bill was lucky enough to be in one of her Harvard classes. Small world.

Home games were the best in the sense of school spirit. We had bonfire rallies on Friday nights before each Saturday game. Most of the school turned out and then packed the stadium for the game the next day. The Rah-Rah enthusiasm for our Wildcats was palpable. One year, my folks came up for a game. Mother made a cheerleader outfit for my little sister Sandy. With platinum curls, blue eyes, and a four-year-old's joyous smile, she stole the show.

Being from New Hampshire, most kids skied. I did not and didn't have the money to learn. While my friends hit the trails on weekends, I worked at the local theater selling popcorn.

In addition to the movie theater, I worked grading math papers to earn money for books and other expenses. During Christmas vacation, I wrapped gifts at Filene's in Wellesley. In the summer, I was an assistant shorthand cook at the local Ford Motor plant on Route 9 in Natick. My friends and I were not old enough yet for the higher paying waitress jobs, as one had to be twenty-one to serve alcohol. In an effort to figure out what I wanted to do after graduation, I worked in a law office one summer, as I had thoughts of going to law school. After proofreading documents for three months, I decided to keep looking. Classes were fairly small for a university. Shakespeare had maybe fifteen students. American history was the biggest; I'm remembering a hundred. Those of us who had Professor David Long were lucky. He was so good at engaging the class that, as big a roomful as he had, he was able to bring us all into the moment. He made learning about our country exciting and made us think and question.

Long reminded me of a teacher I had at Wellesley High. Mr. Raymond Chapman's class required no textbook. Instead, he instructed us to read the *NYT* every day, and in class he fired questions at us about front-page topics. "What did you think of the way that story was played? How do you know it was accurate? The reporter mentioned a law, did you look it up? No? May I show you where the school library is?" He taught us when to raise a red flag, how to dig for information, how not to trust without verifying, as President Reagan would later say.

Both Long and Chapman had a big influence on my learning to think. I was incredibly privileged to say thank you to each in a public way. While a reporter at WCVB-TV, I got a call from Wellesley High saying Mr. Chapman was retiring and would I please host the celebration. I would, with bells on. How great is it to be able to tell your high school teacher that what you learned in his class made you a better reporter?

In 1990, giving the graduation speech at UNH, I had a similar opportunity to acknowledge Professor Long. At the time, I did not know if Professor Long was still living. At the end of the graduation, marching down the aisle, I thought I saw a glimpse of him. It was indeed Long! I turned and ran into the seats to hug him, bringing the procession to a halt.

Seeing Long made up for the worrisome experience of preparing and delivering that graduation speech. As a reporter, I had covered a hundred graduation speeches, none memorable. I didn't want to be the one-hundred-and-first boring speech. As a result, when first asked, I declined. A phone call from fellow Wildcat Marcy Carsey, actually several phone calls, finally persuaded me. She had given the speech the year before and insisted it was fun.

Marcy enjoyed an extraordinary career. She and Tom Werner, now of the Boston Red Sox, formed Carsey-Werner Productions. It was Marcy who convinced Bill Cosby to play the role of Dr. Huxtable in the popular Cosby Show. She went on to be the only person in the history of television to have three independent shows at the top of the ratings simultaneously, in 1988–89. Today, she has created and funds the Carsey Research Institute at UNH, a rigorous research hub with an emphasis on real-world problem-solving. She remains a good friend despite having persuaded me to give that speech which took months out of my life.

In preparation for that speech, I decided I needed to get back on campus to find out what kids were like twenty-five years after my graduation. Driving over that final bridge to Durham flooded me with youthful excitement. I asked my sisters at Alpha Chi to convene a small gathering of men and women so I could learn what was on their minds. I also read two years of the school paper. What I came to realize was that the graduates of 1990 worried about the same things the graduates of 1965 did, that being, "What's next?" That knowledge made writing the speech much easier. Years later, in broadcast news, I would realize again the importance of knowing your audience.

More importantly, I had always felt guilty about not graduating with my class and denying my parents the opportunity to see their daughter in a cap and gown, the first in the family to go to college. At the time, the Vietnam War was first and foremost on everyone's mind. The tension was building, opposition was growing. A draft was in place. Rather than be drafted, able-bodied males had the opportunity to sign up for the army or air force ROTC, reserve officer training corps. As Vietnam escalated, conscription was in place, in the form of a draft which gave way to a lottery system. The United States has not had a draft since Vietnam. Those who fought in later wars were volunteers, often of poorer families. Many will argue where Vietnam divided the country by those for and against the war, it also united the country as every family had a child or friend in uniform.

My relationship with Jake had grown and our decision to marry now centered on when, before or after deployment. We decided, before. So, I went to summer school between junior and senior year to graduate early and accompany him wherever the army would send him. As a result, I missed my graduation. Sadly, my mother had a seat in heaven for the delayed celebration, but my father was there.

I can still remember the fear I experienced standing on the stage as I was introduced as the keynote speaker. While I was able to walk to the microphone, my jaw felt locked, and I feared I would not be able to speak. I looked across the football field filled with graduates and families and suddenly my mind took me back to my cheerleading days sending a wave of relaxation through my body. I said, "The last time I was here, I was a young co-ed in a mini skirt leading the UNH cheer. So give me a U...." and with that I could breathe and regained my composure.

The most lasting memory of my college days was the assassination of our President. It was a cool, clear day November 22, 1963. Walking across the quad, a boy leaned out of his window shouting, "Someone just shot the President!" I didn't take him seriously. But then someone else called out and then someone else. I ran to AXO, as we had a TV there. Many of my sisters were already gathered in the living room. Everyone was crying. We were in a state of shock. For the rest of the week, the whole country was glued to the images on television: Jackie in her pink suit, crawling over the back of the limo to give a hand to a secret service man, the hospital vigil, Walter Cronkite's announcement, Lyndon Johnson taking the oath on Air Force One, hundreds of thousands of people gathering across the country in a collective state of disbelief and fear. The sound of the caissons led by horses marching in Washington, little John John saluting his father's casket, are images seared in the memories of millions. To remember that week is to evoke the same tension, the same hot tears, the same unease.

Jake and I married in a Serbian ceremony in Chicago in May and waited for his orders from the army. I had no clue what career I might pursue. Few options were available for women, so it is not surprising that for many of us, marriage was a bigger priority. The primary opportunities for girls in the mid-60s—teaching, secretarial work, or nursing—did not interest me. I did take my mother's advice and secured enough education credits to be able to teach if necessary. She advised, "Be sure your education qualifies you for work which will allow you to be independent." I don't think I worried about it much at the time. I just thought then, as I often do today, I'll figure it out.

In retrospect, I look back on my UNH days and think of how life was easier then—no drugs, no booze in a dry town, less expensive, less political. Yet a war was building. It would kill my friends. Our popular president would be assassinated. And while some women had professional careers, we women of the 60s would be the generation of women, en masse, to carve out new roles in America, career women, working mothers, military women. We would learn that maybe we couldn't have it all at the same time without sacrifices that could be painful.

We would come to know life would move fast, the unexpected should be expected. Within a few years of graduation, Woodstock, a wild drug culture, and a war divided our country. That bucolic campus of UNH quickly seemed too long ago.

Life had become a giant leap into the unknown.

CHAPTER **4**

Bangkok

Bill "Jake" Jacobson and I were married in Chicago in May of 1965. We had a traditional Serbian wedding beginning the night before with the groom's representatives coming to my home to formally ask my father for permission. This was a formality, as the "bargaining" actually took place days before when the bride and groom's family good-naturedly argued about how much each was worth monetarily. It was all in good fun. I'm told that bargaining in the old days in Serbia served a financial purpose.

On the wedding day, my young brother Billy guarded my bedroom door behind which I stood ready to descend the stairs. At my father's direction, Billy opened the door and looking at the bottom of the stairs I saw my dad, with a sad, pained look on his face. His first child was leaving the nest. I felt for him.

It was a long ride from home in Lake Forest to the Eastern Orthodox Church on Sheridan Road in Chicago as the cavalcade of some fifty automobiles following the bridal car. Chicago traffic is never easy.

The Serbian wedding ceremony is beautiful. Organ music and a full choir filled the cathedral. My bridesmaids and groomsmen marched in. Arm-in-arm, Dad and I approached the altar. My father and my groom traded places and the priest wrapped Jake's and my arms with a holy cloth. We walked around a table three times, in the name of the Father, the Son, and the Holy Ghost. The music and the homily are specific to the marriage ceremony. Following our vows, now a married couple, we left the church and greeted each guest.

Our reception in the church hall was not fancy but full of the joy of the moment and the Popovich Brothers music, the same group that had played for my parents' wedding. They were treasured family friends and years later would play at my father's seventy-fifth birthday celebration.

Seated at the bridal table, I remember being surprised to see my mother and my aunts serving people their dinners. I learned later some of the wait staff had not shown up. The singing and dancing of Serbian kolos went on late into the night. Finally, as is the tradition, all the guests lined up and the orchestra played the Serbian wedding song bidding us adieu, a song that makes everybody cry.

The army sent us first to Fort Gordon in Atlanta, Georgia, where we found a trailer to rent in a field off Tobacco Road. I remember opening the door one day to a couple holding a Bible who said, "We are here to save you." We must have looked impoverished.

Next stop was Fort Monmouth in New Jersey, where we rented a room in Red Bank. I substitute taught at local schools. I found the kids undisciplined, making it difficult to bring enough of a sense of calm to allow me to teach them anything. I knew then that this would not be my career.

Meantime, I was keeping up with my sisters from AXO with a chain letter. Some of us were in Europe, others in various parts of the US, I soon would be in Bangkok. Six of us were part of the chain letter which took almost a year to get around. Contrast that with the instant messaging we all take for granted today.

By December, we were off to Bangkok, Thailand, where we would live for the next two years. We were very lucky, first for Jake to be assigned to Bangkok and not Vietnam, as a first lieutenant in the US Army Signal Corps; and second, for wives to be allowed to accompany the men.

We deplaned in Bangkok in the middle of the night and I didn't think I could breathe. I later learned both temperature and humidity were a pretty constant ninety-eight degrees each day in this country!

When I realized I wasn't dying, I looked around me. I saw men in military uniform, long lines for customs, and among the people in this crowded terminal were beautiful young Thai women, black hair piled on their heads dressed in long flowing Thai dresses. Oh boy, this was going to be a long two years.

Jake and I found an apartment in a high rise. After chasing out lizards and mosquitos, I learned one should keep the lizards as they eat the mosquitos. Since we slept in a bed draped in mosquito netting, I decided the lizards were our friends. The roaches however were another story. They were huge. Every morning before using a fry pan, I had to shake them out and sanitize the pan. We also had to sanitize fresh produce, as Thais used human manure for fertilizer. I would fill the bathtub with water and Clorox and then rinse and rinse and rinse. I eventually got accustomed to it, but I looked for frozen and canned vegetables when available at the PX.

All that aside, Bangkok was an extraordinary experience. It was better than a master's degree in any number of subjects.

I was introduced to an entirely new culture. Thais are Buddhists. As explained to me at the time, Thais believed in reincarnation. We were told that Thai Buddhists believe after death comes Nirvana, provided one lives a good life. I remember that when a girl who worked with us lost her father, she explained that while she was sad to lose him, she knew he was in Nirvana because he had lived a good life. Since then, I have read very different descriptions of Buddhism, some contradicting what I was told. Thais keep the remains of their dead in a sacred vase in their homes.

I found Thais to be quiet, gentle, and kind. I also thought they were passive, especially when matched against the Chinese merchants in the city who seemed in control of most marketplaces.

Monks roamed the streets in their familiar long robes of orange/gold.

I noted that women drove the cars; men were the passengers. My Thai friends explained that driving was a task beneath a man.

Looking for work, I answered an ad for secretary to the manager of southeast Asian operations for Philco-Ford, the company with a US contract to supply communications between Vietnam and the US. Robert Beach was a pleasant fellow and asked if I could type. Of course. Did I take shorthand? Fingers crossed beneath the desk, of course. I got the job.

One day, he was invited to visit with the US ambassador to Thailand and asked me to accompany him to the meeting.

We gathered at the ambassador's residence, where the ambassador and others were explaining to Mr. Beach details about how business needed to be conducted according to the laws of Thailand. I found myself checking out the surroundings and wondering about this man, the ambassador. To me he seemed right out of central casting: short, portly, clothed in white trousers and long white shirt, sandals. I think I had *Casablanca* in mind. My daydreaming was called up short when Mr. Beach turned to me and asked, "Are you getting all of this?"

We got back to the office and Mr. Beach asked me to check my notes on a legal question central to deciding how Philco-Ford would do business. I told him I would write what we had learned. He thought that was fine. He left, I wrote my opinion, and the next day Mr. Beach approved the letter and sent it to headquarters. Perhaps it was here a reporter was born.

Some months later, another position in the company opened up, administrator of a top-secret contract, Seek Dawn. Joe Salute was in charge and hired me on the spot. I was told I could hire whomever I needed to get the job done. We were tasked with getting some four hundred people from the US to Vietnam. We needed people skilled in communications and construction, everyone from forklift operators to microwave specialists and everything in between. Now this is 1967. Just getting a phone call to the US could take hours. Mail, yes mail, as in paper in an envelope, could take a week. And there was a lot of paper. As a result, I needed twelve young Thai women to handle the logistics of mail and phone calls and wires. I hired a woman who was my personal secretary, and yes, she did take shorthand, but made it clear she liked being a secretary and would not create a letter. I must dictate precisely what I wanted said. I'll never forget, here is this woman who could have been my mother's age, saying, "Natalie, if you are as good at your job as I am at mine, we'll be fine." No pressure.

As I look back, I guess I should have found it daunting. After all, I knew nothing about running an office, filling jobs, dealing with US and Thai governmental rules, finding the right people to present to Joe to hire for immediate departure to Vietnam, not to mention we were at war.

At first, I couldn't even get the top-secret clearance I needed because as it turned out my birth certificate had my name as Geraldine, not Natalie. It took my father, who had a friend in Chicago who could fix anything, to get me a correct birth certificate. That caused a delay, but it got done.

And I came to love it all, the job, the heat, the Thais, bartering for material to make drapes, learning to make rice as only a Thai can make it. All Americans hired a maid. They were critical to shopping and just about anything domestic that needed to be done. Rada, a young woman my age, tried to teach me the trick of rice that is always fluffy, never sticky. We would stand side by side at the stove. I did exactly what she did, yet hers always seemed fluffy. Mine? I even got a kick out of knocking those roaches out of my frying pan.

Rada, like many young Thai women, was forced by her parents into a marriage not of her choosing. It was clear she was unhappy and I actually thought we might bring her back to the United States with us. I thought perhaps I could find a Thai community where she might assimilate. It seemed like a good solution but the realities of immigration and of her moving to a new country seemed insurmountable.

I learned a lot living in Bangkok. I learned how another nation looks at us and how our government didn't always take the time to know that nation's customs before making decisions. For example, someone decided it would be a nice gesture to the Thais to leave a PX, the supply ship, unattended with the distinct message it was "open" should someone want to board and help themselves.

I'll never forget hearing a Thai friend calling my name from outside our apartment building. "Come see Natalie, come see." I raced down and saw a Teak R1000 tape machine on the back of his bike. "Where in the world did you get that?" He explained, and with more than a little anger in his voice, said, "Thais don't steal. It is insulting that your government invited us to steal." "Well, you didn't have to take it." "Yes, I did."

I wondered if the ambassador in his white pants and flowing tunic would understand.

I also learned that basic sanitation had not made it to Thailand. The *khlong*, a canal that ran through the city, was used for boating, swimming, bathing, dishwashing, and for waste. Some of those beautiful girls I had seen at the airport were often missing teeth before their twenty-fifth birthdays. People had awful skin issues and God knows what else. Perhaps that has changed now.

And I learned, in a very personal way, that war brings death. Jake and I had a very good friend, Walker Kaiser, a fellow ATO from UNH. We were so excited to hear he was coming to visit us for his R&R, rest and relaxation. Jake and I prepared for days, food, reservations, meetings with fellow pilots. Walker was a fighter pilot. Days passed, he didn't come. We feared the worst but refused to speak it. It was a long time later that we learned he had been killed, and not for even a longer time did we get the details. His fighter jet took a hit, sending him nose first into a tree. I still think of him and remember the goodbye hug at the elevator in Durham as we and his fellow Wildcats bade him God speed.

Through audio tapes with family and the chain letter with my Alpha Chi sisters, I learned more about the fierce anti-war protests going on in the US. Our deployment preceded the height of that movement, and we were home just before the Tet Offensive in 1968, when the brutality of the North Vietnamese was so vicious, they lost the support of some of their own people. The images broadcast on TV also turned many more Americans against the war.

My job with Philco-Ford should have taken me to Saigon and Danang, but Jake was adamant that I would not go. "I got lucky," he said, "and was stationed here in Bangkok. I'm not about to see my wife go."

Each day, life began with an hour-long exercise class and then a visit to the beauty shop before work. These talented stylists could take my long hair and pile it on top of my head, Thai style. When needed, four women, working on my hands and feet, had me ready for work in thirty minutes. It cost but a few baht and was the only way to deal with 100-degree heat and look decent.

Fun after work consisted of dinners at fellow army households or dinners occasionally at the Oriental or Erawan Hotels. The food at those hotels was amazing. Back then, Kobe beef was an honest delicacy. Farmers would massage the herd. I worked for weeks when I got back home to try and replicate the sauces for beef fondue and for French onion soup. The hotels were elegant. We dressed for the venue.

We took rides up that *khlong* on some weekends in a sampan type of boat and saw first-hand how the people lived in these primitive bamboo homes. Children swimming, merchants transporting their wares, and women washing their clothes all made for a quaint scene, but the filth and stench of the river at times was too much.

We visited some of the *wats*, temples, where years back people had carved the most intricate images into the stone of the walls. We did buy a few etchings, which cost almost nothing.

We also took excursions outside the city, Karat for example, where we watched men who toiled for weeks to make a vase of tiny shells. We toured a furniture plant and marveled at the workmanship. Many of our friends shipped home teak furniture that would be way too expensive in the US if you could even find it. We blew that. I guess it was hard to think of furnishing a home when we didn't have one yet and had no idea where we would live or how we would earn a living.

I did take a correspondence course by mail to earn an interior decorating license, so when we got home, I would have something to fall back on. Somehow I never received the actual license. Lost in the mail maybe.

Two years later, when it was time to return to the United States, my wonderful boss Joe Salute took me to lunch and thanked me for a job well done. He added he was glad I was a girl. That was puzzling.

"You see, if you were a guy, I might worry about my job when I got home."

"What do you mean, not that I want your job? I have no idea what I want to do."

"Well, when you get home, you will find few jobs at this level available to women."

I thought he was nuts. Little did I know how right he was.

CHAPTER **5**

Home Again

1967. Driving down Cliff Road in Wellesley, Massachusetts, my sister Jean shouted, "Natalie, I think you want to be on the right side of the yellow line." I swerved quickly to move from the oncoming traffic. After two years of driving on the left side of the road, I found it harder to get back to what I knew than I did learning to drive according to British rules.

And it was cold. Freezing cold. December in Boston never felt so raw. Maybe it's true the blood thins in warm climates. I just couldn't warm up.

It was wonderful to see my family again, my parents, sister Jean, brother Bill, and baby sister Sandy. I hardly recognized her when I got off the plane. She had grown from a little girl of five to a seven-year-old. I felt sad to have missed those two years.

My folks were renting a house in Wellesley, and Jake and I stayed with them briefly as we tried to figure out our next move.

We had returned to our country to find it engulfed in war protests. We clearly had been sheltered from it in Bangkok. What began as peaceful protests among intellectuals and students, led by Students for a Democratic Society (SDS), widened as young people challenged the war and the draft and embraced the drug culture.

By 1967, American deaths had mounted to over 50 thousand, with over 100 thousand injured. The war was costing $25 billion a year. More and more taxpayers were asking, why?

The protests grew in Washington, DC, and in Chicago. Martin Luther King Jr. came out against the war. The heavyweight champion of the world, Muhammad Ali, refused to be drafted.

Just a few months after we got home, the North Vietnamese launched the successful Tet Offensive. It was clear this war was far from over. And that definitely got Americans thinking.

Vietnam has a long and complicated history which did not fit the simple version of anti-communism that was used to justify US involvement.

Vietnam veterans demonstrated against the war, some throwing away their medals. John Kerry famously delivered a blistering anti-war message to Congress. He detailed unimaginable atrocities committed by our soldiers and asked, "How do you ask a man to be the last man to die for a mistake?" It was a speech that would cost him as he sought elective office just a few years later and again perhaps when he ran for President.

By February 1968, the Harris Poll showed only 35% of Americans backed the war, while fully 50% disapproved. President Johnson announced he would not seek a second term. The antiwar activist seeking the presidency, Eugene McCarthy, shocked the party by garnering 42% of the vote to Hubert Humphrey's 48% in the NH primary. Humphrey eventually won the democratic nomination as thousands of demonstrators circled the convention hall in Chicago fighting Mayor John Daley's security forces.

Richard Nixon won the White House that year promising to end the war, but the end would not come quickly. Nixon's lottery draft prompted many to protest, others to flee to Canada. Kent State saw four protesting students killed as the National Guard fired into the crowd. The Pentagon Papers revealed untold secrets, and finally in 1973, Nixon admitting defeat, ended US involvement. The Paris Peace Accord was signed January 27, 1973.

Just after 6 PM on April 4, 1968, Martin Luther King Jr. was fatally shot while standing on the balcony outside his second-story room at the Lorraine Motel in Memphis, Tennessee. He was only thirty-nine. Two months later, June 6, 1968, Robert Kennedy was assassinated in Los Angeles during his run for president. He was only forty-two. To me and millions of other Americans, the country felt as if it were falling apart.

During this turmoil, Jake and I looked for work. Jake had an electrical engineering degree and got work with Westinghouse in Worcester. I had no clue what to do or where to look. I had loved my work with the Philco-Ford Company, but administrative work was not for me; it wasn't a "career." I took a battery of tests at Boston University which I thought would lead me in the right direction, but the list of possibilities of "jobs you might like" was long and varied from politics to social work.

It would be fun to see the results of those tests today, but no matter. While trying to figure it out, I taught school as a substitute, which is difficult primarily because kids can't relate to you as they do with their regular teacher.

I also waitressed at the Red Coach Grill on Route 20 in Wayland, Massachusetts. Now that is a humbling experience everyone should endure at least once. You work hard to be pleasant, get the order right, enter it correctly in the kitchen, get eight orders out at the same time in the right sequence, then watch as the customers fight over the check and the guy who wins leaves you a buck and a half. One of the older waiters urged me to give him the change and tell him he needed it more than I did. I did give the man the dollar fifty but couldn't say anything other than "Here's your change," thinking maybe he made an honest mistake. "No," he said. "Please. That's for you." I had to find something else.

I interviewed with the genius of Madison Avenue, creative director Jim Jordan at BBDO, an ad agency in NYC. I remember this as though it were last week. Jordan, a young, extraordinary talent, took me through the Chiquita Banana ad that BBDO created. "It was a challenge," he explained. "I mean a banana is a banana is a banana." How to distinguish one from the other? They animated the banana, gave her a name, Chiquita, and her very own song and dance.

Campbell's soup was another challenge. Canned soup was not Mama's Sunday best, but people did buy canned soup and who is to say one is better than the other. The kids at Campbell's did. "Mmm good, mmm, good. Campbell's chicken soup is mmm mmm good."

Well, this sounded pretty exciting to me. I always had a vivid imagination and working with this man who was clearly an imaginative risk taker sounded great. Jordan did offer that I might be too old for him. He said he liked hiring people in their early 20s who have not been corrupted by reality, as he put it. I left his office thinking I had to convince him I was not corrupted at twenty-five.

Then I was watching Walter Cronkite one night. Of course, Vietnam was the lead. I got to wondering how this TV thing worked. I mean, how do you get pictures from Vietnam into this little box. I thought maybe I should explore broadcast journalism. Wait, what about newspapers, or magazines, or radio? If it was news that interested me, and it did, why TV? I started thinking: newspapers told the story with words primarily, radio with sound and words, magazines with still pictures and words. TV did all three: moving pictures, sound, and words. And I liked looking at the people being interviewed when they spoke. You learn a lot looking into someone's eyes. I've often thought we listen with our eyes.

I put together a portfolio to convince a prospective employer that I was smart, could write, and knew how to construct a story. I wrote one piece on US foreign policy drawing on my Bangkok experience, taking the position that we should know more about the people and the customs of other nations. I wrote another piece that was fiction, and a third arguing for and against capital punishment.

I called to schedule an interview with channels 4, 5, and 7, the three major locals associated with a network in Boston, CBS, NBC and ABC. Not one would grant me an interview. Finally, one executive at one of the stations said it out loud: "We don't hire girls."

Maybe Joe Salute was right.

Fortunately, a UHF station, Channel 56, WKBG, had started a news operation. I called and got an interview!! Jim Thistle was the news director. He said he was impressed with my portfolio and after our interview offered me a job as a cub reporter. One catch: he wouldn't have it in the budget to hire a cub until next year. Oh well, I'll wait.

By now we were living in Marlboro, Massachusetts, about twenty-five miles west of Boston. Our first house! It was so exciting and a fairly short commute for Jake to Worcester. Still not knowing in what direction to go, I answered an ad for a sales position with Management Recruiters. I don't remember why. The very nice manager of that office said I was the best young prospect he had ever interviewed. I responded, "Great, when do I start?"

"Well, I can't do it," he said.

"Well, why not?"

"We've never hired a girl before."

"You just said I was the best prospect you have met, so I'll be great, and you'll be a hero for breaking new ground."

"No, you are young and married and likely to have a child and then you'll quit."

I didn't have the heart to tell him I would be long gone with a much better job before then, so I just said too bad and left.

As it turned out, another Management Recruiters office, this one in Worcester, had an opening and that manager, Bob Shack, had no problems hiring a female. The logistics worked out since Jake was working in the city. So how about this? I read somewhere that a group of four guys who worked for Digital Equipment Corporation in Maynard, Massachusetts, had come up with a new computer. A company could own it and house it on its own premises rather than rent time on an A Frame, which at the time was Honeywell or Digital. I didn't know a thing about computers—my daughter would say I still don't—but it sure made sense to me that this new product was the future.

I got the names of the men and found out where they were setting up their office and paid a call, pitching to staff their new operation. I also learned they were planning to go public soon under the name Data General Corporation. We had no savings to invest, so I started dialing for dollars. I finally got a few shares through a broker friend. I couldn't convince my father to invest or even loan me money. The stock goes public, opens at $11.00 a share as I recall, and closes early afternoon, on a stop trading order of some kind, at $43 a share. Since I had borrowed the money for my few shares, I cashed out to repay my loan and wasn't smart enough to keep some shares. Maybe we needed the extra money.

The next day I find out that the guy sitting next to me in that office overheard my phone conversations about the stock and called his buddy at Bache, the underwriters, and bought five hundred shares. He quit the day job. I asked why he didn't help me buy some shares. A shoulder shrug is all I remember.

I did well at Management Recruiters and was saluted at a statewide office party as the lead salesman. The fellow who said he couldn't hire a girl was at that event. I just smiled. Small victories.

By then, it had been about a year since Jim Thistle said he would call. One day the phone rings, land line, cells hadn't been invented yet. "Hi, this is Jim Thistle. Do you remember me?" I thought to myself, *Do I remember you? I go to bed thinking about you. I wake up thinking about you.*

"Well, you know that cub reporter job we talked about?"

"Yes."

"I don't have that. But I do need someone in creative services to ascertain the needs of the community, a requirement for our license renewal."

I had no idea what he was talking about, but I said, "Sure, when do I start?" I never asked about the pay, which did not make my husband happy, but I was convinced it didn't matter. I wanted in. I wanted to know how you put pictures and sound and words in that box. And I thought, if this doesn't work for me, I'll figure out the next step.

Sometimes, you just have to go with your gut.

CHAPTER 6

Television

Channel 56 was located on Morrissey Boulevard just south of the inner city of Boston. It was a good hour with no traffic from our home in Marlboro.

The general manager, Bill White, was a kind, tall, good-looking man with an easy smile. Jim Thistle was slight, about my age and welcoming. I could never have known Jim Thistle would be the driving force of news at WCVB-TV not too many years later. I doubt even he could have known how extensive his influence would be, as he would come to lead all three Boston network-affiliated stations as news director.

Also, at this fledgling UHF station, I met the dean of Boston news, Arch MacDonald, who taught me the basic tenets of news reporting: "Be curious, be skeptical but not cynical, double check your facts, be fair. When in doubt, don't."

Arch, who many people thought of as the Walter Cronkite of New England, was a wonderfully warm, kind and decent man, and to my mind the very epitome of what a newsperson should be: honest, inquisitive, factual, and caring. He was WBZ's first news anchor in 1948. I was blessed to meet him at the beginning of my career and will always remember his nightly sign off, "For your hospitality, thank you." How civil. Arch died at the early age of seventy-three.

Thistle was complimentary about my portfolio, and we had a nice get-to-know-you chat. He explained this was a small operation but even so fell under the FCC rules including applying for a license and then its renewal every three years. The dog work was ascertaining the

needs of the community, which needed to be done with personal interviews. I would do those interviews and they needed to include a broad
spectrum of our community.

I started working the phones, setting up interviews, and for the
next six months traveled the city of Boston interviewing many people,
from the mayor to the guy digging ditches. White people, black people, young people, old people, educated and not, immigrants, citizens.
You name it. By the time I was done, I felt I began to have a sense of
who lived here, what made them laugh and cry, what kept them up
at night, what they worked for and dreamed of, what they expected
from their government, what they wanted for their children, why they
watched TV.

I met amazing, creative people. Bob Coard of ABCD, the anti-
poverty agency, was leading all kinds of efforts to help those who needed
it, and individuals pitched in, too. I met an older African-American
grandfather who started an organization pairing retired men with
young black boys who didn't have fathers. He told me he knew a lot of
men his age who, having retired, were looking for things to do. He also
saw a lot of young black boys who didn't have fathers at home, and he
thought, perfect: a win-win. I also met a thoroughly delightful, dimin-
utive but tough and dedicated woman, Lena Saunders, also African-
American, who created My Friend the Policeman. Police, black and
white, partnered with her to create relationships with black kids. She
wanted kids to know that cops were their friends.

I can't imagine a better education for someone who wanted to be
a reporter.

After about six months, I had completed my ascertainments. I
wrote it all up and then, using poster boards, prepared a presentation
to the board of directors of the station. In addition to sharing my
assessment, I offered ideas for programming to address the "needs of
the community."

Standing before the board, I was met with stone cold faces. But I
plowed on and afterward Mr. White asked to see me in his office.

"What do you want to do in this business, Natalie?"

"I'd like to work hard to be the world's greatest TV reporter."

"Well then," he said, "I'm going to do you the world's greatest favor."

Ah, he was finally going to let me into the newsroom, I thought.

"I'm going to let you go."

"What? Did I overstep my bounds at the board meeting?"

"No, that's probably the best presentation those guys ever heard. It is because you did such a good job that I am going to tell you that in two weeks' time, Channel 56 will no longer be doing news. There are twenty-one more experienced people than you in that newsroom who all will be looking for work. You need a head start. Get going."

Oh my. I thought to myself, *thanks, but no one will hire me*. I have all of six months' experience, all of which is "ascertaining the needs of the community."

Mr. White asked where I would like to work if I could. I said WBZ-TV. They were the big boys in town. White, such a nice man, told me to think about how I would present myself. He even corralled a couple of his news people and took me out for a beer so I could practice on them. With his help, I did get an interview at WBZ, and what do you know? Their license was up for renewal. Ha. I likely was the most qualified person in town.

WBZ was intimidating, so big, with such a large staff. The general manager, Lamont Thompson, was kind and reassuring. He made it clear this was not makeshift work. We needed to know our community. He didn't need to convince me.

I already had a rolodex but dug deeper into the growing Hispanic community, adoption agencies, mental institutions. I wrote it up and again presented ideas for programming including PSAs (Public Service Announcements).

I realized if I was going to create any programming, I needed to know how the tools of the trade worked—cameras, lights, sound. So, I asked a few members of the technical staff who worked on weekends if I could come in on Sunday when it was slow so they could teach me what I needed to know. Bless them, they agreed. On Sundays, I would drive from our home in Marlboro to Soldiers Field Road in Brighton to learn the technical tools of the trade.

The engineers taught me to "truck" (move) a camera and "mix" sound. Most important, I learned about lighting, fill lights, spotlights, etc. One of the engineers I ran into in the lunchroom told me he hadn't been asked to use his lighting skills in years and welcomed the opportunity to put his knowledge to use. And we did. I had interviewed the folks at the adoption agency, the New England Home for Little Wanderers. I learned they had over forty children for whom they could not find suitable homes.

I asked the agency to bring me four representative children. I put each on a box. We killed the studio lights. I trucked one camera from one child to the next, spotlighting each, then going to black and coming back up in the spotlight with the next child. It caught your attention. I wrote a script, essentially a very brief description of each child: Sam, six months of age, cleft palette, inquisitive; Marcia, eight months, multi-racial; etc. Jack Cole, a reporter at WBZ had a good deep voice, and I asked him to read my script.

That spot aired and within a couple of weeks the Home for Little Wanderers called to say they had so many good potential adoptive parents, they wanted permission to share their resumes with other agencies in New England. All forty-plus kids found homes quickly, and who knows how many others.

That did it. If I had gone into this TV experiment wondering if this was for me, I now had my answer. If one thirty-second television spot could find homes for all those children, I wanted in. This TV stuff was power of the best kind. It had the potential to change lives for the better.

Energized and encouraged by this success, I created a program, *Que Pasa*, to teach Spanish-speaking kids English. I originally thought we should help adults with English, but one Hispanic woman sat me down at her kitchen table and said, "Natalie, I don't think we would watch because it would be embarrassing to have you teach us English. However, if you were to teach our children, we, as good parents would watch." Bingo.

The public television station, WGBH Channel 2, had a grant of $8000 as I recall, part of which could go to fund the academic part of my effort. Since I had no budget, we partnered with WGBH, and I used the money to pay an educator who would lay out the curriculum. I would then turn that into television. Heaven knows why I thought I could do that. I went walking through the halls of Northeastern to see if I could recruit a Spanish-speaking kid to work with me. I met Jorge Quiroga who was from Colombia. I told him there would be no pay, long hours, and no promise of anything to follow, but we just might break ground and have some fun. I found two other students who, with Jorge, were willing to give it a try.

Together with the help of the art department and techs at WBZ, we created a set that resembled a park in the South End of Boston. Our characters were Pepe El Magnifico, a Puerto Rican squirrel; Sidney, a Brooklyn rabbit; and Ollie, a wise old tree. The three Northeastern students were the puppeteers and the voices of the characters. We wrote a loose script. I called various schools in the city and asked them to send me a group of young children to play in our park with our characters, all as a backdrop for learning English. I also felt we needed a hook, someone the Hispanic kids knew and admired. One such person was Joe Kapp of the Boston Patriots, known as the toughest Chicano. Kapp was delightfully engaging with the children and of course they were awed.

So, we taught school in a park with Pepe arguing with Sidney about proper pronunciation, etc. The schools were ecstatic, and we also produced a curriculum for them. Mr. Thompson, who ran the station, was happy to pioneer such an effort, and by golly we all did have fun. I don't recall exactly how many episodes we did, but I do remember being told years later that schools in the southwest of the US and the Caribbean island countries used our series as a teaching tool. I felt proud and honored. (Jorge and his wife would come to be dear friends and Jorge an outstanding reporter for WCVB, which had yet to be born.)

The late 60s were pioneering days of television, when TV news was defining itself. And I still had not made it into the newsroom.

Ok, I thought. I'll lift from the newsroom and create a news show called *For Kids Only*. I asked schools to send me four smart sixth-graders who would form a panel and ask questions of an expert in any particular field. We had three segments, the news topic of the week, sports, and whatever else came to mind. Each segment was introduced by a clip from the newsroom that had aired that week. The powers to be liked my idea but insisted I add an adult to the panel to shepherd the discussion. Bruce Schwoegler, one of our meteorologists, was assigned. He was great.

The kids were perfect and asked the questions adults would be embarrassed to ask, such as, "What is the Dow Jones?"

For Kids Only went on long past my time at WBZ.

"Now can I have a shot in the newsroom?" I asked Win Baker, the new GM.

"Not yet."

An experienced producer and I teamed up and created *First Person*, a one-on-one interview with someone famous like Art Buchwald and our Jack Cole. With Buchwald, we set up in a small private dining room at Locke-Ober, a famous Boston restaurant. I learned big cameras needed much more space to move around than a tiny dining room, and promised the techs we'd be more careful. *First Person* became a popular show.

"Now?"

Mr. Baker still wasn't ready to give me that shot. "Well, we are thinking we want to create a consumer report. Why don't you create that programming and give it a try."

Bess Myerson, former Miss America, was head of New York City's newly created Consumer Division. I called and got some tips and then wrote up a bunch of consumer reports for us. I now was the person on the TV reading my own script.

Mel Bernstein, who was program manager, Bill Hillier, news direc-tor and Wynn Baker, GM succeeding Mr. Thompson, loved the whole concept but said I was not to be the consumer reporter. Why? In Mr. Baker's direct style, he said, "I don't like you on air."

Well chew me up and spit me out.

CHAPTER 7

Honoring the Promise

Across town, the Herald Traveler Corporation, which owned a television station, radio station, and newspaper morning and afternoon editions, was in a fight for its life, first with the *Boston Globe*, and later with a group of Boston businessmen.

Calling themselves Boston Broadcasters Inc. (BBI), this group of successful businessmen from various fields decided they were ready for a new challenge and wanted to own a television station. They began what would be a protracted fight to take the license from the Herald Traveler Corporation.

The story became the subject of several books, including *The Hundred Million Dollar Lunch* by Sterling Red Quinlan, and later a memoir by Robert Bennett, *How We Built the Greatest Television Station in America.*

BBI promised local programming, the quantity and quality of which no one believed they could deliver. I decided to look into this new station to see if they would consider me. I was up front with Messrs. Baker and Bernstein, saying I wanted to be a news reporter and since they didn't "like me on camera," I would look elsewhere. I don't think it mattered much to them, as I kept working while I looked for work. Early in 1972, I think, or late the previous year, I was invited to interview for a job as a news reporter with this fledgling station that was still waiting for the go-ahead from the FCC.

What an interview. It lasted several days. I was grilled on a variety of topics, by the news director, Larry Pickard; programming director,

Dick Burdick; and two reporters they had already hired, Mike Taibbi and Jim Boyd. I was asked to argue for and against a controversial issue of my choosing. I was given a set of circumstances and told to have a story ready in fifteen minutes. It went on and on.

I thought if a company was going to such lengths to hire a reporter, they must be gathering some really good people. In the end I got the job and would start when they got the license, whenever that might be. I can't help but think, TV news today would be so much better if candidates today were put through such a rigorous interview.

BBI hired Robert Bennett from Metromedia in New York to run the station. I think they gave him 5 percent of the company with the mandate to make this the greatest television station in the country. The value of the company at that moment was zero.

Bennett must have thought he had died and gone to heaven. This board of directors of Boston Broadcasters Inc. held their meetings in a conference room at the end of the hall, thirty feet from Bennett's office. None of them knew much about running a television station, which was fine. They just hired a guy who knew a lot about television. The board essentially agreed to whatever he wanted, and what he wanted was everyone's best.

BBI was made up of men who were all successful in their own right. Leo Beranek for example, was an acoustical genius; his book *Acoustics* is still considered the Bible on the subject. Bolt, Beranek, and Neuman was the firm hired to investigate that eighteen-minute gap in the Nixon tapes after Watergate. Others included, Bill Porvoo, Harvard Business School Faculty; John Knowles head of Mass General Hospital; Oscar Handlin, noted historian. The list went on.

March 19, 1972, at 3 AM The Boston Broadcasters group led by Leo were all drinking champagne and celebrating a long-fought victory in an office of the new Channel 5 in Needham. Those of us about to begin reporting for the news department were down the hall watching a test pattern on our television sets as ownership changed from the Herald Traveler Corporation to Boston Broadcasters, Inc. WHDH was now WCVB.

I would later learn that across town on Morrissey Boulevard, WHDH employees were in mourning. Tom Clancy, the general manager, had fought hard to keep the television station, and now, as the WCVB-TV test pattern filling the screen made clear, the fight was over.

The technicians were all coming to the new Channel 5, as were most of the on-air talent. Jack Hynes, John Henning, Don Gillis, Bob Copeland, Bill O'Connell, Chet Curtis, Bill Harrington, Bob Clinkscale, Frank Avrush, and others; all experienced, well-known people in greater Boston; would be the face of the new channel. It was not an easy transition for many of them. I can understand that. They were now employed by the enemy. But they were pros and adjusted and gave it their best.

I seem to remember being in awe, a little nervous and a lot excited. I felt a sense that something big was beginning. Little did I know.

I had an unwelcome surprise that very first Thanksgiving with Channel 5. Larry Pickard, the news director, asked who was anchoring the newscasts on Thanksgiving Day. He was told that the regulars, Jack Hynes, John Henning, and Chet Curtis, had the day off. So, who was left? I happened to walk by, and Larry asked if I was working tomorrow. I was.

"Good, you will anchor our 6 and 11 PM newscasts tomorrow."

Oh my. I was not an anchor. I was just learning to be a reporter.

Tomorrow came and I sat in the anchor chair, petrified. The opening music and credits played. I could not speak. This is just great. Mine would be the shortest-lived career in television history.

Cameraman Tony Towa peered around his big studio camera. "What's wrong?"

"I can't talk," I muttered through clenched teeth. "I'm scared."

Tony smiled and said, "You read a story every day for this newscast, don't you?"

Yes, I thought, *one story, the one I reported and wrote*. But here I was holding fifty-five pages. I just wanted to be anyplace but here. I looked at Tony.

"You know, Natalie, you can only read one story at a time."

With that I heard the announcement, "And now, NewsCenter 5 with Natalie Jacobson substituting for Jack Hynes." My mouth opened and words came out. God bless Tony.

I would come to know that life in television news moves fast. Perhaps only a trading floor moves faster. At times, I felt the need to schedule a few minutes to reflect on what had happened that month, or week, or day!

I found the television newsroom to be unlike any other place of work. Minutes evaporate at warp speed. New information pours in, from the wires, the telephones, police radios, reporters. Before computers, typewriters were constantly clicking. Ringing phones and loud voices accost your ability to think. The clock never stops. Deadlines loom. 6 o'clock ready or not. And it seems everyone smoked. So, you had to learn to cancel out the noise and take up smoking if you didn't smoke already.

I would come to learn the crux of news is how it is defined and reported. What is news, what isn't? To answer that question, we considered relevance. Who cares? Should they care? Why is this important, and to whom? Is the information honest, factually correct? How do you know what you think you know? Who is your source? Can you trust it?

During our morning meetings we would ask ourselves and each other, what do the people NEED to know? Today that question often has changed to "What will they watch?" The change in question changes the content. They need to know their taxes are going up. But would they rather watch a tiger maul his trainer? I personally would opt for the tax story.

On the table to consider are the events of the day, the continuing stories, new information, unexpected happenings, new ideas. What's new? Why is that important? The better you know your viewers, the better your decisions. And the more curious you are, the better chance you have of asking "Why?"; often uncovering information one might not have guessed.

For example, thinking back to 2004 after the historic Red Sox win, if you didn't know Johnny Damon's agent was talking to the New York Yankees at 8 o'clock Tuesday night and John Henry was out to dinner and not taking calls, how would you know you shouldn't eat that second slice of pizza? You would have no clue you were going to be sick to your stomach when you woke up in the morning.

Now, one could get upset and argue that Henry et al. didn't handle that well, but I wanted to know why they didn't handle it well. As a reporter I get to ask Mr. Henry why and then I get to tell ninety gillion Red Sox fans what he said. Then we could all be sick to our stomach together, which is more comforting than being sick alone.

As a reporter you would need to defend your idea before other reporters and your producers and news director, who have the final say. With only so much time in a newscast, not everyone's idea wins. So, you have to be a good salesman.

Above all, in my opinion, to be a good reporter, you have to care about the people about whom and for whom you report. You need to know your viewers, their needs, their lives. You are not the story. Opinions were labeled as such.

Where the subject was controversial, the Fairness Doctrine of the Federal Communications Commission required all sides to be addressed, as accurately and fairly as possible. Let the viewer make up his/her own mind based on solid information. Some subjects are more complicated than others, but it is still easy to be fair.

For example, I believe it was during the 80s when across the country agencies sprung up to help people who had been adopted find their biological parents and, vice versa, parents find their children. Many parents were very uncomfortable with this growing phenomenon and so the story grew.

How should we at WCVB handle it? Being local, we told the story through our viewers who were grappling with the issue.

Legal questions were at play, as some adoptions were sealed with the promise of secrecy. What of the ramifications? What would happen if and when you learned who your biological parents were? Could you handle it? What if the biological parents didn't want to meet you? How would the parents who raised you feel? Did they tell you about being adopted or is this news to you? How will you handle the news? Forty years might have passed.

Some of the people I interviewed said it was worth whatever problems might arise to conduct the search. Others said, no way. They did not want to look. As a reporter, I felt it was out of line to expose anyone who didn't want to be exposed. So, there were no surprise interviews. Instead, if the person searching, either the parent or the adult child, chose to speak about it, and if both sides agreed, I would interview them on camera and allow them to tell their stories as they saw it, experienced it, and now lived with it.

This is not a story I would have gone looking for, but it was a movement across the country and as a news reporter you couldn't pretend it wasn't happening. It seemed the best way to deal with it was to let the people affected deal with it as they chose and publicly share their experiences or not. I personally learned how complicated and varied these situations can be. I hope our audience did, too.

Of course, there are many such examples: gun control, birth control, abortion, immigration, education, etc. I remember preparing a five-part series on abortion, to this day a divisive topic. I received letters from people accusing me of being pro-choice and letters accusing me of being pro-life. With a fairly equal number of each, I figured I fairly presented the opinions on both sides.

I believed then and now that while you might not agree with an opposing view, understanding why that person embraces that opinion allows for people to coexist in a civilized society. How is it that some college students and their deans deny speakers a platform just because they offer a different point of view. What are they afraid of? And why spend tens of thousands of dollars to attend a university if you only want to associate with people who agree with you? You could stay home and look in the mirror. You would save a lot of money.

The phrase "fake news" has come into common use today. Fake means not genuine. But the term has come to mean untruthful, a lie. And sadly, too often fake news isn't an error, it is deliberate.

During the Trump administration, we all witnessed the vitriol of the mainstream media fueled by a hatred of Trump. Commentators could not spew their venom into their microphones more forcefully. Those who supported Trump saw this as more evidence of the "deep state," a hidden government. Conspiracy theories confounded reason. The partisanship has taken on a degree of hatred and sanctimony so sharp it divides the country. It is so broad it spreads through our congress, our intelligence branches, our judiciary, even our families. Today it is difficult to find "just the facts." We seem to have difficulty engaging in meaningful conversation without resorting to name calling and thinking people who express opposing views are stupid or deplorable. This does not serve our democracy.

I could not have imagined this scenario when I began in news. We believed a news reporter's job is to inform and enlighten, to gather information the average citizen might not be privy to, and then to present it to the viewers for them to think about. We felt you have every right to expect the news your read, hear, or watch to be truthful, honest, actual—not opinion, assumption, hearsay, rumor, fabrication, lies. Commentary used to be labeled such. TV stations aired editorials which were the opinions of the person speaking, not necessarily the opinion of the station or the reporters. Of course, there is room for intelligent commentary, based on reason and truth. We can learn from them. I personally like to read a newspaper's editorial page as I look for insight into a viewpoint I might not have known or considered.

We saw news as a team effort. I loved that. No one can claim singular credit for anything. You count on your colleagues to do their jobs and they count on you to do yours. Even if you write a brilliant essay, as our Critic at Large Chuck Kramer often did, he still needed to work with the film department, the art department, the cameramen, an editor, the show producer, and the technical staff, beginning with the director.

Reporting from the field, a reporter is teamed with a photographer. In the 70s, we sometimes had two photographers, as one shot with a large heavy camera that recorded pictures and sound on film and another smaller camera which only recorded pictures. Technology moved fast, from black and white to color, from silent film to sound, from tape to digital, all of this in one lifetime. And today anyone can shoot video from a mobile phone and share it in an instant!

I never took a journalism or television course in college. And perhaps it was just as well, as covering news for television was an evolving experience. I learned it was the reporter's job to take charge of the content, make the calls ahead of time to gather information, set up interviews, get approval for shooting in private places, and sharing the mission with the photographer so he or she knew what to shoot. Producers and the assignment desk were an important part of the process. Teamwork.

Returning to the studio, film, in the early days, was processed, then the reporter was teamed up with an editor to cut and splice the film together to marry with a script which the reporter writes. The producer of the show tells you how many minutes you have for your story—never enough.

If you are the anchor of the show, you read everyone's scripts if possible and write or edit the introduction to each story.

In the 70s, the news department and the programming department of this fledgling station often worked together. Formerly a Caterpillar factory just off Route 128 in Needham, WCVB was a boiler room of creativity filled with energetic, smart, imaginative people. It felt as though we were launching a new show every day. Boston Broadcasters had made a lot of promises in the fight for the license to operate Channel 5. Therefore, all ideas were welcome. I didn't know much, but I had a lot of ideas as did almost everyone who worked there.

The talented people at Channel 5 churned out new programming the likes of which was not seen before or since. We aired more local programming in the 70s and 80s than any other station in the history of television. No topic was too controversial. The *New York Times*, referring to WCVB, wrote, "This may be America's best television station."

WCVB-TV was one of a kind. We created television shows as no one else did, from a kids show called *Jabberwocky* to a sitcom, *Park Street Under*, which became a prototype for *Cheers*. Viewers loved the newness and the energy and so did advertisers. It was good television and good business.

We aired a ninety-minute show on women's health, novel at the time, calling it *Adam was a Rough Draft*. Back in the 70s, people didn't talk about intimate body parts on television. It is hard to imagine today, but the words vagina and penis were not spoken. Jane LaPriore, now a dearest friend, did a masterful job with her colleagues producing this show, which was instructional and favorably received. Janet Langhart and I were assigned to anchor along with medical expert Dr. Timothy Johnson. Dr. Johnson was key to keeping our discussion on a comfortable, clinical level. As a result, there was no embarrassment about anything, and we gave women information they might otherwise not have had. We broke barriers and continued over the years to provide viewers with a new source for health information.

Just as great teachers often don't come from "education" schools, good journalists can come from many fields.

Dr. Timothy Johnson illustrates my point. Dr. John Knowles, then head of Massachusetts General Hospital, was also on the board of Boston Broadcasters, Inc. Knowles knew Johnson from the medical world and recognized in him a good doctor and so much more. Knowles recommended Dr. Johnson to Dick Burdick, then programming director at WCVB. Dr. Tim as we later called him, joined us to host *House Call*.

House Call went on the air our very first Monday in March of 1972. Tim, never having worked in television, asked for advice. General manager Bennett said, "Look at the camera; when the red light goes on, just be yourself."

I think Tim mumbled something like, "Who else would I be?" Every Monday at 8:30 AM more and more people began their day with Dr. Tim, and when the show ended Tim would go to the hospital for his real job. By the fall of 1972, the popular *House Call* was moved to Thursday nights.

Tim studied to be a minister before turning to medicine, and those two hats gave him a perspective on people and medicine that was unique. Combine that brilliant mind with his sympathetic nature and you have our very own *Dr. Welby*, a popular TV show during the 70s, only better and for real. It didn't take long to realize we needed Tim in the newsroom. I loved working live with him because I learned he could take the complicated and make it understandable to everyone. Equally important, I always learned from him. And to have an intellectual debate with him on or off the air on the merits of, say, universal health care, was a great education.

It didn't take long for ABC to want him, too. Bennett had put the bug in the network's ear. Tim agreed, but only after ABC agreed he could continue to work with us at WCVB. Loyalty was another Johnson trademark. To this day, I treasure our friendship.

The atmosphere at Channel 5 was ripe for innovation. Someone heard this bow-tied lawyer, Arthur Miller, conduct a class at Harvard and thought he was a hoot. Some called him wacky. Whatever the adjective, we knew he would be great as a real lawyer on a TV show, *Miller's Court*. You never knew what he would say to provoke you, make you question. And you learned, maybe for the first time, how a courtroom worked. Miller was a brand unto himself and *Miller's Court*, like *House Call*, was a huge success.

One of the most far reaching and long-lasting shows created in this era was *Good Morning*, a daily ninety-minute live program featuring whatever was happening in New England. With Boston as the hub of a six-state region, there was never a lack of material. The original on-air team gave way to John Willis and Janet Langhart. They clicked, as did the show, which lasted eighteen years on WCVB and later was syndicated to seventy-one markets.

I remember substituting for Janet for six weeks! That was in addition to my job in news. And then for one week I also was anchoring the 11, as the regular anchors, Jack Hynes and John Henning, were on vacation. So, I was working from 6 AM to midnight. I can remember sitting on the set of *Good Morning*—cameras rolling—and noticing that John Willis was talking to me. His lips were moving but I couldn't hear a thing. I was so tired my brain had shut down. His lips stopped moving. He must have asked me something. I had enough battery power to call for a commercial. I was happy when Janet came back to work so I could concentrate on news.

Channel 5 relinquished the title *Good Morning* to ABC and we became *Good Day*.

In my opinion, WCVB would never have risen to its extraordinarily innovative heights without Bob Bennett. Bob was a salesman at heart. Like my father, Bennett came from humble beginnings. Bob grew up in Altoona, Pennsylvania, where his grandfather worked in the rail yards. I loved that once Bob became successful, he returned to Altoona to donate $270,000 to complete the Altoona Roundtable project in honor of his grandfather, Harry Bennett.

Bob Bennett was handsome, smart, a fighter. He actually was a boxer once. He was a good listener. He had no patience for stupidity, laziness and whiners. He had a good sense of humor and had an insatiable desire to win, at everything. Laughing came easily to him. He was my dream of a manager. His door was always open even to rookies like me. He was a risk taker and encouraged his people to be innovative. You could propose a show and if it failed, you lived to try again.

For example, early in 1972, I was assigned to host *Sound Off*. True to its name, we invited some eighty people that first show to sound off on the hottest subject of the day, busing. A federal court order was pending to integrate Boston schools by busing children from one neighborhood to another. Parents in both black and white neighborhoods were fearful of what was to come. Boston is a city of neighborhoods, East Boston, primarily Italian; South Boston, primarily Irish; Roxbury, primarily black, etc. Neighbors were tight-knit, churches and schools were central to their identity. Busing would change everything.

People were angry. What a nightmare. I was the host trying to moderate a discussion, which turned into a screaming match with people gesturing and threatening and coming at me as though I was a ring master, and they wanted my whip. I was powerless to do anything.

Sitting in Bob Bennett's office the next day, I didn't know what to expect from him. "What do you think, Natalie?"

True to his inclusive style, he invited my opinion and we talked for a long time about whether to change the format of *Sound Off* or drop it. I don't know what the producers of the show told him, but he decided we should try again. He liked the idea of giving a voice to the people. Our job was to provide a structure that allowed people to actually be heard. How do we get them to listen? We more or less figured it out and it got better.

Bob decided Hollywood should not have all the fun; he wanted to make movies. He directed the staff to send out the word to New England writers to send us a script for a movie. We would choose the best and produce it. Six hundred New Englanders submitted scripts!

The result was *Summer Solstice*, starring Henry Fonda and Myrna Loy. No local station had ever done anything like this. And what a gift to our technical crew, which had a chance to stretch its skills to new heights.

One notable show remains forty years later, *Chronicle*. The brainchild of Phil Balboni, it is our *60 Minutes* in terms of relevance and endurance. It was called *Calendar* at first, not really sure of its identity. I was among those who reported for and anchored it. True to its ultimate name, it serves as a nightly chronicle of life in New England, covering stories from fishing to mom-and-pop restaurants. I liken it to *Sunday Morning* on CBS. You always learn something. Paul La Camera, later our general manager, was a prime mover of its inspiration and growth. Peter Mehegan and Mary Richardson were the early anchors with Peter roaming New England in his trusty '69 Chevy. Now Anthony Everett and Shayna Seymour continue this ratings winner and great example of good story telling. You are introduced to neighbors you never met, ideas that fascinate you, places to visit you might not have known of. For my money, *Chronicle* is the best local TV show in New England.

Balboni succeeded Jim Thistle as news director of WCVB from 1982 to 1990 and is a prime example of the innovative minds of WCVB. It was Balboni who conceived of and led the Hearst Corporation to join with Cablevision to create the 24-hour cable station NECN, which he ran with Charles Kravetz, its founding news director. With both a business and news mind, Balboni went on to create two digital sites, Global Post and Daily Chatter. Kravetz would go on to run NECN and then succeed Paul La Camera as head of WBUR radio in Boston. All three leaders earned their stripes at WCVB-TV, and without them the station could not have continued to succeed.

They would agree that the primary value of any company is its people. Right from the beginning in 1972, the Channel 5 newsroom was loaded with talent, beginning with its new news director, the legendary Jim Thistle. Yes, that guy that hired me a few years before at Channel 56. He was to the news department what Bennett was to the station. A unique leader.

Thistle was the newsman's newsman, a legend in his own time. Skinny, chain smoking, brain always in high gear, nothing could stop him from getting a story on air. Once the news van broke down. No problem, Thistle jumps out and changes the tire.

Another time during a live program celebrating America in 1976, I'm on a rooftop in New York overlooking the Statue of Liberty. It was a clear, cool night embracing New York Harbor. I was consumed with the awe of the moment, the Revolution, our independence, our longevity, our blessing to be Americans. My fingers remained poised over the typewriter and not a letter was pressed. Thistle looking at the clock asked what was wrong.

"I don't know, I can't focus." He moved me out of my seat and wrote it, whatever "it" was. I felt embarrassed, but gratitude prevailed. I think I got it together for the anchoring ad lib part of the broadcast.

To prepare for a live broadcast, it is necessary to learn more than you might ever have time or need to share while on the air. I came to enjoy reporting special events from the anchor chair. Unscripted, it was an opportunity to report the big picture and together with the rest of the team put the pieces into an encompassing story.

I even liked doing the homework. In this case, I read everything I could find about the Statue of Liberty: how tall is it, can you go inside, is there an elevator? Why did France give us this statue? What is her real name? Et cetera. My mantra is, one can never have enough information at your fingertips. Good ad-libbing is telling people what they don't know, or expanding on what they might know. I believe people like to learn and like to be able to pass on information to others. "Hey Joe, did you know the Statue of Liberty has 354 stairs?"

Among our many talented people was Chuck Kramer, a brilliant mind and gifted writer. He was the best of art critics. His "Ode to Christmas" is legend. Chuck strung together materialistic aspects of Christmas in a humorous, fast-paced poem that challenges the true meaning of Christmas: "*Lord...and Taylor. Anne Taylor. Ann & Hope, Anne Klein, Calvin Klein, Cuisinart...*" Google it. It's a classic.

In a piece on art critics, Chuck said something to the effect of: When the show is bad, a good critic laments that it missed its mark because he loves the medium, respects the art, and cannot help but root for its success. A bad critic finds joy in its missteps. He likely said it much better than that, but I have never forgotten the message. I can't help but wish we used this as a standard when criticizing anything.

Clark Booth was perhaps the greatest utility player in all of news. Sports, religion, politics, he could cover it all and do it better than most. He had a great mind for history, and few knew more about the Catholic Church than Clark. He was the best writer on the team. As Joe Fitzgerald of the *Boston Herald* said in writing Clark's obituary, "Clark was born to be what he was, a sharp-eyed observer with a fertile mind and a golden tongue."

You can imagine my trepidation, when years later at the 1980 democratic convention in New York, the management in Needham sent word they wanted a recap of Ted Kennedy's political life. It was late in the afternoon. Clark refused to do it. He said he couldn't possibly do a competent job on such short notice. I figured he spoke for all of us at Madison Square Garden, but no. The producers insisted we needed that piece in the 6 o'clock news. Well, if Clark can't do it, nobody can.

"Natalie, you will do it."

Panic. And I had a lot more to do to prepare for that broadcast. Fear is a great motivator. I wrote a summary of Kennedy's political life story off the top of my head. There was no Google back then. I called my friend, presidential historian, Doris Kearns Goodwin and read it to her. She said for a brief bio, it worked. "Was it accurate?" "Yes." I'm sure Clark would have done it better.

Before long, and way too soon for me, I was assigned to anchor the midday news. I hated it. It took me out of the line-up for covering the big stories. Usually, the big story of the day begins in the morning—making calls, reading the wires, rechecking the newspapers, setting up the interviews. While I still covered a story every afternoon for the 6 PM news, the midday was a major interruption as I saw it, as it kept me off the lead stories.

So, I decided to bring something new to the half hour. Since this whole operation was an exciting experiment, why not? A new national tennis league was forming. Boston would field the Boston Lobsters with Roy Emerson and Martina Navratilova, Greer Stevens and Tony Roche. They needed publicity and I needed content, so I asked if they would give tennis lessons, which we would air on the midday news in segments over a period of weeks. They agreed. If you're into tennis, this was pretty cool. My lasting memory was of Martina, who did a basic lesson on net play. Some months later, she was playing in a big tournament and while she had been struggling of late, she won. She actually called me to say thanks for asking her to do the lessons. It was her net play, she said, that had been costing her.

Returning to basics brought her game back. What a classy woman to make that call.

On a daily basis, I often found myself being assigned boring stories—weekly school committee meetings come to mind—or soft stories in which I had no interest, such as a piece on a local fellow, Louis Gordon, who invented a way to grow hair on balding men. Sorry, Louis.

Well, I figured, *OK. You are the rookie. It is only right that you pay your dues.* As time went on, I suggested stories I wanted to cover. I don't think I realized it at the time, but I was an oddity. I was female. I was the only woman other than clerical and administrative staff at the station for almost two years. Anne McGrath, who had been hired before me as a reporter, had quit before we went on the air on March 19, 1972. In the city, the only other women reporters I can remember, Shelby Scott and Sarah Ann Shaw, were at WBZ. When I called to set up an interview, I almost always got it. I wonder now if it was in part because people were curious, who is this "girl"?

As the only woman among the reporters, I came to realize pretty quickly that when you are in the minority you need to step it up. You need to prove you are worthy.

I felt the pressure to produce and present stories that were a cut above the average. I had to show I was smart, a good writer, had a flair for getting to the heart of the matter. First, I had to convince myself I could do all these things.

Once the preparation was done, the story in the can, film shot and edited, I had to present it with a professional face and voice, absent vestiges of femininity—no dangling earrings, plunging necklines, tight fitting sweaters, not too much makeup. I felt I wanted to be the conveyer of the information, not the on-stage presenter.

As time went on, I like to think I earned the respect of my male colleagues and superiors. Women's groups approached, wanting me to champion the cause of women to gain opportunity, equality. Yet, I sensed that rather than carry a banner, I could help the women's movement best by being good at my job. I hoped I would earn the right for people to see me as a competent reporter. I confess, though, the thought that I represented, very publicly, my gender, always lingered in the recesses of my mind.

Now years later, I believe I was right. I believe by being honest and caring and good at my work, I and other women did advance the cause of women in the workplace. I believe we are seen as equals today. No one would think to send a "girl" out to do a fluff piece on hemlines, just because she was female. At the same time, a woman today would not feel demeaned to do a story on fashion because it is not the only type of story she covers.

In my private life as a friend, wife, mother, and daughter, I was free to express my female side. And for all the times my father said, "If only you were a boy," I hope before he died, he realized being a "girl" did not handicap me.

All in all, I was a happy duck. I finally was in the newsroom learning how to marry those three ingredients that brought me to TV in the first place: pictures, sound, and words. More importantly, I was learning to know what news was and wasn't. I learned how to construct the story, how to present it so it was relevant, honest and fair. And I was meeting hundreds of interesting people.

If you think about it, the old-fashioned mantra taught in school to tell a good story—*who, what, when, where and why*—is as relevant today as ever. For example, if you tell me that for twenty years the state of Massachusetts has been updating its plan for vaccinating the public in an emergency, and then tell me the government abandoned that plan during COVID-19 vaccinations, what is the first question you, the reader or listener might ask? Why? The story I read did not ask or answer, why? It left me, the consumer of that news, frustrated.

As to relevance, if I as a Boston reporter tell you General Electric is cutting back its workforce nationwide but fail to relate that news to the company's jet engine plant in the Boston area, I have left out the most important part of the story to my viewers.

For me at that time, among the difficult local stories to report on a daily basis involved the politics at the state house or city hall. You really need to develop a knowledge about the elected officials, the history of a particular bill, etc. to know what is true and what is being fed to you for political purposes. You also need to know the players. One day when our highly regarded state house reporter, Bill Harrington, was off, I was sent to cover a story at the state house and never felt more incompetent. Sure, I did what homework I could in the limited hour or two I had, but at that time in my career, I lacked his knowledge and contacts. Heck, I had to ask directions to the ladies' room. So, while my report was factual, it lacked the nuance and relevance Bill would have known to give it.

Speaking of Harrington, I was lucky. He was among the many more experienced people in the newsroom from whom I learned a lot. I remember his noticing me fidgeting in front of my typewriter, getting more nervous as I kept looking at the clock.

"What's wrong?" he asked.

"I have so much information, I don't know where to begin."

Bill calmly advised, "When faced with a myriad of facts, think: Why is this a story? The answer leads you to the peg. The rest supports it."

God bless him.

As I was learning to be a reporter, I was also facing the sad truth that after seven years, my marriage was coming to an end. Jake is a good person, but as time went on, it was clear we were a mismatch. We married too young, before either of us really knew ourselves or our goals in life. Somehow at twenty-one, it had seemed enough to be in love.

It is good that work was as busy and all-encompassing as it was. It made getting through a painful time a little easier. Truth be told, I couldn't wait to get to work in the morning. It reminded me of my days at UNH when I couldn't wait to fall asleep to start the new day.

CHAPTER 8

The Offer of a Lifetime

In 1974, CBS News president, Dick Salant, invited me to New York. He was tall, slender, and imposing. He was also kind and inquisitive, fatherly in a way. He included his number two man, Bill Small. We had lunch somewhere in Manhattan. I was anxious to say the least. I couldn't believe I was talking to the president of CBS News, the home of Walter Cronkite. Me, the Serbian kid from Chicago.

Mr. Salant talked with me about working for CBS and specifically *60 Minutes*. Don Hewitt created the show and was giving Americans an entirely different form of TV news—investigative journalism.

In addition, Mr. Salant asked what bureau I might like to work in. I had no idea but answered Washington. "Well, that is the most competitive of our bureaus, another choice might be a better way to start," he cautioned.

I left New York completely overwhelmed. Was I over my head? Was I good enough to do this? Who might I speak with about this? I couldn't think of anyone. I couldn't talk with anyone at work. I didn't have any close friends who weren't at the station. Why I didn't include my parents, I don't know.

In addition to having doubts about my ability to do the job, I had a personal angst. I really wanted to have a family as well as a career, and how could I do that if I was working for the network? There were no women mentors to ask.

So, what to do? While working for CBS was an incredible opportunity, I did love my job at WCVB. I was comfortable there. I knew

Boston. New Hampshire was part of my life. I found myself thinking I could combine career and family if I stayed local. If I went to New York or Washington, I might have to wait till later in life to get married and have children. Perhaps I was young enough.

Salant's office called to say Mr. Salant wanted to meet with me again. So, I flew to New York and was offered a job. I don't remember the salary, but it was a lot more than the $11,500 I was making at the time. The thought of working on *60 Minutes* was really the draw. Don Hewitt was someone I would be lucky to work with. And a shot at a bureau, perhaps overseas, was appealing. I went back to Boston promising to call in a day or two. I was scared to death.

I really didn't know what to do. If ever I needed counsel, it was then, and I just didn't know where to find it. Looking back, I realize nothing in my upbringing prepared me for such an opportunity. So perhaps it is not surprising that I called and turned down the offer. Mr. Salant himself was on the phone. "You come here to NY and tell me to my face you are not taking this position." Oh My God. I went. It had to be among the most frightening days of my life.

I told him the truth, that I wanted both a career and a family and I didn't know if that was possible working for the network. He just couldn't believe it.

"If the president of CBS had offered me what I just offered you, I would have been here in a second."

In his limo on the ride back to CBS, he did acknowledge that he understood it was different for women, in that if we wanted both a career and a family, women had to fill those roles in a way that men don't, especially men married to women who did not work outside the home.

We got to the curb in front of CBS. "I am going to ask one promise. If you change your mind, you will call me first. I don't want to hear you have gone to another network."

Of course, I promised. He got out of the car and I felt I had just made the mistake of my life. I bawled all the way to LaGuardia.

Now every Sunday night, I allow myself sixty seconds to remember, and even allow myself to wish that I had accepted, not because I didn't have a wonderful life as a TV anchor and reporter in Boston, but because if I had taken that job, I'd probably still be working at CBS. Local news changed but *60 Minutes* retains its in-depth reporting. And, unlike most of television in the country, the network values the experience of its *60 Minutes* staff.

So, having walked away from the offer of a lifetime—what now?

CHAPTER 9

The Wars That Changed Us

Fortunately, there was plenty of news to keep me busy.

During the early 70s, the Vietnam protests continued. The seemingly senseless war would not end. More and more young men returned in body bags. It seemed a week did not go by without reporting yet another New England death.

Covering Vietnam was a challenge. As a local reporter, there was no picking up the phone and asking Lyndon Johnson why he was sending troops to Cambodia and Laos or asking Richard Nixon or Henry Kissinger why US troops were being withdrawn as the US Air Force was dropping bombs from B52's on North Vietnam.

Yet, while the shots were called in Washington and we were in Boston, this war touched every American, primarily because we had a draft. Everyone either had a family member in the war or knew someone down the street who did. We have not had a draft since, which perhaps made it easier for Congress to pass legislation authorizing funds for sending troops to Iraq, Afghanistan, Turkey, Syria, and Libya. There was a long period when not a single member of Congress had a child in these wars.

The lack of a draft also made it easier for some Americans to simply ignore those later deployments. They were far away and too few knew the young men and women fighting. As a result, it wasn't personal anymore.

Vietnam was very personal. My worst nightmares were realized when the news producer would send me to a family's home to talk about their hero son or daughter who had been killed. The only thing that made sense to me was to offer sincere condolences and ask if they would like to share stories about their wonderful child. Some parents were eager to talk about what a great kid he was and could somehow manage it through their unimaginable grief. Others would just say, "I'm sorry. I just can't." I was always relieved to be able to walk away.

I also found covering the protests conflicting. While people who were honestly opposed to continuing the war certainly had a right to express their opposition, many young people we met at these protests joined just to be part of a protest, part of the chanting, bottle throwing, sit-ins. I see a similarity among some who join the Black Lives Matter protests of today. Most upsetting, without any real opinion on the war, there seemed little appreciation for the men and women in uniform. It's hard to imagine fighting for your country in a foreign land and knowing you did not have the support of your fellow citizens. Tens of thousands of Americans were dying there, so many more wounded. And life for most of them would never be "normal."

Somehow every story took me back to Bangkok, waiting for Walker Kaiser.

When the war was finally over in 1973, there was no ticker tape parade for our soldiers. There was not enough of the help they needed to reenter life at home. Now we were covering suicides and men without legs trying to find a job, and marriages dissolving amid the emotional nightmares these young men carried home. Agent Orange, a cancer-causing defoliant used by the US military, kills men to this day.

It took years before we really knew the history of Vietnam and how five US presidents made fateful decisions that kept America in a war for twenty years.

The Vietnam War was America's longest continuous conflict. US advisors were there in the 50s, during the Truman and Eisenhower administrations. In 1961, President Kennedy sent jet fighters, helicopters, and armored tanks. In 1964, Johnson retaliated against the North's alleged attack on US ships. Congress all but unanimously passed the Gulf of Tonkin resolution, giving Johnson carte blanche in the fight. By 1969, we had half a million soldiers on the ground. Russia was pouring in support for the North. In 1973, the US gave up. The cost in human life was too much, the outcome still uncertain, and the American people had enough. Over 58,000 Americans died there, many thousands more injured, and over 2 million Vietnamese died, North and South. Stories of the barbaric fighting involving the Viet Cong and Khmer Rouge are hard to read. The depth of injury to American soldiers and our county itself remains unquantifiable. Peace was officially declared in 1973. But to those of us who lost family and friends and see the physical and emotional struggles that still exist, Vietnam, like all wars, never really ends. Today, Afghanistan continues to haunt us.

It was interesting to learn Ho Chi Minh had lived in Boston and worked at the Parker House Hotel, where he reportedly was a cook. It was even more interesting to read the beginning of his Declaration of Independence from France was word for word from our own Declaration of Independence from England. The United States was seen worldwide as an anti-colonial power. While Minh was clearly a communist, he apparently appreciated at least some of our ideology. Some historians have written that the US perhaps missed a chance to help Minh win his country's freedom from France. They note that in 1919 Minh went to France for the signing of the peace treaty at Versailles. He petitioned President Woodrow Wilson for support in his fight against the French but was ignored. It is not known if Wilson even knew of his effort. The vicious fight to unite North and South Vietnam as one communist nation continued past Ho's death.

Ho Chi Minh, born Nguyen That Thanh on May 19, 1890, was the ruler of North Vietnam from 1954 until his death September 2, 1969. When Saigon fell to the Vietcong, the city was renamed Ho Chi Minh City in his honor.

In 1995, the US resumed diplomatic relations with the country of Vietnam.

Meantime, closer to home, a different kind of war, racial fury, was building in Boston.

The schools, then predominantly white, with a growing black population, had a problem. Schools in black districts didn't have the same benefits—from books to teachers—that the white kids had. The school committee deliberately set policy that hurt black students. Facing an intransigent school committee, black parents filed suit, Morgan vs. Hennigan.

The case was assigned to a federal judge, W. Arthur Garrity Jr. The word was, he was going to order busing children among city schools to achieve racial balance. I called the judge and asked why he was going to bus kids rather than order the school committee to be fair with its policies and resources. He invited me to a brown-bag lunch in his chambers. As I remember, he had a small office outside the courtroom and took only twenty or thirty minutes for lunch, that day a small sandwich and an apple.

I found the judge to be soft spoken and gracious. We chatted a bit and then he asked:

"So, Natalie, what was your question?"

"Why bus kids around just to mix up blacks and whites. How is this going to make education better for anyone?"

"Education is not the issue before the court," he explained, "segregation is."

"But no one would be arguing about race if the black schools weren't being short-changed," I argued.

"The NAACP believes if whites have to attend these schools, improvements will come."

"But what if the whites leave the city?"

"Well, there is nothing I can do about that. I will order busing as a means of desegregating the schools."

I couldn't let it go. "I have talked to many black parents who are not comfortable sending their little children on a bus. They would rather have a good school in their neighborhood. The mothers I talked with don't care about segregation as much as they want good education for their children. And they like the security of having their kids nearby, same as white parents."

"That may be," he acknowledged, "but that is not the case before me."

I left the judge's chamber dumbstruck. I understood his legal argument but was sorely afraid of what was to come. And even more, I was angry that the innocent children of Boston were going to be pawns, moved around the city, not to be better educated, but to sit next to a classmate of a different color. There had to be a better way.

What followed was a nightmare. Precious children, white and black, being bused around the city in a crisis of epic proportions. Hatred, violence, and fear continued to dominate our city for months. Busing was the lead story night after night.

We interviewed parents, educators, and politicians in an effort to put a human face on this.

I'll never forget one day when black mothers, opposed to busing, called a news conference late in the afternoon. I was sent with a black photographer and his assistant, also black, who told me he was very anxious about my safety because I was white. I was surprised at his concern and did not share it. When we got to the location of the meeting, I saw I was the only white person among the news people. We were jammed into a dark, small space for what seemed an interminable period of time. Finally, the doors opened into a large brightly lit room where a group of children came running toward us shouting. It was like driving out of a dark tunnel into the sunlight. At first, I was bewildered but then realized they were asking me for my autograph. I was stunned. One of the mothers said, "You have to sign each one. We will not begin the news conference until you do."

This was embarrassing. My colleagues from the other stations were not pleased and, honestly, I knew this put us all in jeopardy from a time perspective. We were tight against our 6 o'clock newscasts. "Could we have your statement first and then I'll stay and sign?" "No." The woman was insistent, so I signed a lot of autographs as quickly as I could.

Racing back to the station, my cameramen and I were in a bit of awe at what had just happened. The producers were barking at us through the car radios anxious about our getting back in time. We explained what happened. Their response, "You're kidding."

Over time, the whites who could afford it left, leaving the city schools predominantly non-white. There was no way to achieve racial balance, then or now.

Almost fifty years after court ordered busing in the city of Boston, the question remains, what was accomplished? And today black and white parents are begging for neighborhood schools.

On the fortieth anniversary of busing, I got a call from an old friend, Joe Dotoli, who said he had written a book from a different perspective on busing. He had been a teacher at English High during this period and after interviewing hundreds of students, teachers, parents, and administrators, he had written *A Piece of Chalk*. He paid me the compliment of asking me to write a foreword.

Dotoli tells the story of America's oldest public school. He writes, "English High School was an exam school at the time and was racially balanced, perhaps even color blind, before the court order. Competitive in sports and academics, English High attracted kids who wanted to learn."

Dotoli writes that the school committee began its most egregious racist ruling, instituting a middle school system that hurt black kids, and then designating English as an open enrollment school, dropping the exam. English became the school not of first choice, but of last resort.

Much has been written about busing in Boston, generally from an ideological, legal, political or racial view. *A Piece of Chalk* takes us into the minds and hearts of the people at English High who lived it, survived it, and were changed by it.

I think back to the brown-bag lunch and wish that the judge had found another solution or that the plaintiffs had given him a suit dealing directly with educational balance rather than racial balance. Maybe, rather than talking about de jure segregation, we would have been talking about de facto opportunity for all children to succeed.

CHAPTER 10
Chet

For the better part of two decades, Chet Curtis and I were the face of Channel 5. We anchored our Monday through Friday evening news broadcasts and virtually all of the specials that we aired. Rarely were our last names used; people referred to us as "Nat and Chet" or "Chet and Nat."

Chet Curtis was born Czeslaw Kukiewicz in Amsterdam, New York, an upstate town perhaps best-known at one time for making carpets.

His mother died giving birth to him. His father died when Chet was in high school. He tells the story of waking up concerned that he would be late for school. His father drove him and his friends each morning. He tried to rouse his father, could not, and realized he had died in his sleep.

Chet's uncle Whitey, his dad's brother, took him to live with him and his wife, Mayme, a warm, smart, loving lady.

Chet was given to telling people about his parents' deaths. It was part of his identity. He wanted to share that. He liked to refer to himself as an itinerant reporter from upstate New York. He also liked to tell people about his Catholic upbringing and how the sisters made everyone toe the line.

I met Chet when he and the rest of the team came from WHDH-TV to WCVB-TV in 1972. I came to know him, Jack Hynes, John Henning, and Bill Harrington as smart news people, easy to work with. Chet was charismatic and loquacious. He loved to roam the halls and chat with anyone and everyone. He had a good singing voice, and years later he and Eileen Prose, later a host of *Good Day*, who also can sing, would ham it up on and off the air.

Chet was intelligent, well read, and thanks to the sisters in Catholic schools in Amsterdam, had an excellent command of the English language. And more than anything, Chet loved flying. He had a pilot's license and read everything ever written about planes and flying.

I appreciated his love of flying because of an earlier chance dinner with our New York advertising agency, Harrington Richter and Parsons (HRP). The group was in town for meetings and invited me to join them for dinner. The only topic of conversation that entire night was flying. It turned out each person at the table had a pilot's license. At first, I thought this was going to be boring; not only was I the only woman at the table, but the only one who didn't fly. But as the evening went on, I got to thinking, what is it about this flying thing that has all these bright men hooked?

It didn't take long for me to understand. The next day, I got up early and went to Norwood Airport to take a demo ride. When we landed, I immediately signed up for lessons. I was lucky to have a teacher who figured me out pretty quickly in terms of how I learn. He told me later, "I knew immediately you would best learn how to fly by flying."

He would put us into a spin and with my stomach leaving my body, he pulled the yoke toward him to show that only tightened the spin. To get out of it, he pulled the power briefly, applied the opposite rudder, pushed the yoke forward, and then released it to let the plane do its thing, fly. Now that is a lesson you do not forget.

Another time, we were taking off from a little airport south of Norwood, and with me in the pilot's seat on take-off, he asked me if I was planning to go over or under the electrical wires in front of us. Oh, oh. I had not noticed those wires and with only a second to decide, I went under them. My reasoning, as I explained later, was that I had no idea if the power of this plane was great enough to get me over the wires in time, but I was pretty sure I could maneuver safely below them.

I never again forgot to check for high tension lines. I also decided I needed to get better acquainted with the engine on the Cherokee 140.

No pilot ever forgets her first solo flight. I was to fly from Norwood Airport to Ayer, Massachusetts. I did my homework, memorizing the runway coordinates, and off I went. It was a beautiful day and while a little nervous with no one sitting to my right for the first time, I was enjoying the left seat. You see, the reason I was never nervous flying before with my instructor was that I was sure he was not suicidal, so I figured he would handle whatever I did wrong. Well, there was no one to handle it now. I looked down, saw the field and gave the necessary information to Unicom, the system used at airports without towers. Coming in for a landing, I suddenly noticed this airport had a tower. Oh man—I was at the wrong field. This was a military base. I was committed to landing and being totally inexperienced did not trust my ability to abort. So, I landed and the military guys came charging at me. No way I was getting out of that plane. I smiled and did the "dumb babe" routine. After another call to Unicom, I took a runway and left.

Now I had to get my book signed, so I flew to the correct airport, which was right next door and had the same runway configurations. No wonder I messed up. I landed, got my signature and flew back to Norwood. Phew.

My instructor asked if I had had any problems. Nope. Everything was perfect.

"Well," he said, "Maybe not."

Some years later, in 1980, I had the rare privilege to fly with the Thunderbirds, the US Air Force precision flying team. These are among the most gifted pilots in the world along with the US Navy's Blue Angels.

First, I needed to go through a test at Pease Air Force Base in New Hampshire, where I would be placed in an air chamber to see if I could handle the pressure changes. We filmed that. On the day of the airshow, I was to get myself to a field in New York where I would join up with the Thunderbirds for the flight to Hanscom. We filmed the critical meeting just before show time among the pilots. Their serious concentration was palpable. I felt the professional tension.

They strapped me in to the seat behind the pilot of the T38 Talon. The ride to Hanscom was quick and soon we were in formation. I will always remember listening to the lead pilot's calm assertive voice giving commands. I was struck by my pilot dropping down from altitude and tucking in behind the others just above the tarmac and never needing to touch his throttle to adjust his speed. Amazing. The sixth plane, in this case carrying me, does not participate in the formations for obvious safety reasons. If you have ever been to an air show you likely remember some of these formations—Diamond, Delta and the spectacular Starburst.

I'm sorry to tell you of a sad epilogue to this story about this team I flew with. In January of 1982, they suffered a catastrophic loss during a preseason practice outside Nellis Air Force Base in Nevada. The lead pilot experienced a mechanical failure during a maneuver which put him in a dive from which he could not recover. Later reports said he likely didn't know until he was at the point of no return that his stabilizer had jammed. The three men behind him followed as they are trained to do and had no chance to pull out. The only survivor was the pilot of that sixth plane I had been in. I believe he became the new leader.

The Air Force held a memorial at Hanscom Field in Bedford. Chet and I went. As pilots ourselves, albeit nowhere near the Thunderbird level, we were overwhelmed with sadness. These are the elite pilots of the Air Force who train at a level unimaginable to most, who put faith into their mission without reserve, and who trust their lives to their leader, always.

Flying played a role when Chet and I were getting to know each other. We learned we had much in common, from our basic values about people and life to our ethnic backgrounds.

We each had been married and divorced. Unlike me, Chet had two young children, Dana and Dawn. Their mother remarried and moved to Rochester, New York.

We traveled one weekend to the upstate New York town of Amsterdam where Chet was raised. I remember the ride through the town. It was clear these were not good economic times for Amsterdam. We stopped at the cemetery where his parents were buried and then went to the apartment building where members of his family lived.

We climbed up to the second floor, the doors flung open. His surrogate parents, Mayme and Whitey, were in one unit, and Aunt Lucy and Uncle Steve lived across the hall,. I could feel tension inside me. The scrutiny was understandable, but uncomfortable just the same.

Their apartments looked just like the ones I knew in Chicago where my grandparents and aunts and uncles lived. Sparse, old furniture; uncomfortable chairs; tub, toilet, and sink; no shower. It was familiar and somehow comforting.

Chet told me when he was younger, he played the accordion and hoped to make singing his life. He said he auditioned with someone in New York but didn't get the job. With no one banging down his door in entertainment, he turned to television news and worked in Washington for a number of years before moving to Boston.

With Mayme and Whitey, talk centered on food and the similarities in Serbian and Polish cuisines: filo dough, stuffed cabbage, and homemade bread. Uncle Whitey asked if I could cook. I told him I had learned from my mother and, eager to please, went to the store and brought back the ingredients for bread which I made while they watched. Hours later when the bread came out of the oven, I looked at Whitey and saw him smile. Auntie Mayme said, "See." I would come to love this woman and treasure the times she would live with us for weeks at a stretch. She and my mother seemed to share something special too. Aunt Mayme taught me to make pirogi and I took her shopping for clothes she insisted she didn't need. But I saw her smile when she looked in the mirror.

In addition to our ties to our respective ethnic backgrounds, our Christian faith and our similar childhoods created a bond. By going to college, each of us had been given an opportunity our parents did not have. There was an unspoken appreciation within each of us of feeling lucky to have had the love of family, but also of moving on.

In 1975, Chet and I decided to marry. We wanted a church wedding, but what church?

One possibility was the Eastern Orthodox Church but there was no Serbian church in Boston, only Greek and Russian. Aside from that, we learned that Chet would have to convert from Catholicism to the Orthodox church. My mother suggested that having been brought up Catholic, Chet would find that difficult. Of course, she was right. He was grateful. The Catholic Church was out of the question as the church did not recognize divorce unless a priest annulled the first marriage. That was unacceptable.

Our quandary regarding a venue was settled when President Gerald Ford, on the eve of the two-hundredth anniversary of American independence, led the bicentennial celebration at the Old North Church in Boston.

He delivered a televised speech to the nation from the Old North Church on April 18, 1975:

> *The Declaration of Independence has won the minds and it has won the hearts of the world beyond the dreams of any revolutionary who has ever lived. The two lanterns of Old North Church fired a torch of freedom that has been carried to the ends of the world.*

To mark the occasion, he gave the church a third lantern, which remains there to this day.

Chet was covering the event for us at the church. I was working the story from the studio. At one point in the evening, I got to thinking maybe the Old North Church could be our wedding venue. It is an Episcopal church, so the creed and basic tenets of the faith were essentially the same as what we learned from our respective churches. I had always thought of the Old North Church in historic terms, but now I wondered if it was still active. I called, not really expecting anyone to answer with the big celebration ongoing, but a lovely lady answered. I asked her if Old North was a working church, with weddings, christenings, funerals. She said it was.

That night, we talked about it and the next day called the vicar, the Reverend Robert Golledge. He agreed to meet with us and spelled out an education program that would be necessary for him to consider marrying us. We agreed.

On May 24, 1975, the Reverend Robert Golledge married us in this historic Boston church. It was a small gathering; just our closest friends and family were with us. After the ceremony, we celebrated aboard the *Peter Stuyvesant* at Anthony's Pier 4 on the harbor.

It all seemed wonderful. A whole new life had begun.

CHAPTER 11

Boston Celebrates

Boston is a daily reminder of our American history. In addition to the Old North Church, the first American commissioned warship, the USS *Constitution*, sits in Charlestown adjacent to the North End of Boston. I looked at it every day when I lived in the North End.

I love walking through the Boston Common, the Public Garden, and the adjacent Commonwealth Avenue, pausing before the statues depicting Boston's history. I would try to imagine life as it was then. Legend has it the narrow streets of the city, curving without beginning or end, are just paved-over cow paths. The poet Ralph Waldo Emerson wrote in 1860, "We say the cows laid out Boston. Well, there are worse surveyors." There are more logical explanations, but I like Emerson's.

When you live in a city with a history that traces back to the American Revolution, it is easy not to notice. Boston Latin, the first public school; Harvard, the first college; the Olde Union Oyster House, the first American restaurant; Fenway Park, the oldest major league park still in use; Boston Common, the nation's first public park; the Boston Public Library, the first free public lending library—all still exist. The Paul Revere statue, Breeds Hill—all are testaments to the beginning of our country as we fought the Revolutionary War to separate from England.

So, in July of 1976, when the Queen of England decided to pay Boston a visit to celebrate America's Bicentennial, Channel 5 made history with an eight-hour live broadcast. No local television station had ever attempted such an extraordinary broadcast.

News Director Jim Thistle laid out our coverage. We were going to field eleven live cameras and cover her from the minute she stepped off the HMY *Britannia* to when she retired for the night.

The enthusiasm exploding in the newsroom about this upcoming broadcast permeated the entire station. Everyone pulled his or her weight and then some. Our techs pulled off feats that probably surprised even them. I don't know much about technology, but clearly fielding so many cameras, transmitting via microwave transmitters (no satellites then), was a major undertaking. So much could go wrong, such as a piece of equipment not working. But our team did it. Across the country, the world of broadcast television took note.

We were going to use the queen's visit as an American history lesson. Chet and I were chosen to anchor the coverage. We had not anchored together before. We began at 9 AM and were on the air for over eight solid hours. At each of the queen's stops, we had a reporter and cameraperson describing what was happening at that location. From our anchor position, Chet and I related the stories of two hundred years ago. I never crammed harder for any exam than I did for that broadcast. It was a blazing hot day as we sat on the roof of city hall. Backlit by the sun coming up in the east and flooded with countering lights in our face, it had to be 110 degrees before we started. Every ounce of water in me must have been drained, as I never left that chair until we signed off at 5:30.

It was truly a broadcast to be proud of. Our team of reporters and photographers at each of those stops was fantastic, following the queen and her entourage from place to place. We filled those hours with history, humor, and a clear sense of the here and now. I think we all sensed that we were recording another chapter in the history of America and England.

I still remember us all watching with anticipation as Boston Mayor Kevin White greeted the queen. He had been told never to touch her. It just wasn't done. Well, anyone who knew our demonstrative mayor knew that he likely was not going to keep his hands in his pockets. He was Irish. He talked with his hands. We took bets. Initially he bowed his head to Her Majesty, but he couldn't help himself; how could he escort her without taking her arm? It was too funny. The queen took it all in stride.

But perhaps the best part of all was the next day when we learned that hundreds of people had left their homes in New Hampshire, Vermont, and Maine to be part of this historic moment in Boston. As one viewer put it in a letter to me, "My family and I had to come. Your coverage was wonderful, but we had to be there, to see it, to taste it, to fill our senses with this incredible moment, the queen of England celebrating America's independence from England!" The irony was lost on no one.

Another "Ah ha" moment for me. Yes, television was where I belonged.

Bennett loved it. And he apparently also liked the pairing of Chet and me as anchors. And maybe Chet and I were each surprised and pleased as well. This was our first event together. He teased me at home about all the time I put in to studying the history of exactly what went on at each of the places where the queen would stop, such as Faneuil Hall, Old City Hall, and Boston Harbor itself, where her ship the HMY *Britannia* would dock. I couldn't believe Chet wasn't cramming as well. But I came to learn that was Chet. In that broadcast, he was the play-by-play guy. I was the color. I think we complemented each other. For whatever reason, it was easy. And more than that, it was fun! I loved it all, even being so hot I was stuck to the chair.

Chet and I eventually would be paired on the evening news. Before that, I anchored with Jack Hynes, at times with John Henning, and later with Tom Ellis. I read an article which noted that I was the first woman to anchor the evening newscasts in Boston. I don't think I even thought about that at the time.

Across America, the bicentennial celebrations continued throughout 1976. On the Fourth of July, I can't imagine a better seat in the country than on the rooftop of 100 Beacon Street overlooking the Charles River Esplanade. The Hatch Shell was ablaze in light.

The Boston Symphony Orchestra was tuning up, and an estimated four hundred people were hauling their blankets and coolers to celebrate. This was the first of what would become a yearly tradition of the Boston Pops on the esplanade.

I was anchoring this part of the 6 PM broadcast from that roof. Chet was anchoring from the studio in Needham. The star of our newscast was Arthur Fiedler, conductor of the Boston Pops Orchestra, who took the baton in 1930 and led the BSO for almost fifty years. Fiedler was a celebrated and gifted musician. Born in Boston to musicians, Fiedler traveled the world and as head of the Pops was the best-selling classical conductor of all time, selling over 50 million discs.

Bostonians knew him not only as the conductor of the Pops but also as president of the Boston Firefighters Fan Club. He would go to fires to watch the men work. He owned a Ford Pumper Fire Truck. Boston firefighters made him honorary captain of the department.

And when it suited him, Arthur Fiedler could be a curmudgeon. On this night July 4, 1976, it suited him.

It was minutes before the six o'clock news. We were the lead and Fiedler was going to be my guest. The station kept asking, "Is he there yet?" The minutes ticked down to sixty seconds. No Fiedler.

Maybe thirty seconds before air, he finally appeared. I was ecstatic, welcomed him, tried to give him a hug, asked if he was excited. He answered with a grunt. Oh, boy. "What a moment for Boston," I said. Grunt. "Look at all the people who showed up!" Grunt.

"Maestro, you and I have talked before. I know you can be charming and tonight I need you to be charming. You cannot just grunt." My stomach was in knots. I knew very well if he wanted to, he could just grunt.

With that, I was on the air, setting the scene and hoping I was hiding my anxiety. I turned to Fiedler, who had a bit of twinkle in his eye—or did I imagine it? —and offering the sentiments of the moment, I put the microphone to him. He gave it a very, very pregnant pause, and then, he was charming.

Anyone who was there will never forget the *1812 Overture* and the spectacular fireworks display of that night. And no one will forget Fiedler. It was hot. The maestro had shed his jacket. He puffed his cheeks to the beat of the music and mugged for his musicians. Arthur Fielder was having the time of his life. And once again, WCVB was bringing history into the homes of our viewers.

Channel 5's relationship with the Boston Pops and the entire orchestra continued long after Arthur Fiedler. Leo Beranek, president of WCVB, was also on the board of trustees of the Boston Symphony Orchestra. He offered our services once a year for an entire weekend of fundraising for the orchestra, which Chet and I hosted. It was good entertainment that raised a lot of money thanks to the efforts of many, especially our talented producer Stella Gould, a musician herself.

As a result, we got to know some amazing talent, beginning with John Williams, who succeeded Arthur Fiedler as conductor of the Pops. I addressed him as Mr. Williams. He insisted on John. His attentive eyes, his soft speaking manner embraces you. Williams' modest smile belies the energy of the man. Perhaps the most prolific writer of music for film and stage of all time, John Williams is an American treasure. You know his work—*Star Wars, Jaws, ET*, the first three Harry Potter movies—the list extends to over one hundred films.

He and I once talked about trying to capture his relationship with producer, Steven Spielberg. I thought maybe we could put each on the phone, Spielberg in LA and Williams in Boston, with a photographer on either end. (Facetime had not been invented.) Spielberg would tell a story, Williams would put it to music. Can you imagine? Williams called Spielberg who agreed to do it. How I wish we could have pulled that off. I cannot remember why we didn't.

I felt sorry for Keith Lockhart, who followed these legends, but I needn't have. Harry Ellis Dickson, associate conductor of the Pops, called him "the kid." That then thirty-five-year-old is still a kid, twenty-five years later still leading the Pops with his inexhaustible energy.

Boston could boast of yet another musical giant of the world, Seiji Ozawa, who came to Boston as conductor of the Boston Symphony Orchestra in 1973 and became the longest serving music director in the BSO's history, twenty-nine years.

I fell in love with him the first time we met backstage at Symphony Hall during our fundraiser. He was thin, shy, with giant brown expressive eyes, bushy black hair and a childlike impish smile. He spoke not a word of English and did not want to address the audience. With the help of an interpreter, I convinced him all he would need to say is "welcome." We practiced. "Welcome." "Welcome."

He agreed and standing on stage before a packed house with Arthur Fielder, Chet, and me, he proudly said, "Welcome."

We had some fun over the years, cooking pasta during one interview in his kitchen, just the two of us sitting in Symphony Hall reminiscing just before he left us for Vienna. But the moment seared in my memory is during a rehearsal at Symphony Hall. I was standing on the floor just beneath the stage looking up at him as he took the baton. He smiled broadly at his orchestra, seemingly taking each musician into himself. Then, standing ramrod straight, he bowed, folding himself in half, his hair dusting the floor. When he moved upright, his countenance had changed. It seemed he was someplace else. Raising his baton, the music played.

I asked him about that. Did I imagine it, or did he transport himself to someplace beyond? He told me he disappears into the music. He does not use a score. He can hear every note from every instrument. Positively extraordinary.

To have the opportunity to get to know people like this is among the many incredible gifts of this reporter's life.

CHAPTER 12

The Blizzard of '78

February 1978. Chet and I drove home from the train station, just a mile and a half away. Snow was coming down furiously and our driveway, full of snow, maybe four-feet high, greeted us as we skidded down Old Greendale Ave. Chet decided to plow into it. It was late. We were tired. We would deal with it in the morning.

The next morning, I opened the garage door and looking at me was a façade of snow as high as the garage door itself. I ran to the front door of the house calling for Chet to come look. Again, I could see nothing but snow. The same was true at the back of the house. We were trapped.

Only half kidding, I suggested we jump into the snow from the second floor. And then in the distance, on the main street, Greendale Avenue, we could barely make out a man turning onto our little street. He was riding a plow of some kind and worked for hours to free us. Imagine someone doing this! Finally, we were able to make it to the main street where police officers gave us a lift to the station. They knew we had to get to work. Needham was like that.

If ever I felt as though our work was critical, it was then. Little did we know this would be among the many times we would be reminded of our partnership with our viewers.

We got to the newsroom, a noisy hub of voices, typewriters, and ringing phones. What we learned was mind-blowing. What began as "Wow," became "Oh My God!" The blizzard stretched through central and southern New England, and before it was done killed one hundred people, injuring forty-five hundred others. Hurricane force winds seventy-nine to ninety-two mph gusting to over 118 mph flooded the coast, destroying two thousand homes and damaging ten thousand more from Marblehead to Plymouth. One flood tide ran into the next.

The wind and water destroyed the *Peter Stuyvesant* at Anthony's Pier 4, the venue of our wedding reception.

The saddest story was a five-year-old girl who was swept from her mother's arms as they were being rescued by firefighters in a skiff. Little Amy Lanzikas and a neighbor, Ed Hart, trying to help with the rescue, drowned. I still cry thinking about them.

The snow had stranded five thousand cars and five hundred trucks stretching for miles beginning just below us on Route 128. Fourteen people died of carbon monoxide inhalation. People slept in pews at St. Bartholomew's Church in Needham, just two miles from the station and around the corner from our home.

I walked down the hill to Route 128 with a photographer. People were keeping up with news on their radios and were desperate to hear what we knew. Needham neighbors brought the stranded drivers food and drinks. I've seen it often; in a crisis, people are moved to help. Throughout the area, people were checking on neighbors, providing shelter where needed, getting people to hospitals. It was an extraordinary picture of people at their best.

Trees were down. Power was out throughout much of New England for a week. Homes were destroyed, all roads were blocked. This was an historic catastrophe still in the making. The snow continued for an unprecedented thirty-three hours, sometimes at four inches an hour. The winds created drifts twenty-feet high.

Thousands of people were stranded at work. Hockey fans watching the Beanpot Tournament at the Garden ended up surviving on hot dogs and sleeping in the bleachers.

Much to his chagrin, Boston Mayor Kevin White was in Florida, with no possibility of getting back to Boston. Governor Michael Dukakis was on the WBZ David Brudnoy radio show when he heard of panic in Revere, and from that microphone began calling for people to evacuate. Dukakis brought out the National Guard and, wearing one of the now-famous cardigan sweaters, kept a public vigil for a week.

We went to work making calls, desperate for details to give to viewers who still had power and could watch us. We were on the air around the clock for days.

When the winds subsided, I was sent by helicopter to the coast. We flew over Hull, where we could see homes that had been emptied out by the surge of water. We managed to land and found the owners of one home who told their frightening story. Sitting on a couch, they heard a sound, then looked up to see what must have looked like a tsunami break right through their windows and carry them out the back of the house, breaking the walls in its wake.

Anchoring a story as it is happening is a challenge. There is no opportunity to put anything in perspective, as you don't know what is next. You and the viewer are one, both watching events unfold at the same time. On the plus side, the continuing coverage felt like a long conversation with each person in New England. Our photographers and reporters in the field, soaked and cold, captured the storm in human terms.

Many of our team stayed at the Sheraton Hotel across the street over several nights. I actually cannot remember when Chet and I went home again. We were lucky we lived so close by.

When the snow stopped, and the wind receded, people started coming out of their homes to assess the damage. I took a crew into nearby streets looking for aftermath stories. We came upon a Fourth-of-July-type party in the streets between mountains of snow, drifts twelve feet high. The air was full of the smell of charcoal and hot dogs and hamburgers. Dressed in snow parkas, people had brought out their grills, and baseball bats and frisbees. It was the block party of a lifetime. Some people met their next-door neighbors for the first time! It was good to report some fun and happy stories amid the numbers of casualties and damage this storm had brought.

I like to think of WCVB as the people's television station. We had been producing programs, telethons, town meetings, and PSAs, for umpteen causes and charities for six years now. We and our competitors were the information arm of the community. We weren't stars, or celebrities. We were news people. That humility came naturally and was critical to the connection with our neighbors. Compared especially with cable TV of today, it was a hometown, "we're here to help" kind of place.

CHAPTER 13

Darker Days

1976. The phone rang early one morning. It was my father.

"I need to speak with you in person." This couldn't be good.

Dad came over. We sat at the kitchen table and I held my breath.

"Your mother has breast cancer."

She would need a mastectomy. She was only fifty-six and the picture of health. She would tell me later that she had complained to our family physician of pain in her breast. He said not to worry because cancer did not cause pain. Initially, he did not do any testing—no mammogram, no ultrasound. The cancer progressed until it was too late.

The surgery was frightening but the treatments to come seemed worse. My memory is filled with the daily trips to the hospital following the mastectomy. I accompanied her to her chemo treatments, which made her sick for days afterward, and then radiation, which caused her hair to fall out.

I remember taking her to a place where they sold silicone fillers for your bra to fill the missing space. The closet sized space looked like a storage room. We went to another equally depressing place to try on wigs after the radiation. It was so impersonal and demeaning. You felt like this was something to be ashamed of. You wouldn't want to tell anyone. And worse, my mother told me, "I don't feel like a woman."

It was dreadful, but I kept saying, "It's OK. This is the worst part. We'll get through this and life will be normal again."

I remember our wonderful neighbor calling Mom. Mrs. Mercer said, "Dawn, you'll be OK. I've been flying with one wing for years." God bless her. She really lifted Mom's spirits.

For the next three years, Mom valiantly and optimistically battled the cancer. Then, Christmas 1978, we got the news we all had been praying for. Dr. Rita Carey, oncologist at Massachusetts General Hospital, told us Mom's cancer was gone. What a blessed Christmas.

A month later in January of 1979, Chet and I were vacationing in the Windward Islands of the Caribbean, on a tiny island called Petit St. Vincent (PSV), where we had vacationed before. On a beautiful sunny day, sitting at an outdoor table overlooking the boat filled harbor having lunch, I suddenly experienced the excruciating pain I knew one day would come. But here, now? I raced from the table to our cottage and found myself throwing my body against the lava walls, substituting one pain for another.

I had been experiencing abdominal pain for almost two years and been seen by the best of Boston doctors, but no one could figure out what was wrong. A sharp pain would buckle me, then my abdomen would extend and then it would stop. At first this lasted thirty seconds, but over the months grew to extend up to an hour. I lived in fear that whatever this was would show itself eventually. I remember one attack just minutes before the 6 o'clock news. Jim Thistle caught me as I was collapsing and yelled for someone to take my script and anchor the news.

Now, here we were in paradise, several plane rides from home when it hit. I can remember saying to Chet, "Please get me to Boston and if I don't make it, don't blame yourself."

Quickly, Hayes Richardson, who owned the resort, and his wife, Jennifer, had me lying down in a small motorboat as they raced us to the nearest little airport on Union Island, about a half hour away. They tried to get me on a plane to Barbados but that took a while and I kept passing out and coming to.

Eventually, we got to Barbados with hopes of getting a flight to the United States. I remember lying on the tarmac. No plane. Chet took me to a Catholic hospital on the island. The cab ride seemed like an eternity as I moaned and screamed in extraordinary pain. I woke up in the hospital as someone was about to inject me with something. I asked where I was and what was I about to be given. I can still remember the medical person saying I had no right to know, and as I screamed for Chet who was not in the immediate vicinity, the needle went in. I'm sure it must have been some kind of pain killer, but I was scared to death and didn't trust anyone.

The next day, we got a flight to New York. In order to be allowed on the flight, I think Chet had to sign some paper stating he would not sue the airline if I died en route. At JFK, I was forced to walk through customs. About to pass out, I remember looking at the agent, who gave up questioning me and moved us along. I think he too feared I would die on his watch.

Chet had arranged for a friend to fly from Norwood Airport to pick us up in New York. I remember sitting in that little plane and listening to Chet and our friend chatting in the cockpit. I passed out again and woke up in my bed in Needham. "Chet," I begged. "Please get me to a hospital."

Instead, our doctor came over, as did my parents. He gave me a shot of morphine. Later, in the middle of the night, I was again throwing myself against the wall and screaming for an ambulance. Finally, Chet got an ambulance and the next time I woke up I was met with a truly surreal scene.

It was a big room, white, brightly lit, and empty. There was no sound. I wondered if I had died and this was heaven. A hazy figure in a white coat walked toward me. He looked human. I asked him where I was. Boston City Hospital. Ah. I wasn't dead.

I remember a lot of white coats and a bucket filled with green liquid which I saw was coming from my abdomen. Then another. I must have passed out and when I awoke again that same doctor was back. He said I would need surgery.

The next time I woke up, I was in a patient room and a nurse came to me and asked if I understood what that doctor had said to me. I was not able to think clearly. When I asked for my husband, I was told he had left the hospital. I asked for a phone, called home, and got no answer. Finally, I reached my mother and begged her to come to the hospital right away and bring Dad. People were asking me questions and I was too sick to make any decisions.

My next wake up was in a small room with a doctor examining my belly and saying, "I think I know what is wrong." The next time I gained consciousness, I was being wheeled into an operating room. My parents and Chet were there, and Mom handed me a pen saying I had to give approval for the surgery.

And then, after two long years, it was over.

I had an "intussusception," a condition where one part of the intestines telescope inside another part. I was lucky because when they finally opened me up, about four feet of intestines were gone, dead. I later was told I had come within hours of the intestines being destroyed, which likely would have ended my life. The reason no one could figure this out over two years I was told, was because the pain and the intussusception were not in the same place. It was referred pain, they said. When I was given a barium enema, the intestines would release, so when they took a picture, everything looked normal. I remember a gastroenterologist at Lahey Clinic saying I had to consider this was all in my head.

One day, I was with Dr. Tom Durant of Mass General Hospital, who had examined me at least once before. Dr. Durant was known as a brilliant diagnostician. Suddenly, as we were talking, I had an attack. He was ecstatic, as he had been just as baffled as his colleagues and thought now he would be better able to see what was wrong. The next thing I knew I was on a hospital table under dazzling lights, looking up at a half dozen white coats. Once my body calmed down, Dr. Durant, disappointed, said that they could not figure it out.

Apparently, an intussusception is not uncommon in two-year-old boys, but unheard of in a thirty-five-year-old woman.

Now recovering at Boston City Hospital, I was the happiest girl in the world. I would live.

But my joy was short lived as, with my parents in the room, a nurse came in and handed my mother an envelope with what we thought were my test results. Oddly, I was in the same room where my mother had been when she had her mastectomy. My mother said, "This must be for my daughter." Looking grave, the nurse replied, "No, Mrs. Sala-tich. These are your test results."

We held our breaths. Dear God. The cancer was back. And within a day Mom was in the hospital again, this time at MGH. Every night after work, Dad stopped to see me at Boston City and then Mom at Mass General. So many wonderful people had sent me flowers and each night I gave Dad some of them to take to Mom. What a nightmare.

God was not ready for me, but he was waiting for my wonderful mother, who did go home in February only to return on Father's Day in June, never to leave Mass General until September. We all visited every day, and I was absolutely convinced she would beat this.

On Labor Day weekend, we were all gathered in our Needham yard having dinner—my father, brother Bill, sister Jean, sister Sandra, Chet, and I—when we got the call.

God had sent his angels for our mother. She was fifty-nine.

That sucking sound returns as I write this, the feeling of life being drawn right out of you. I think part of each of us dies when we lose someone so important to us. I long for her to this day. She was my constant. She was always there.

When I was a child and there were no children in the neighbor-hood to play with and she was busy with the new baby, she bought me a doll. She helped me care for my "baby" as she tended to my sister Jean. She made me her ally. We were mothers together, she at twenty-six, I at four.

When I went to school and the kids made fun of me because I didn't speak fluent English, she would pull me into her lap, and hug-ging me, read to me in English.

Standing on a chair to reach the sink, I was her sous chef, her assis-tant in that dark basement laundry, holding the sheets as she ran them through the ringer. I was her purser in charge of the transfer tickets on the streetcar as she balanced two babies now.

When she fixed her hair and colored her lips, she would lend me her comb and her lipstick. I wanted to be just like her.

Many years later when I had my own baby, I had to mother alone. God must have needed Dawn Trbovich Salatich badly, but not before she suffered those years of chemo and radiation. I picture her still, sitting in the sunshine, without a wig, smiling as the breeze embraced her bald head. She was ever strong in spirit. So, we weren't sad. We knew she would beat this beast.

Even so, we were all scared. I remember lying beside her on one of her last days at home and asked her if she thought I would be a good mother. "Am I too engrossed in my work to be the mother you have been to us?"

I will remember forever her turning with difficulty to face me and with the assurance that was her mantra, said, "Of course, honey, you will be a wonderful mother." "Are you sure?" "Yes, Natalie, I am sure."

Well, my Lindsay Dawn, who would be born two years later, never knew her grandmother. But because of my mom, I know love, the kind of love that asks nothing in return, love that is ever present, the kind of love that you always want to share, with people, with animals, with nature, the kind of love that allows you to smile at your daughter, even when you are dying.

CHAPTER 14

Boston

The Mass Pike was still there. Route 128 looked just as it did the last time I saw it. You might think I had gone to Mars and was reentering Earth for the first time in decades.

We were returning to our home in Needham after my two-week hospital stay. Escaping death, narrowly, made me appreciative of every living thing. Even the traffic was comforting.

Recuperating from extensive abdominal surgery took time. Walking upstairs was painful. Yet I was careful to ease off the medication as quickly as possible because, to tell the truth, a dose of Demerol was too nice. I can see how people in pain get hooked on drugs; pain can be chronic and drugs can bring peace.

When I returned to the anchor desk after four months away, I was surprised at how uncomfortable I was. I felt self-conscious somehow and couldn't breathe properly. Whoever thinks about breathing? I would swallow to catch my breath, I guess. I couldn't figure it out. What was different now compared with the thousands of times I sat in the anchor chair before?

At one point, I actually thought I should leave television and see if I could get a job at the *Boston Globe* if they would have me. Eventually, after many months, this passed.

By the fall, with Mom's passing and my recovery, life started to return to normal, albeit on a very sad note. I took a real estate broker's license course on weekends to be able to help my father with the sale of his home. Dad was planning to move back to Chicago, where my siblings lived at the time. I wanted to buy the house. For me it was a way of keeping my mother alive, not to mention it was a much nicer home than we had. But Chet was adamant that it would be depressing to live there. I reluctantly acquiesced and we made plans to expand the house we had in Needham.

It was quite by circumstance that I spent my professional life in Boston. Yet, if I had a choice of any city in the country in which to work as a reporter, I would choose Boston: small enough to be called a town, big enough to be a city, important enough to be the hub of a six-state region.

Logan Airport and the commercial shipping terminals are the entry point for the region and much of the country. Boston's medical institutions, colleges and universities, and biotech companies are second to none. The city draws people from around the globe. The fishing industry feeds a nation.

It is a city of neighborhoods, each defined by its dominant immigrants, each still with its own character. The uniqueness of South Boston's Irish culture served as the theme of the Academy Award-winning *Good Will Hunting*. Ben Affleck and Matt Damon's portrayal of "Southie" boys is a classic. Both Affleck and Damon are Boston area boys, though not from Southie. They went to school together at Cambridge Rindge and Latin High School and lived two blocks from one another.

I remember going to Hollywood to report on our local stars just before the Academy Awards. I met Ben at a posh hotel outdoor terrace. It was too funny. Here I am a bit in awe of a star in the making and he, thinking I'm big stuff from home, is equally starstruck. What a hoot. Both Matt and Ben took their mothers as their dates when they collected their first Oscar.

The city boasts four major-league teams, all fodder for countless stories—especially the curse-breaking Boston Red Sox of 2004.

And too, the Boston Celtics, the Boston Bruins and the New England Patriots. What a privilege to watch the greats—Bob Cousy,

Bill Russell, Larry Bird, Bobby Orr, Phil Esposito, Kenny Hodge, Terry O'Reilly. And today the Patriots, without Number 12, perhaps the greatest quarterback of all time, Tom Brady. When Bill Belichick arrived in Boston as head coach in January of 2000, people wondered who he was. He rarely revealed his thoughts. I was intrigued and after checking with Mike Lynch to be sure I wasn't stepping on his toes, I called Belichick and asked if I could do a brief interview. He agreed and I met him during a practice session. I asked him about the big Miami game which the Patriots lost. He said after the game he gathered the team and passed around a shovel. As a team they dug a hole, then passed the game football around and buried it. That's it. That game is over, past tense, move on. He also told me he took the team to the Museum of Science in Boston where they watched the movie about the Shackleton epic, a team surviving a South Pole disaster. The film reinforced a Belichick mantra, teamwork. No one person can win the game. It's teamwork. As it turned out both stories were "news." As a reporter it is always fun to bring something new to light, especially when it is about your hometown team's new coach.

The lifeblood of Boston, incessantly pulsating through it all, is politics.

Four presidents and seven US House speakers hailed from the Bay State, including John McCormack and Thomas P. O'Neill, each of whom served five terms. Boston has had its share of colorful mayors, including James Michael Curley, who remained enormously popular even while on "sabbatical" in prison.

More recently, three men who won their party's nomination for president hailed from Boston: Governor Michael Dukakis, Governor Mitt Romney, and Senator John Kerry. And it was in Boston that Barack Obama was catapulted to the national stage.

In 2004, Senator Kerry chose the Boston Garden as the location for his convention. He asked a first-term senator from Illinois to be his keynote speaker. Barack Obama was young, handsome, fit, and black. And he hit it out of the arena. My eyes scanned the room. People watched with their mouths hanging open. Some were crying. Others clutched their chests. The crowd kept interrupting with applause. I caught sight of Ted Kennedy, smiling as broadly as I had ever seen him. I remembered Kennedy upstaging Jimmy Carter at Carter's convention. In my opinion, this newcomer had just done the same to John Kerry.

Security conscious, many would argue, overly so, the Secret Service and the Boston Police Department essentially shut down the city of Boston to host the Democrats' convention. It was a ghost town. Merchants were furious. I remember walking home from the North End to the South End that night after our broadcast around midnight and the only people I saw were Boston cops.

Kerry lost that election to George W. Bush, who was elected to a second term by three million votes. Four years later, Kerry's keynote speaker of 2004 would be the first black man to be elected president of the United States.

Most of the time, our political reporting involved the local pols. Beloved mayor Tom Menino was as colorful as they come. The press called him "Mumbles," as he didn't speak clearly. But his constituents understood him just fine.

Governor Frank Sargent was tall and lanky, with a ready smile and dry sense of humor. He had heart surgery, which needed a redo. In his hospital bed, we reporters asked him about the need for a second operation. Sargent, in his inimitable style, answered, "Well, that's what you get when you take the lowest bid."

Kevin White was the opposite. The can't-sit-still mayor was the embodiment of perpetual motion. His piercing blue eyes darting around the room, seemed to take everything in. He was near-sighted though and hated the look of his glasses. I remember shouting a question from the back of the room at City Hall during a press conference and he had an assistant bring me to him so he could see up close who had asked that question, which he did not like.

In the 60s, White had endured a bitter battle with Louise Day Hicks, the anti-busing candidate, and went on to serve as mayor for sixteen years. Early on, he wanted a decentralized administration, creating "little city halls," as did Mayor John Lindsay in New York. But eventually, White was drawn to the trappings of power and consolidated the machinery into his domain at *his* city hall.

White trained his innate energy on trying to create a world-class city, as he put it. He endorsed the multi-million-dollar Park Plaza Project, which originally was designed to be a multi-tower, varied-use project along the south side of the Boston Common and Boston Public Garden. There was opposition from just about everywhere. Unions, environmental groups, businesses, and residents who would be displaced were up in arms.

60 State Street was also a work in progress. White said no 60 State without Park Plaza. In the end, 60 State was built, with modifications. Park Plaza was not.

White was responsible for the creation of the new Quincy Market, adjacent to Faneuil Hall, home to great orations by Samuel Adams, Daniel Webster, and Frederick Douglass. White promised various incentives to businesses to get them to open shops at the Faneuil Hall Marketplace. It worked. To this day the food aisle is busy, but the retail shops have come and gone, and changed from small businesses to chains. It lost its unique charm.

Among the gifts of being a reporter in Boston is the reserve of rich history from which one can draw. Faneuil Hall, usually pronounced to rhyme with Daniel, is also pronounced to rhyme with panel. I was intrigued with the pronunciation. On a slow news day, my cameraman and I went to the Athenaeum, and with the help of the librarian looked it up. Imagine our surprise when it turns out Peter Faneuil pronounced it Funnel, as in tunnel. It made for a fun kicker on that night's newscast.

The Charles Restaurant, 75 Chestnut Street, at the base of Beacon Hill, was the hangout for pols, media, and athletes, and just about anyone who knew Tommy. Managed by the excitable, impatient, irascible, yet effusively welcoming Tommy Mirasola, the Charles became home base for Chet and me several nights a week during the late 70s,

Bob Bennett, founding general manager. He encouraged each of us to be the best we could be.

News Director Jim Thistle. A man of energy and vision.

Natalie's final broadcast.

The Boston Marathon. Joan Benoit Samuelson, Natalie, Mike Lynch, and Billy Rogers.

Nat and Chet celebrating a successful charity event.

1980's news team.
Reproduced by permission of WCVB Channel 5 Boston.

Chet and Nat with Jack Hynes.
Reproduced by permission of WCVB Channel 5 Boston.

Dick Albert, Natalie, Chet, and Mike Lynch; friends on and off the air.

Nat and Chet, co-anchors for over twenty years.

Nat and Dick Albert.

"Five is Family."

Dick Albert, Tom Ellis,
Don Gillis, Natalie, and Chet.
Reproduced by permission of WCVB
Channel 5 Boston.

Natalie accepting the Governor's Award at the Regional Emmys.
Reproduced by permission of WCVB Channel 5 Boston.

Natalie and Jennifer Haskins. It was love at first sight.

Natalie and Master Chef Jasper White. "What Your Cookbook Doesn't Tell You."

Anchoring live coverage of the Tall Ships in Boston.

With *60 Minutes* correspondent Mike Wallace accepting Emmy awards.
Reproduced by permission of WCVB Channel 5 Boston.

Nat and her baseball hero, Ted Williams, hosting a fundraiser for lupus.

With Red Sox President Larry Lucchino in 2004. The curse was broken!

In Hollywood with Ben Affleck, *Good Will Hunting* Oscar winner.

Fenway 2007. Throwing out the ceremonial first pitch at a Yankees-Red Sox game.

Anthony Athanas's ninetieth birthday,
Pier 4 Boston.

Natalie delivering the 1990 UNH
commencement speech.

John Williams, America's most prolific
composer.

With new Patriots' coach Bill Belichick.
Reproduced by permission of WCVB Channel 5 Boston.

Riding on the Concorde's first US flight from
Florida to Boston.

With Speaker of the US House of Representatives Thomas "Tip" O'Neill and Ted Williams.

Boston Symphony Orchestra Director Seiji Ozawa and Boston Pops Maestro Arthur Fiedler.

Cooking with Julia Child on her last day in Cambridge.

Nat's mom, Dawn, helping with the graduation cape at Babson College. No kinder soul.

Natalie's dad—from cab driver to Gillette president.

Tramp, bringing home the morning paper.

Natalie with her maternal grandmother, "Baba" Trbovich, Chicago.

Aunt "Teta" Rista, on her one hundredth birthday. Natalie's lifetime hero!

Breezy, who sat beneath the anchor desk.

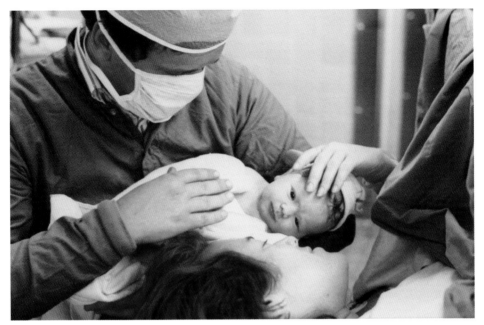

It's a Girl! Lindsay Dawn Curtis enters the world.

Proud and happy parents with Lindsay Dawn.

Lindsay and her mom cheering on the Heart Association's "Go Red" campaign.

Lindsay and sisters Dawn and Dana.

With Lindsay at a horse show.

To: Natalie,
G Bu

Salem State College Lecture Series. Natalie with President George H. W. Bush and CBS's Walter Cronkite.

Talking marathons and Bosnia with President Bill Clinton.

Texas Governor George W. Bush and Producer Linda Polach, at the Republican National Convention in California.

Natalie with candidates Joe Biden, Hillary Clinton, and Barack Obama in the 2008 presidential primary.

Olivia and James,
"Baba's" treasures.

Lindsay, Eric, James, Olivia, and Ozzy.

before our responsibilities included the 11 o'clock news and before our daughter was born in 1981.

For reporters like us, it was a great place to get the scoop on people, bills, feuds, etc. Everyone respected "off the record." And while never violating that trust, information gleaned from those casual conversations proved invaluable in gaining perspective on many stories.

There was a basic trust and respect among reporters and politicians back then. The vitriol of today did not exist. Partisanship was respectable and respected. Reporters were expected to be fair. Our mission was to deliver information, not our opinions. Most people I speak with today wish it were still that way.

Tommy treated everyone as the most important person in the world. The food was great. The booths which he reserved for his regulars were intimate. One actually had a drape in front of it for people who didn't want to be seen.

One colorful man who knew Tommy was Joe Savino, owner of several entertainment venues in the Combat Zone, home of pimps and prostitutes. Joe was married to Betty Biddle, formerly the hot stripper at the Old Howard Theater in Scully Square, now City Hall Plaza. Coincidently, Biddle was the name of a wealthy family in Pennsylvania. They did not like their name being paraded on a burlesque stage and reportedly got her to change her stage name to Sylvia Star. We knew her as Becky.

The Pilgrim Theater originally was the Grand Olympia Theater, and in the early 1900s could seat 2,500 people. By the late 60s, it had become home to sex films, and in the 70s, Savino tried to bring back burlesque. Chesty Morgan was his star for a time, but the big story coming out of the Pilgrim was Fanny Foxe and the powerful House Ways and Means Chairman, Wilbur Mills of Arkansas.

In October of 1974, Mills and Fanny had to be fished out of the Potomac in Washington. Reportedly, cops stopped Mills car, driven by someone else. Mills was in the back with three strippers from the Silver Slipper Club in DC. Fanny reportedly bolted from the car and jumped into the Potomac. Mills jumped in after her. The story dominated national news for weeks.

And in Boston, the story took on a sequel. Billing herself as the Washington Tidal Basin Bombshell, and commanding $3,000 a week, Annabella Battistella was the highest paid stripper in the country.

Joe Savino brought Fanny Foxe to the Pilgrim. Wilbur Mills could not stay away from her. One night, Mills visited her in her dressing room and then, totally drunk, he decided to join Fanny on stage. That did it. Mills was subsequently removed from his chairmanship and chose not to seek reelection.

Savino was a frequent visitor to the Charles. You could never pay the tab if you were at his table. One night, he asked Tommy to get some money out of his jacket which he had hung on a hook near the front door. Mirasola came back screaming at him as only one Italian can do to another. He shoved a fistful of money at his friend, incredulous that he would leave so much cash where anyone could have stolen it.

Another night, Savino didn't have any money but still would not let any of us pay. He called Becky and directed her to a particular shoebox in his closet. Poor Becky had been ready for bed and had to bring dear Joe his shoebox only to be chastised for bringing the wrong one. This one had thousand-dollar bills. He wanted the one with hundreds.

Perhaps prompted by Savino's stories, I asked a couple of Boston cops working the Combat Zone if I could ride with them to try and understand who these "streetwalkers" were. Newspaper stories about pimps and prostitutes were common. What I saw were young girls reaching right into the cars when they slowed. Who were these girls?

With the help of one of the officers, I secured some private time with a young woman who struck me as quiet and very sad. She had no family and no money. She was at the mercy of her pimp, a man she feared more than contracting any disease from her clients. She did not see any future for herself and was resigned to what she figured would be the end of her life here in the street. We aired her story, keeping her anonymous.

It is so easy to label people, and I wanted our viewers to see at least this one girl as a person. Every life is a story.

Among the regulars at Tommy's was Bill Harrington, Channel 5's statehouse reporter. Unassuming, bright, amiable, Bill knew everyone on the hill. And he was a character. A bachelor, Bill had a different lady for different activities. He explained that it was unreasonable to expect one woman to enjoy all the different activities he did. So, one woman was his companion skiing, another his date for the theater, etc. He was up front with each of them about his other dates.

At WHDH, Bill was Bozo, then Nozo, on the very popular kids' show, *Romper Room*. He was married to "Miss Jean" and together with Frank Avruch was another example of the multi- talented people WCVB inherited from WHDH.

Harrington lived in a modest apartment on Beacon Street across from the Boston Common and had a roof garden. He would invite a bunch of us to the roof, have us pick our vegetables, and bring them in to the kitchen. He would prepare the main course. The guests did the dishes.

One of his specialties was a grilled sirloin which he seasoned and then slathered with powdered sugar to make it burn. His charcoal was red hot and he would add a small log to make it even hotter. That was the secret; the sugar burned off, searing the meat. It was a fabulous dinner under the stars on Beacon Hill. Bill was a close friend. I learned a lot from him. He was an honest reporter, no bias, no taking sides or trying to do someone in. He had the earned respect of the hill. Sadly, he died of cancer when he was only seventy-five.

Bob Caulfield had been the news director at WHDH. Chet knew him well, having worked for him at the old Channel 5. Caulfield was thin, wiry, impatient, a library of information. Chain smoking, a recovering alcoholic, Bob read basically every word in every newspaper he could find. If he talked about something and you didn't know your facts, hadn't read that particular story, look out.

That said, he was a good man. I learned a lot about reading newspapers from him and also how to read the tea leaves, that is, deciphering truth from fiction. "Be skeptical until you have proved you needn't be." He too died too early.

Years earlier, my first encounter professionally with Caulfield—everyone called him Caulfield—was not so friendly.

That very first year at WCVB-TV, I was assigned to cover the fifth congressional district. John Kerry, the Vietnam veteran turned anti-war advocate was making his maiden journey into electoral politics. He was young, my age, tall, Lincolnesque. He talked fast, walked fast, devoured a conversation. He was sure of himself. "This war is wrong."

My first interview with him was at the Charles, where Tommy secured us a table in a quiet corner. Kerry had an air about him, confidence maybe. But in the Fifth District, some saw it as elitism. No one used that word, but in this blue-collar town, people would say, "He thinks he's better than we are." "He's not a patriot." The very eloquent anti-war speech in Congress came to haunt him.

It didn't help that the White House, under President Nixon and his attorney Charles Colson, pushed the Kerry anti-American image. The *Lowell Sun* was against him. The combination hurt.

If Kerry was worried that night of the election, he hid it well. I was sitting at the Sheraton Hotel coffee shop with Kerry's campaign guy, Mark Trbovich.

We each were looking over our own informal polling data and at the same time we looked across the table at each other, both realizing the same thing—Kerry had lost. It wasn't 8 o'clock yet. Mark bolted from the table. I found a phone booth and called the station and told the producers, Kerry would lose the Fifth District to Republican Paul Cronin.

Caulfield who probably knew more about politics than I would ever know, was running our campaign coverage. When I told him Kerry would lose, Caulfield berated me, calling me a know-nothing rookie and a few other compliments. I finally got the powers-that-be to promise me, they would not call the race for Kerry. At least give me that much. As I walked into the Sheraton ballroom, fitted out with the usual balloons and screaming music and oversized TV screens, Channel 5 came on the air. Silence. Anchor Hynes or Henning called the race for Kerry. The crowd cheered but Kerry's key people knew he had lost and looked at me as though I were an idiot.

I was embarrassed. This may have been my first race, but I had worked that district for six weeks. And Kerry's own man confirmed my evaluation. Caulfield eventually apologized and became a good friend. Chet asked him to be his best man at our wedding.

We all missed the camaraderie of the Charles after Tommy left. He died inexplicably following elective surgery shortly afterward. New owners named the restaurant 75 Chestnut, but for most of us, The Charles died with Tommy.

For all the politics we covered, entering the political arena myself was not on my radar screen. My brother often suggested I should run for the US Senate, but I didn't give it much thought. I liked being a reporter.

Then one day, I arrived home to find several men from the political world in Massachusetts standing in our family room talking with Chet. I wondered why they were there. They said they came to ask me to run as a Republican for the US Senate against Ted Kennedy. This was 1993. Well, that was right out of the blue!

They felt Kennedy, despite his popularity, was vulnerable at the time, and in their opinion, I had a good chance of beating him. Never mind that Massachusetts is as Democratic a state as any in the union, never mind there is not a single Republican in Congress from the Bay State in either branch, never mind that the state legislature is overwhelmingly Democratic. We used to joke that Republicans in the Bay State could hide out in a phone booth.

They said I would not have to hold a single fundraiser. One of their group would pay for the entire campaign, whatever it took. That meant I would be beholden to no one, including that one donor.

Campaign finance reform and term limits were hot topics of the day. I did agree with the need for both. Many saw both houses of Congress as exclusive clubs. It was hard to defeat an incumbent. Lobbyists were running the show. It seemed that for too many on Capitol Hill, money and power trumped public service.

I had learned some people run for congress to gain the access to benefit them as a lobbyist where they could make a lot of money. What if we had a law that dictated a ten-year wait before one could make such a move? What if Congress passed a law that kept political contributions to a limit that could not be bypassed by loopholes?

The ultimate correction would be term limits. Two six-year terms for US Senate and three two-year terms for the House was one suggestion.

I was not a politician. I was neither a Republican nor a Democrat. What chance did I really have, first of winning, and secondly of effecting changes if I did win? This group actually thought I could win. It was hard to fathom. The honeymoon period would help. A local Boston reporter beats the Lion of the Senate. There would be a lot of publicity for a while and an opportunity to push for term limits and campaign finance reform. How successful could a novice be?

Chet and I talked about it. He was strongly opposed, primarily as it would dynamically change our lives. I was worried about leaving a young teen for long periods of time as I traveled to Washington. And what did I know about being a US Senator? Once again, I wondered with whom I could consult.

In the end, I declined.

As it turned out, Mitt Romney did challenge Kennedy that year. I covered the debate between the two at Faneuil Hall. The debate was divided in two distinct sections. First, reporters would ask the questions in a traditional timed debate. Second, the candidates would question each other.

I thought Romney scored better in the first part but blew it in the second. Then in the town meeting later in the campaign, he seemed unable to connect with the people, while Kennedy was in his element.

Watching Romney carefully, I thought, *could I have done this?* I remember feeling I would have been very nervous in the debate, but probably comfortable in the town meeting.

My "At Home" interviews with Romney and Kennedy that year were revealing. The Romney home was a buzz of activity with his five sons. Ann Romney is warm and friendly. She suffered from MS but felt it did not inhibit her as her husband ran for office. Romney is measured when he speaks. He smiles and laughs easily. He is intelligent, is data driven, and sees things in practical terms. Logic trumps emotion. As a Mormon, right and wrong are clear to him. As the son of a Michigan governor and presidential contender, George Romney, politics seemed a natural career.

Gathered in his kitchen, as I was preparing to leave, I asked him what he planned to do about the group of Kennedy supporters who were arriving the next day from Indiana. They were a group of men who had lost their jobs when Romney's investment company, Bain Capital, bought their company and sold it. Romney said he had no plans to do anything as this did not involve him.

"But these workers believe it definitely involves you. They feel you cost them their jobs."

Romney saw it as a business transaction, not anything personal.

It is not appropriate for me to give advice to a candidate. With everyone in the room staring at me, wondering why I asked this question, I filled the silence by simply saying, "I might rethink that."

The Indiana contingent had its desired effect. In a carefully orchestrated campaign move by the Kennedy people, Romney was seen as anti-worker. He lost to Kennedy by 17 percent and Kennedy went on to serve a sixth term in the US Senate. I made an appointment to see Romney after the campaign and asked if he thought he had made a mistake in not addressing the workers' concerns. He said, simply, "No, I don't."

Six years later, Romney would go on to be the governor of Massachusetts, instituting what would be called Romney Care. Some saw it as the precursor to Obamacare, which didn't sit well with some Republicans. In 2012, Romney won his party's nomination for president. He was defeated by a popular vote margin of 4 percent to incumbent Barack Obama. As of this writing, Romney is a US Senator from Utah.

As you might expect, Boston is home to many immigrants who found success in America. Among them is Anthony Athanas, who came to America at the age of five from Albania.

The youngster who earned a few dollars stoking coal stoves eventually created one of the largest grossing restaurants in the country. I came to know and admire Anthony, another immigrant embodying the American dream. He, like my dad, was honored with the Horatio Alger Award. At one time, he employed some eight hundred people at his restaurants. He was proud to be able to give people a job, but some of his employees would say, be glad you are his friend and not an employee. I'm told he could be tough, expecting perfection. I guess I could relate to that. One of my favorite stories he shared involved an idea he had to get more customers. He closed his restaurant on a Saturday night, as I recall, and invited all the Boston cab drivers and their wives to a multi-course dinner as his guests. He then opened a coffee stand just outside his front doors for the cabbies. Now where do you think those cabbies took their riders at Logan when customers asked for a restaurant suggestion.

Pier 4 became the place for pols, the rich and famous and for anyone who loved great fish and hot popovers. Chet and I went often, and I was honored to be asked to be the MC for Anthony's ninetieth birthday party. Anyone who was anyone in Boston was there.

Jimmy Doulos, another immigrant, gave Anthony his best competition. Jimmy came from Greece at the age of fifteen. His hole-in-the wall lunchroom became the celebrated Jimmy's Harborside just up the street from Pier 4, attracting a similar crowd of pols, athletes, businessmen and media folk. For my money, Jimmy's had the best Greek salad and fresh scallops in the city. Chet and I loved the place. I remember back in the 70s, waitresses in the bar area telling me they made $200 a night. I couldn't help but wish I had worked there rather than the Red Coach Grill in Sudbury, where on a good night I was lucky to take home fifty bucks. After Jimmy died, only in his early 70s, his family continued with the restaurant. Years later, his grandchildren tried to reinvent it, but in the end, Jimmy's closed.

Now that whole area is a crowded second city within the city of Boston. Some call it the Innovation District, others, the Seaport, home to many restaurants, most of them chains. I for one miss the charm and camaraderie of those two uniquely Boston institutions.

I suppose many people share a pride of their hometown. I had the distinct privilege of representing my city on a national television show which included anchors from around the country. I remember extolling many of Boston's distinctions. It was a point of pride for me and I felt lucky to do it. Wherever I land, I think, for me, Boston will always be home.

CHAPTER 15

Cooking

Anthony's and Jimmy's Harborside excepted, Boston was not known as a city of restaurants in the 70s. To be sure, every neighborhood had its popular eateries, often catering to its particular ethnic group. The North End, for example, was known for its Italian food, pizza, "gravy," and bakeries.

As I remember, there was one gourmet restaurant, 21 Broad, and then years later Jasper's. And then seemingly overnight, Boston became a mecca of culinary innovation. Chefs became rock stars. Now there is a plethora of restaurants, both chains and originals.

My mother used to say, "If you know how to read, you will never be lonely." She was right. You can transport yourself to anywhere in the galaxy, meet interesting people through biographies, introduce yourself to other people's ideas, learn more about history or among the fiction collection, get lost in spy novels.

I learned something similar. If you learn to cook, you will never be bored. When you are alone, cook something. Make it up. Pour a glass of wine and turn on some music. You will be fully engrossed. When your nerves need calming, head for the kitchen. Make your favorite food. I just made two loaves of bread. (I had to take a break from writing this book.) When you need to take your mind off something, check your stock. Be creative. It will take all your mind and push that other stuff aside. If you like your creation, write it down as you might not remember it next time. My niece, Nicole, saved many of mine, thank goodness.

My daughter, Lindsay, is finding joy in experimenting as well.

When she asked me to help her learn, I said, "Open the pantry, the refrigerator, what do you see? Anything interesting? Now close your eyes, breath through your nose. Are you starting to smell something inviting? Finally, move your tongue across your lips. Taste anything? Sauté an onion and garlic. Go for it."

I love to cook, especially creating a dish. I usually follow a new recipe the first time and then likely will alter it, simply for the fun of experimenting. Many of my friends used to ask me how I could make this or that. "Where do you start?" they would ask. So, I decided to create a video teaching the techniques of cooking and to dedicate it to my mom, because that's where the love started.

My father used to say Mom didn't know how to cook when he married her. Well, true or not, she taught herself to be a great cook. With little money, few fresh ingredients, she could turn nothing into something we loved to eat. She did know how to cook the Serbian foods. Her mother must have taught her. Especially difficult is working with filo dough. We used to make our own. If you ever want an exercise in frustration, try stretching a grapefruit-sized ball of dough across a big dining room table. It wouldn't take much to stretch it too much and at times you had to start all over again. And to add to it, the weather played a big role. Damp weather, dry weather, you had to adjust your stretch. Then you had to slice it into sheets and keep the sheets separated. Finally, you line the baking pan with eight-to-ten sheets separated by melted butter which you sprinkled on each sheet using a fork. The center was filled with a cheese/spinach mixture (make sure you squeeze every ounce of water out of the spinach) or with fruit, depending on the dish.

I tried this when we lived in Bangkok. Impossible. It was way too hot.

She also made bread. We did not have a stand mixer, so all the kneading was done by hand. When I was at UNH, a few girlfriends and I decided to impress our dates by making dinner. I volunteered the bread. Well, if you dropped my bread on the floor, I think it would have made its way down to the basement. I took a lot of ribbing. I asked mom about that when I came home. We went over the recipe. "Did you remember to let the dough rise a second time?" "What? Mom, it wasn't on the recipe you sent me." "Oh, perhaps I forgot to write that down. But you should know, after all we've made it together." Live and learn.

What I took from our time in the kitchen was the fun it was to invent the meal. How about a little of this, or a little of that? Way better than following a recipe, is creating one.

I asked Jasper White, a master chef, if he would like to make the video with me. He agreed. It is a lot easier to learn cooking techniques by watching rather than reading instructions, so we created a video encyclopedia of techniques. I wanted to do this in my kitchen, as I thought it would be more user-friendly than a restaurant kitchen. We used my old pots and pans and utensils. I laid out a list of topics to be covered from carving a turkey to braising a stew. We did not work from a script.

Jasper's gourmet restaurant in the North End of Boston, Jasper's, was the place we and many friends went on special occasions and actually any time we wanted a unique meal. We used to dress for it. It was that special. His duck salad was over the top. I once asked him why he would share his recipes in a book. He said it was the best way to protect his authorship of them.

For the video, I wrote up a "To Do" list of sorts. We winged it for a week and had a ball. I hired a crew to shoot it and then, renting space at a nearby edit facility, I edited it, working several hours every morning before heading to work. It took a lot longer than I anticipated and stretched even my limits to the edge. But we got it done and called it, "What Your Cookbook Doesn't Tell You."

Long before cooking videos and TV cooking shows were popular, people relied on cookbooks for recipes. Those recipes rarely included techniques. So, for example, if your recipe said: "Sauté the veal medallions in clarified butter, deglaze and reduce," you might be stuck if you didn't understand those instructions. Our video offers the way to sauté, deglaze, and reduce.

Men really appreciated the turkey-carving lesson, as they are often called upon at Thanksgiving to do the honors. Rather than hack away on Mom's favorite tablecloth, Jasper suggests you parade the beautiful bird intact before the crowd then disappear into the kitchen to carve it.

Even men who don't cook are often called upon to grill the entrée over an outdoor charcoal grill. Jasper had great advice for making charcoal fires allowing for different temperatures on the grill. And he had some tips on judging the internal temperature of the meat using your fingers. Now many people have gas grills, but many of the same techniques apply.

We also went "shopping" for fish, meat and produce. He taught us how to check for freshness. Fish for example, should not have a fishy odor. That comes with age. And did you know, leaving fish in a hot car for even one hour can age it three days?

The video is packed with that kind of useful information.

Jasper and I conducted live demonstrations to sell the videos. We drew crowds at Filene's, Bloomingdale's, Jordan's, and others. Interestingly, men loved watching the video as much or more than the women.

Our effort was a lot of work but fun. Unfortunately, I never sold enough to cover my costs. Technology changed, forcing me to transfer from VHS to DVD and now I still need someone to digitize it! Still, I'm proud of it and happy I paid tribute to my mother. If you can get past my hairdo, it still has value.

Jasper decided he had enough of gourmet, which involves getting to the restaurant early in the morning to make the sauces and staying late at night to finish his masterpieces. He opened the opposite kind of restaurant, Summer Shack, and eventually had a chain of them.

One year, an independent producer approached me and asked if I would be interested in working with him on a TV show he created called *Food New England*. Each half hour involved cooking at a famous chef's home, then having a nutritionist give us the facts about the food, and a wine expert give us his picks to go with the dish.

I loved the whole concept and working with the chefs was a treat. They, of course, rarely cook at home, so it was funny to watch them trying to maneuver in unfamiliar space. Plus, their interviews were enlightening. As I recall, Julia Child and Jacques Pepin had opposite techniques for risotto. We included most of the restaurant chefs in the greater Boston area. What a treat for me to meet and cook with such a talented group.

When Lindsay turned thirty, my gift to her was a cooking lesson with Gordon Hamersley at his bistro in the South End of Boston. We learned some of his trademark fish recipes and a few techniques from a master. Gordon was known for his famous garlic-roasted chickens. Combined with the roasted potatoes, it was my favorite dish. Gordon was kind enough to join me at the Nantucket Wine & Food Festival one year, and together we presented some of his favorite dishes to an enthusiastic crowd.

One year, Channel 5's *Chronicle* program offered me a chance to produce cooking shows while they let their staff off for vacation. I invited people like the enthusiastic Chris Schlesinger to cook with me and, in his case, share his knowledge of grilling. If you love to grill on charcoal, an hour with Chris Schlesinger is a major treat. He has a number of cookbooks, my favorite of which is *License to Grill*.

Todd English was a creator of the unusual. He would mix ingredients I might not have considered compatible. We prepared a salad involving greens, grilled vegetables, sauteed garlic and onions and a vinaigrette. It seemed complicated but tasted terrific.

When Julia Child decided to leave her longtime home in Cambridge, Massachusetts, I called and asked if she would spend some time with me so her many fans could bid her adieu. She agreed. Our timing couldn't have been better, as the day after our interview the Smithsonian Institute arrived to take her kitchen to Washington. Julia truly was one of a kind. She didn't learn to cook until her husband was sent to France, and she told me she took up cooking because she didn't have anything to do and was bored. So, she learned to cook and took her knowledge to new heights, becoming the first woman to use television to teach those interested how to cook. Her large frame, unusual voice, and devil may care attitude brought her lasting fame. Julia Child authored many cookbooks, of which the first, *Mastering the Art of French Cooking*, is a classic.

During that final interview, I asked her why she was moving to Santa Barbara, California. She said, "To get my kids off my back."

Then in her late eighties, they were worried about her living alone at her age, so she signed up for an assisted living place of sorts. She had no need for assistance, she explained, but the children will be mollified.

When the country paid tribute to her on her passing, I was thrilled to be able to offer Gordon Hammersley a copy of my video of that final interview in her kitchen for him to play for his customers that evening. Gordon's restaurant was a favorite of the Cambridge crowd, so it was the right venue.

Cooking is about more than eating; it captures your senses, titillates your creativity and engages your time. It can make your day.

I love to read cookbooks, especially the introductions where the author shares her or his thoughts about food. There is much to be learned there. For example, Schlesinger in his introduction to *License to Grill*, talks about differences among cooks and authors in their relationship with food and cooking. He says that some cooks stress technique, others the quality of ingredients but that he asks, "Was it fun? To me that is the most crucial part of any food experience."

That speaks to me.

CHAPTER 16

America Held Hostage

The year 1979 is hard for many people to forget. The energy crisis of 1973 returned, bringing OPEC into everybody's garage once again. Gas lines were long, gas was rationed, and now Americans would be held hostage in a prolonged Iranian drama that would cost Jimmy Carter his presidency.

Most Americans had probably never heard of the Organization of Petroleum Exporting Countries, then Iran, Iraq, Kuwait, Saudi Arabia, and Venezuela. The 1973 oil crisis developed when OPEC decided to retaliate against the US for its military support of Israel in the 1973 Arab Israeli war. The Arab nations were still demanding a return of the land Israel previously acquired in the '67 war. The dispute over that land continues to this day. OPEC decided it would reduce oil production by 5 percent every month until Israel returned the land. The price of oil shot from $3.00 a barrel to $12.00, more than compensating for the decreased production. In the US, a national 55 mph speed limit was imposed to save energy, and Americans came to realize how dependent our foreign policy was on foreign oil.

Environmentalists began a concerted effort to find an alternative to oil, and by 1977, under the Carter administration, the Department of Energy was created. Today, with fracking, we now produce our own oil and natural gas and even export it, freeing us from the shackles of OPEC and others. But now, we are moving toward solar and wind. People are still afraid of nuclear power. The need for energy only grows.

In 1979, Iranians, fed up with the Shah, Mohammed Raza Shah Pahlavi, revolted. The Ayatollah Ruhollah Khomeini, an elderly cleric, became both the spiritual and political leader of Iran. President Jimmy Carter neither supported the Shah nor embraced the opposition. The Shah, suffering from cancer and then exiled in Mexico, sought medical help. President Carter allowed him into the US for humanitarian reasons. That enraged Iranian revolutionaries.

On November 4, 1979, a group of Iranian students seized the American embassy in Tehran and held sixty-six Americans hostage. Thirteen were released, then one more when he became ill, but for fifty-two Americans, life would be hell for 444 days. In the US, we watched the nightly update on ABC at 11:30 PM on what became known as *Nightline* with Ted Koppel. Again, Americans were being reminded of our dependence on foreign oil.

President Carter's effort to free the hostages failed, costing American lives. Carter was at the nadir of his political career. His standing with the American public was so low, a fellow Democrat sought to challenge him for the nomination to a second term, Senator Edward Kennedy of Massachusetts.

Kennedy had some baggage of his own. The tragedy of Chappaquiddick, ten years before, remained on the table. And while he and his family were beloved in Boston, he was not so popular in other parts of the country. Many saw him as privileged and not in tune with their lives. Contrasted with President Carter's upbringing in a house with no heat, Kennedy was of another class.

But Carter was vulnerable. He seemed not in control, uncertain.

Kennedy and his wife Joan were thought to be estranged. She struggled with alcoholism, enduring a vicious cycle of victories and failures.

Seeing this as one part of the story that was local and germane to Kennedy's presidential ambitions, I like many journalists across the country, sought an interview with her. After about four months of trying, I finally got the call that she would talk with me. The person who called said that Mrs. Kennedy trusted that I would be fair.

I met her first at Lesley College (Lesley University since 2000), where she was studying for her master's degree in education.

She was a little nervous, but open and friendly, and she seemed sharp.

We were together an hour or so as I tried to get a sense of her, but I felt we needed more time. I had not yet asked about her husband, whether they were living together, how she felt about stories about him with other women, "Chappy." It just didn't feel right at that moment. And truth be told, I was uncomfortable asking. I'm a private person, and I respect other people's privacy, but it was a legitimate story. Americans had a right to know if there would be a first lady in the White House if her husband won. And somehow it seemed important to know if she was OK with it all.

I asked if we could meet again and she agreed, this time at her apartment on Beacon Street in Boston. Noticing a magnificent baby grand, I asked if she would play for me. She did and I could see her relax. She is a talented musician. We talked about family and her children, and when it seemed appropriate, I asked those questions.

She opened up about her addiction, about the hurt regarding stories about her husband, and about the possibility of her being first lady. She spoke passionately about her children, so proud of each of their accomplishments in life. Could she handle that very public role? Would she live in the White House? Could she beat the beast, alcoholism? She thought she could.

I cut a rough draft of the multi-hour interview and drove to New Hampshire, where we were in the middle of covering the first in the nation presidential primary. I showed it to our news director, Jim Thistle, and asked what he thought. I hoped he might give me eight minutes, which is an eternity in a thirty-minute newscast. He watched it carefully, turned off the tape machine and called the station. "We're wiping the newscast and airing Natalie's interview for the entire broadcast." The rough cut was about nineteen-minutes long. I begged him not to do it. It was a rough cut not at all ready for air and did it really deserve the entire newscast? I was appalled.

But say what you will, Thistle knows a news story when he sees it, jump cuts and all.

Here I was in Manchester, New Hampshire, as the primary was beginning. I was surrounded by all these national stars of television and politics. I was uneasy. After the newscast, I asked Thistle if he thought he had done the right thing. "Did you see anyone doing anything but watching us?"

But it wasn't until the next day when the networks were calling, asking for permission to air parts of our interview, that I realized we had the interview everyone else in the country had also tried to get. I have to say, that felt good.

Many years later, in 2011, Joan and Ted's daughter, Kara, died of lung cancer at the age of fifty-one. I read the news in the paper and felt that gut horror any mother might feel. I was walking through the South End of Boston and rounding a corner, I saw two women coming toward me. I was startled because one of the women, with a scarf around her head, looked like Joan. When she looked up, I knew it was she. I wasn't sure what to do. So, I asked quietly, "Joan?" She looked at me, tentative at first, then hugged me. Neither of us wanted to let go. She had buried her daughter just the day before. I remember walking away in tears and somehow feeling grateful for that moment.

While some saw Joan as a liability in Kennedy's quest for the White House, it was Kennedy himself who lost it. Roger Mudd of CBS News conducted the first personal interview of the campaign at the family compound in Hyannis. Mudd asked a straightforward question, "Why do you want to be President?" Kennedy rambled and didn't answer, at least not to anyone's satisfaction. If you wanted to postulate that the campaign ended there, I would agree.

How interesting that ten years later, when I would ask a candidate who wanted to be governor of Massachusetts, how he might describe himself in terms of his strengths and weaknesses, Dr. John Silber could not answer that simple question. It had the same result.

In August of 1980, Madison Square Garden was on steroids. This was my first political party convention. We were on the air every day for four days on every newscast with convention news.

Edward M. Kennedy had just delivered the speech of his life. "...And the dream shall never die." Jimmy Carter had been nominated for reelection, but he did not have his party in his corner. That night, EMK controlled the hearts of those at the convention. And one could argue that sentiment killed President Carter's chance for a second term. He would get whipped by Ronald Reagan.

Two moments remain with me after all these years. The first was Kennedy's speech, especially the conclusion: "For all those whose cares have been our concern, the work goes on, the cause endures, the hope still lives, and the dream shall never die." In the opinion of many, it was his best. It made delegates almost sick that he wasn't the nominee.

As someone quipped, "Amazing how much they love you when you're done."

I also remember after President Carter delivered his acceptance speech, he waited on stage for what seemed like an eternity. I later learned it was actually twenty minutes before Ted Kennedy joined him for the traditional unity salute. Not only did Kennedy embarrass his party's president by making him wait, but when he finally arrived on stage to a long and loud applause, he never joined Carter in that unity gesture.

I couldn't help but wonder, what was Kennedy trying to prove? And where were Carter's people? Why did they allow him to stand on that stage so long? It was embarrassing. If Mr. Carter was looking for unity, he didn't get it.

One personal moment, I will never forget. It had been an exhausting, however exhilarating, week. By midnight, our duties came to an end with our reports on an extended edition of the 11 PM news.

Tired as we were, Jack Hynes and I and our crew were ready for a beer. Plus, it was my birthday. I mentioned to Jack that earlier in the week, Speaker Tip O'Neill invited me to join him at the Sign of the

Dove where he was holding court with a few friends. It was now about 1 AM so I thought maybe it was too late. Jack suggested we drive by and see. So, we did. The restaurant was clearly closed but we knocked on the door anyway. The darkness of the night exploded into bright lights, music, laughter, and the unmistakable voice of the speaker. "Natly dahling." He never did get that second *a*. Suddenly I had a drink in my hand, was hoisted to the top of the baby grand, and Tip was leading the room in a raucous version of "Happy Birthday." Without a doubt, my most memorable birthday ever.

CHAPTER 17
Lindsay Dawn

I didn't know it then, but likely I was pregnant during that convention. Chet and I had been hoping for a baby from the time we married in 1975. In the fall of 1980, I visited my doctor and at the age of thirty-seven got the news I had prayed for.

I had a speaking engagement that afternoon at a Jimmy Fund Luncheon but figured I had just enough time to run across Route 9 in Chestnut Hill to buy a pair of booties. I raced back to Needham and asked the guard at the guard shack in the parking lot to ask Chet to come out and give him this box with the booties. I hid behind a car to watch Chet's reaction. He opened the box and smiled broadly looking around for me. We hugged and I asked him to promise not to tell anyone, as I was only six weeks pregnant. He promised. With that I raced up to the North Shore for my speech. I was dying to share my good news, but I held back. Chet returned to the newsroom and told everyone.

That night, concluding the 11 o'clock news which I co-anchored with Tom Ellis, Tom made a thinly veiled reference to my being pregnant. I wanted to kill him. And there began the longest public pregnancy ever.

My poor colleagues had to deal with people asking every day for the next seven months, "Did Natalie have the baby yet?"

And it became national news. Jacqueline Smith of the popular TV show *Charlie's Angels* was also pregnant. Smith, a year or two younger than I, was the cover of a *Time* magazine story on older women having babies. At thirty-seven, I was among others included as examples. One night after the late news, a talk show host at a radio station in the northwest called to ask what it was like to be my age expecting a child. I think I gave some snappy response like, pretty good for a woman over eighty! I probably just wished I had said that. I'm sure this sounds archaic today as women well into their forties have babies, but then it was unusual.

In fact, I was being cared for by a doctor, Henry Klapholz, who gave up mechanical engineering to become an obstetrician specializing in "older" pregnancies.

As a woman anchor, I was in the minority. To be pregnant and on the air was novel. And of course, the baby was late, by my calculations two weeks late when during the 6 o'clock news with me sitting between Chet and Tom Ellis, I felt a pain. I wrote the time, 6:03. Five minutes later, again, 6:08. I tilted my script to show my timing notes to Chet. Neither of us could remember what news was in that broadcast.

After the newscast we stopped home briefly to pick up my already packed bag and headed to Beth Israel Hospital. It proved to be a long night. I had the good fortune to have a strong authoritative nurse assigned to me. She walked me up and down the halls all night. I saw Dr. Klapholz and asked why he was there. He said he had things to do, but I was sure he was there for me and that alarmed me. An internal monitor showed the baby in duress. I was quickly moved to an operating room and my nurse told me the umbilical cord likely was wrapped around the baby's neck. They were going to give me an epidural and take the baby by C-section. I begged them to just take the baby. Forget the epidural. I wouldn't die of pain, but the delay could cause damage to my baby.

They had trouble getting the needle in the spine and the whole procedure took forever. Eventually I was on a table. I was truly scared for my baby. Finally, they draped a curtain between my head and abdomen so I could not see them cut. Chet could and, clearly having difficulty, buried his face in mine. I told him everything would be all right.

And then I heard Dr. Klapholz say, "Ok, we have unwound the cord, once, and again and one more time, three times!" He lifted my baby and now I could see her. He had warned us not to be concerned if she didn't cry right away. In fact, that was preferable as it allowed them to remove the mucus from her throat before she swallowed. I remained dead silent. Chet, frightened and forgetting what the doctor had said, shouted, "She's not breathing, she's not breathing!" With that our little baby cried out loud and the doctors had to work hard to extract the mucus. When they finally handed her to me and lay her on my chest, I felt a spiritual peace unlike anything I had ever known.

They wheeled me into a private room. I could not take my eyes off my little baby. I was enthralled as I watched her eyes find mine. I think it is only when you have a baby that you understand how much your mother loved you.

She had brown hair, which later would turn to platinum blond; deep, bright blue eyes; and a red face. When the medical team finished cleaning her up and we were alone, I unwrapped her and saw she was perfect. I brought her to my breast, and she latched on as though she had done it a million times. Her suck was so unexpectedly powerful, I flinched.

The connection is unlike anything I have ever known. Love, mother for child, child for mother, has no match. It is a bond so strong, nothing, no one can ever break it. And it never changes.

Chet had gone down to the hospital lobby to meet with reporters. I saw in the paper the next day that someone had given him a cigar. It was a cute picture. And I learned he had named the baby!

We had not decided on a name. I had been conflicted because I always wanted to name a daughter Dawn after my mother. Chet had two daughters, Dana and Dawn. We had figured once she was born, one of the names on our short list would fit.

"How did you decide on Lindsay?"

"I've always been in love with Lindsay Wagner."

Lindsay Dawn Curtis. We stayed in the hospital for several days because of the caesarian. Flowers poured into Beth Israel. I asked the sweet nurses to distribute them to other new mothers and then to pretty much everyone in the hospital. The outpouring of affection was so beautiful. I felt a hundred hugs.

For five years, I kept a daily journal for Lindsay for when she became a mother. I guess I thought it would be instructional, but when I pulled it out for her when her baby was born, I realized I hadn't said anything in that journal that was helpful at all. Page after page after page, one sentiment: I love you so much.

Coming home was an adjustment. My father had cataract surgery and moved in for a while. My sister Jean came from Chicago to help with Dad. Dana came to help as well.

It was all too much confusion for me, so I would escape to our bedroom with my baby. I could hear nothing but her coo. I could see nothing but her eyes. I could feel nothing but her powerful sucking, her tender soft skin. What a miracle.

I brought the bassinet next to me. I lay awake for hours and when I did fall asleep, I would wake up frightened. Is she OK? Chet would bring her into bed to lie next to him. As soon as he fell asleep, I put her back in her bassinet. I was scared to death he would roll over and smother her.

I don't think I have ever stopped worrying about her, even now, when she is my age at the time of her birth and has two babies of her own.

There was only one thing missing during this happy blessed time, my mother who had died two years before. I had a hundred questions. How do I know she is getting enough nutrients from my milk? She didn't poop today, is something wrong? She won't stop crying. Is she in pain? How do I know what is wrong? The doctors say to lay her on her stomach for sleep. Is that what you did with me? How can I be sure I won't pinch her when I safety pin the diaper?

Mothers and grandmothers who watched Channel 5 pitched in. They knitted baby hats and blankets for Lindsay. There were so many beautiful handmade blankets we packed them up and took them to the maternity wards at area hospitals. I was sure those wonderful mothers would be pleased.

One night after the 11 o'clock news, I opened a package containing a doll made out of the items one might include in a layette, cloth diapers, safety pins, baby bottle, thermometer, baby powder, booties, onesie, and a tiny toy. And with this "doll" this woman included a letter, beginning with, "If your mother were alive, she would tell you these things." I couldn't stop crying. But I had to try.

WCVB was introducing a new midnight talk show that night with the popular radio personality Matt Siegel, and I was scheduled to talk with him in a welcoming interview at midnight. Red eyed, mascara washed away, I greeted Matt. He looked aghast and asked what was wrong. So, I explained. All this on live television. Oh dear.

We wrote to each of these wonderful women. How can you adequately thank someone for reaching out in such a loving, motherly way?

There was yet another gift that came from our viewers. About two dozen couples wrote to say they had not had luck in getting pregnant and the tension that brought had some of them at the point of considering divorce. It was not a secret that we had been trying to have a baby for several years. When these couples saw us, thirty-seven and forty-one years of age, finally having a child, they wrote that it gave them hope. For years after, those that did conceive sent me photos of their children at every birthday. To think that our example had been such an inspiration made me feel wonderful.

We took Lindsay to Chicago at six weeks of age to be christened in the Serbian Church. A christening is a very big affair among Serbs. The church ceremony is filled with Orthodox Christian pageantry, much like a wedding. The baby in her Kum's (godfather's) arms follows the priest around the table three times, to honor Father, Son, and Holy Ghost, and the baptism often includes a full dunking in a giant urn. Or worse, a pitcher of holy water is poured over the baby's head. Lindsay howled through the whole thing and it was my fault. I should have fed her first even though that would have meant holding up the proceedings.

Following the ceremony, the Popovich Brothers, a full Serbian orchestra, and a table laden with traditional foods greeted us at my dad's house. We danced the Serbian kolos, sang the Serbian songs, and devoured the Serbian food—pita, lamb and baklava. Perhaps a hundred family and friends were there, including some of Chet and my dearest friends from the East Coast who made the long trip. Their friendship was pretty wonderful.

After the christening, Chet and I went to our home in Nantucket. Usually a calming place, Nantucket would, we hoped, be a respite from the emotional high of the previous month. But our baby was colicky, miserably so. And it lasted six weeks. Her pain became mine. It was agonizing not to be able to comfort her.

"I'm watching what I eat. I must have missed something. I'm sure this is my fault."

The constant crying unnerved Chet. He was beside himself and suggested I take her to the hospital. I suggested he go fishing with his friends. There is a reason women bear the children.

Lindsay was born in May, and I had planned on returning to work after Labor Day. I didn't want to leave my baby. I thought maybe I should quit and stay home until she was in grammar school. Chet and our news director prevailed, and I finally did return at the end of September. It was awful. We had hired a woman to take care of Lindsay, but I was not comfortable with any of it. And on the set, while anchoring the news, when I thought of her, the milk came pouring out. I had adequately protected myself and wore a jacket but still. It was another sign I should be home!

While I eventually adjusted, leaving my baby was never easy. After having to redo my make-up once I got to the station because my tears made a mess, I finally learned not to even bother with the mascara until I got to work. To this day, I can see her little nose up against the window as I pulled out of the driveway, tears filling those big blue eyes. I still feel guilty.

One day we were playing together, and Lindsay asked, "Mommy, do we have to hurry up and have fun?" Dear God.

I know my colleagues had their share of angst about leaving their children and we talked about it. But I stood alone among these mothers in being tormented.

Why was that? Maybe because I was older. Maybe because I had a stay-at-home mother. Maybe because I wanted children more than anything else in the world. Why else did I say no to CBS? Some things just are. There isn't always a simple explanation.

I used to walk through the house with my little Lindsay in my arms and show her the photos on the upright piano. I named each person, Aunt Jean, Uncle Bill, Baba, Jedo, etc. I noticed her eyes always returned to the picture of Baba, my mother.

When she was a little older and able to talk, she said, "Mama, I know Baba."

"You do? How do you know Baba?"

"I don't know. But I know Baba before I know Mama."

Did that mean she saw my mother before she was born?

I have thought about that ever since.

My colleague and friend, Martha Bradlee, had Greta a few months earlier and she seemed much more comfortable leaving her baby. Martha had a Mormon girl from Utah and through her found another Mormon girl for us. We flew her out, and we were to meet her at our Needham home. She arrived when we were still anchoring the news. When we got home, we found Wendy, a young, slight blonde, sitting by the pool drinking a beer and smoking a cigarette!

We went through our difficulties with Wendy, but she was good with Lindsay, sweet, kind, and protective. And Lindsay took to her.

Eventually we had to part ways and my friend Edie Duggan suggested her sister Maureen might fill in while we looked for someone. Maureen was a happy, fun person, and I wished she would want to stay, but she had other plans.

Then we got lucky and met a young woman who had been working with older people but decided she would prefer to care for children. Kathy Vigliano was an energetic, confident, loquacious, young woman.

Lindsay was three when Kathy came to us, which was a perfect age, as Kathy loved the outdoors and never was at a loss for fun things to do. Lindsay came to love her, and to this day we consider Kathy a member of our family.

Another plus, Kathy wanted to learn how to cook. As I love to cook, teaching her was fun. When I didn't have time to prepare a meal, it was a gift to be able to count on Kathy. As time went on, she felt comfortable experimenting and taught me new dishes. Perfect.

We had the good fortune to meet the McAnulty family. They had six children, lived in a tiny house in Dedham. Fred worked two jobs, day and night. When did he sleep? Kathy somehow managed all those children with the most upbeat, positive attitude you will ever know. Lindsay and their two oldest children, Katie and Erin, became fast friends along with another preschool friend, Meghan Vicidomino. They filled a big gap, as I was concerned about Lindsay being an only child. I had hoped we would have more children. It was not to be.

One day, I remember going to Scorby's Photo Shop in Needham to drop off a few rolls of film to be developed (digital had not yet been invented) and out from behind the counter scrambled five of the cutest little puppies I had ever seen. They were white, floppy-eared, bushy-tailed babies. The fellow at Scorby's told me they were bishons, bishon frise. I had never heard of the breed. I fell in love and began a search.

Chet and I both thought a puppy would be good for Lindsay, especially during these changes in caregivers. A puppy would be someone constant for our three-year-old, someone who would not leave.

Well, none of those cute ones I had seen were available, so we hunted for a breeder. Bishons were pretty rare at that time. Finally, we did find one and were told the babies would be ready in a few months. We told Lindsay she could name the puppy and since she was enamored with Disney's *Lady and the Tramp*, she chose the name Lady. When we went to the breeder to pick up our puppy, we were told we would get the male dog. So now what would we name him?

Without missing a beat, Lindsay said, "That's OK mommy, we'll just name him Tramp." That certainly made sense from her point of view, but naming that adorable roly-poly puppy, Tramp, didn't seem to fit. Ah, but Tramp it was. And Tramp was indeed an all-time champ!

Just as we had hoped, Tramp became Lindsay's best friend. She included him in everything, from tea parties with dolls to jumping fences as though he were a horse. By now, several friends and my brother had fallen in love with Tramp and found bichons for themselves. Little Tramp was the inspirational sire to many.

Every year on Tramp's birthday, we invited bichons and their families to celebrate. Lindsay filled little cupcake wrappers with treats. We had party hats for each and of course we gave them ice cream. Chet teased that Tramp was a dog and we were humiliating him. Not true. Tramp was definitely a person.

Kathy eventually married James O'Neill and had two children. I remember being concerned about her ability to care for her children and mine. She tossed that worry aside. "Jim can change diapers and feed the children as well as I can." Ah, the next generation.

Lindsay had a perceptive, smart teacher in the second grade at the Broadmeadow School in Needham. The class had children from many ethnic backgrounds, so she gave each child an opportunity to illustrate their culture. They could bring someone in with them and do whatever they liked—play music, show pictures, share food. The kids learned a lot about diversity, long before anyone was talking about diversity.

As a teacher's aide and chaperone, I noticed the kids referred to us as TV people and that made Lindsay uneasy. With the teacher's permission, I invited the class to Channel 5, which was just up the street. I wanted the kids to see that Lindsay's parents were similar to their parents. The only difference was people got to watch us doing part of our jobs.

The cameramen were great and allowed the children to sit at the anchor desk and see themselves on TV, and of course they thought it was a hoot. Young kids are great. They got it. Their teacher told me later she thought it made a difference. Lindsay was just one of them now.

However, when she left Broadmeadow for middle school and sixth grade, her teachers called us in and told us she was very quiet in class and rarely participated. We were surprised as she was an outgoing kid with a lot of spunk and laughter. Did this have anything to do with being a child of public people? Her teachers suggested we look into private schools where the classes would be smaller. We did, and in the seventh grade she began attending school at Noble and Greenough. I had mixed feelings about her leaving public schools.

When Lindsay was six years old, we took her to Disney World. You could pay a dollar and run around the pony ring with your child. Well, about ten dollars later, and a huffing and puffing Dad, Lindsay was hooked on horses.

About a week later, I happened to be shooting an introduction (called a stand-up) to a story I had prepared using a horse farm as a prop behind me. Seeing a boy who looked to be about Lindsay's age riding a very big pony, I spoke with his mom and explained our daughter could talk about nothing but the pony at Disney World. The woman said six was a good age to start, so I asked if Chet and I could stop by over the weekend. We did, and that was the beginning of Lindsay's love of horses and riding.

From then until she went to college, horses dominated her life and ours. I tried to get her interested in tennis and Dawn's talented friend was kind enough to give her lessons, but Lindsay was not interested.

She definitely had a way with animals. Good thing. It is no small matter to think about a sixty-pound child on a thousand-pound animal. We took her to various barns and eventually enrolled her at the Dana Hall Riding Center. Every day after school, either Chet or I drove her to Dana Hall in Wellesley.

It didn't take long before she was competing in equestrian competitions, and we were off to horse shows throughout New England almost every weekend and Florida in the winter. She got to be a good rider, so good that in her later teens she earned the right to compete in the ASPCA Maclay Finals at the National Horse Show at Madison

Square Garden; at the Nationals at Harrisburg, Pennsylvania, in the Medal Finals; and also the National Prix des States. It was no small feat, from maybe five thousand kids nationwide, a small fraction made it to the finals.

By accumulating points during competitions throughout the year, Lindsay earned the right to be part of a four-person team representing New England in a national competition.

I can still feel my insides churning. Lindsay was on her horse, Costello, barn name, Elvis. He and the other three horses rode two rounds and were tied with California. A jump off was needed to determine the winner. It was already huge to be in a jump off because California usually took top honors. But New England wasn't done yet. You were scored on time and clean jumps, meaning, getting over without knocking them down.

The other girls had younger, more expensive horses, and they had more than one. But Lindsay had Elvis. "He was the horse of a lifetime," Lindsay would say. "He knew what I was thinking and could move before I asked. We had a bond, a trust, that is beyond anything I had ever known. I knew this night, was our night."

I looked at the entrance of the ring. I thought Lindsay looked a little nervous. Elvis looked raring to go. Did he really have another round in him?

"Riding for New England, Lindsay Dawn Curtis, on Costello."

Jump one, clean, next, clean. Time, how's the time? Next jump clean. How many seconds? Clean again. Double clean. She made the jumps in the time allowed. Oh man! The whole team was fantastic, but it was Lindsay's double-clean round that sealed it. New England beat the vaunted California team for the first time.

As a mother and spectator, what stays with me after all the competitions, is the extraordinary bond between horse and rider. Trust takes time. It comes with hard work, day after day. Maybe most of all, it comes from caring for your animal. Riding is a small part of the time spent with a horse. Grooming him, feeding, walking him, sleeping in his stall when he is sick, standing by his side as he is shod, calming him just before the ring, allowing him to calm you, hugging his big neck, watching his ears talk to you, his nose nudge you. You could hear Elvis whinny in the barn when Lindsay arrived in the parking lot!

Imagine the trust it takes for a horse to jump a six-foot fence, unable to see what is on the other side: precisely the challenge at the Puissance. The first time I saw the Puissance, I wasn't sure my heart would keep beating.

Financially, we were out of our league in that horse-show circuit, which meant we couldn't buy the number or quality of horses Lindsay's friends could buy. We knew it put her at a disadvantage. But she worked hard and made the best of what we could provide. We couldn't have been more proud of her. Both Chet and I cried when she was selected by trainers and fellow riders to win the Sportsmanship Award at Madison Square Garden in her last year of competition. That might not have been the same as a blue ribbon, but to us, as her parents, it was gold.

CHAPTER 18

I Am Woman

Until Lindsay was born, my career in broadcast journalism was my focus. My work directed my thought, my schedule, my goals. Chet and I talked about how lucky we were to be in the same industry because our professional lives were so consuming. We could understand the other's concerns.

Motherhood changed everything. Compromise became a daily art which I struggled to master. Balancing work with time with my child was an hourly challenge. More than organization, I faced emotional angst. I just didn't want to miss a minute with my baby girl. I wanted to hear her first word. If she needed hugging, I wanted to be the one to hug her for as long as she wanted and not hurry off to work.

It wasn't that news was no longer important to me, it was. It still was more a calling than a job. But after nine months of carrying a growing life within me, the baby that emerged filled my entire being with joy, compassion, concern, with a love as I had never known it. I wish I were a better writer as even these words cannot describe my passion. And today, with the gift of two grandchildren, all of that wonder rushes through me just as it did in 1981. Motherhood IS grand.

Lindsay today is a senior vice president of a global sports marketing company. Her thoughts about combining career and motherhood illustrate how much has changed in forty years.

"I think I am a better mother because I also have a job. When I'm with the kids, I'm present. While my children are my number one priority, there is a part of me that needs the professional stimulus. Being a working mom, and just a mom in general, is the most humbling and rewarding part of my life. Our children are mini reflections of us and sometimes you may not always like what's looking back at you. But for now, I'm holding onto the moments when they crawl in my lap and look at me as though I am the most important person in the entire world. There is no better feeling than that."

Between Lindsay's birth and that of her children, life changed dramatically for women in the United States.

At WCVB-TV in 1972, I was the only woman among the ranks of reporters and editors for two years. I was one of the first women on television in the country to be pregnant at the advanced age of thirty-seven. I was the first woman to anchor the evening newscasts at 6 and 11 PM in Boston. Pretty quickly, more women began to fill the newsroom. The hard-fought battles of the 60s and early 70s were paying off despite a very tough anti-feminist movement led by Phyllis Schlafly.

Among married couples in the 50s and 60s, primarily the man worked, the woman raised the children, and in my limited world, whatever the man was able to provide had to be enough and people lived accordingly. When I was a child, we did not have a car or a TV. We did not go to restaurants. My mother bought food she could afford and made it stretch. I remember she had an envelope system. Each envelope accumulated the cash to pay the bills, electricity, rent, food, gas, etc. She kept one little jar for herself and deposited a dime every week. When she had enough in that jar, she bought something like a tube of lipstick.

As an adult, I straddled the old and the new in that I did get a college education, but I also married early and wanted both a family and a career. Few careers were open to women. As I saw it, I could be a teacher, a nurse, or a secretary, not a superintendent, or doctor, or president of a company. Nothing wrong with those professions, they just didn't interest me. Getting married and living overseas for two years was a lucky break in that supply and demand put me in demand for a position I likely would not have had access to in the US.

Today, not only does a woman have a chance to be president of our country, many women are presidents of major corporations, many create and run their own businesses, as does my step-daughter Dawn. A woman for the first time is the vice president of the country and another is speaker of the US House of Representatives. Women captain commercial airplanes. I'll never forget climbing into the cockpit of a light plane and hearing a group of school children express surprise.

"Look that's a girl going to fly that plane."

I got out of the plane to say hello and to tell those little girls, you too can learn to fly a plane if you want to.

Women have been working for years to provide the necessities of life, food, and shelter. Women certainly proved themselves every bit as capable as men during WWII when they had to take over the jobs of the men who were now fighting overseas. But when the war was over and the men came home, many women who could returned to their earlier roles as "domestic engineers," as my mother would say. The 50s were an *Ozzy and Harriet* time, *Father Knows Best. Madame Secretary* could not have been imagined.

The 60s saw the Women's Movement flower. Birth control gave women independence. In the 70s, the federal government suggested none too softly, that companies receiving any federal assistance needed to be more inclusive in hiring women and minorities.

Until the mid-70s, men thought hiring a woman was a waste because they would marry, get pregnant, and leave. I was turned away from jobs for just that reason. My own father thought the woman's place was in the home and saw no reason for me to go to college.

While there were women of my parents' age who worked in professions, it was my generation of women who, en masse, would prove women could do both.

But we would learn, careers are one thing. Motherhood another.

Children were not part of the feminist discussion in the 60s, opportunity in the work place was. So, as we got jobs and then husbands and children, it didn't take long for many of us to shout, as *MS Magazine* did in 1971, "I want a Wife."

Judy Brady's satirical look at the duties expected of a wife became a classic.

Why do I want a wife? I would like to go back to school so that I can become economically independent, support myself, and, if need be, support those dependent on me. I want a wife who will work and send me to school. And while I am going to school I want a wife to take care of my children. I want a wife to keep track of the children's doctor and dentist appointments. And to keep track of mine, too... who wouldn't want a wife?

Then some twenty years later, in 1990, the cover of *Time* blared: THEY WANTED IT ALL – NOW THEY'VE JUST HAD IT. IS THERE A FUTURE FOR FEMINISM?

To give Phyllis Schlafly her due, she was ahead of this issue in the sense she worried that women, who will always be the bearers of children, and usually the chief caregivers, need certain protections. Women without degrees would be wiped out in a divorce without the alimony rules in place at the time. And that did happen to many women when states instituted no fault divorce. "Not all housewives want to be Hillary Rodham Clinton," Abigail Shirer wrote in the *Wall Street Journal*.

Women are not a homogenous group and neither are children. Every mother figures out what works best for her and her family.

My step-daughter Dawn, now fifty-five, says, "Of course, it was emotional to leave my children with a nanny in the beginning, but I didn't dwell on it because I knew I had to work, I wanted to work; I trusted our nanny, and I knew my children would be okay and possibly even have more experiences because there were more people in their lives to love and care for them.

"I'm not a person who ever wanted to be a stay-at-home mom. I struggle sometimes with friends that are so focused on mothering.

I've always wanted my kids to be independent and need me less and less. I embrace their independence because I am not solely defined by raising them."

Dawn's work allowed money for childcare and today she runs a business entirely of her making.

Her sister, Dana, now fifty-eight, had different priorities.

"I had always hoped to have a few years to be with my children full time, to answer their questions, to see what made them laugh, to help them be individuals, and to teach them to be kind and curious. I felt lucky to have those years and then to be able to return to work that I love."

Dana's husband's salary allowed for her to stay home until her youngest son started middle school. She has returned to her work at Harvard Business School and Wellesley College as a career advisor.

Nothing is black and white and what works for one generation might not work for the next. Times change. For example, rules limiting the number of hours women in factories could be required to work was seen as protection at that time. Today it is viewed as limiting.

Title 9 was created to give girls a better opportunity in sports. But now, in the gender-neutral age, transgender boys are allowed to compete with girls and women who say that just doesn't work because while you can change your gender identity, you can't change your muscles. Girls ask, "Who do you think will get the athletic scholarships?"

I found Schlafly's views regressive back in the 70s and prescient today. I bet my mother would have supported her protective stance for women, since my mother was a housewife raising four kids. Mom saw that women whose husbands did not make enough money worked in menial jobs. I could understand that of course, but also saw Schlafly's positions as limiting women like me.

Schlafly herself was a lawyer and the mother of six children, all now professionals. She died in 2016 at the age of ninety-two.

Many younger women don't give much thought to this because it is normal now to work and have children and to hire help if you can afford it. Some mothers are lucky to have their mothers help with the children, a gift for all three generations. For many women who work in either blue collar or professional jobs, there is no choice. The family often cannot make it on the man's salary. And we see a growing number of women as single mothers, either by choice or circumstance.

And something else has changed. Men. My father, God bless him, couldn't boil water. Moreover, he saw everything related to the home as my mother's responsibility. My husband, Chet, God bless him too, wasn't much different when it came to housework and maintenance, but he got pretty good on the grill and was more involved in Lindsay's life than my father was in mine. I wasn't around when Dana and Dawn were younger, but Chet was devoted to them despite the difficulties of separation that divorce created.

My son-in-law, Eric, thirty-nine, is of another generation. He pitches in at home and is very much engaged with the children. "In addition to teaching my children how to perform physical things like riding a bike and throwing a ball, I want to instill the value of learning how to educate yourself to problem-solve on your own. Education too often is confused with strictly learning 'school math' such as algebra as opposed to managing your money. Learning is a lifelong quest to enhance your view of the world and prepare yourself for engaging with situations of challenge or discomfort."

Lindsay will say she is lucky to have a husband who sees parenting as a job to be shared. Since the children were babies, they took turns getting up at night, and to this day they take turns putting the children to bed. That said, she admits, "Moms have more on their minds about home and kids, everything from groceries to doctors' appointments to school projects to 'is the epi-pen current?'"

I'll never forget sitting on a dais with my then general manager who was receiving an award. I introduced him and he said to the audience, "I'd like to thank my wife for raising our children. I didn't have much to do with their growing-up lives, because I was working." I thought how awful. But that was his generation.

As women have moved into what were men's jobs, men today are employed in what once were considered primarily a women's jobs: nurse, teacher, flight attendant, secretary, house cleaner, etc. So maybe the women's movement also gave men more choices and brought them into the home to better share, if not housework, parenting?

And men have moved into the kitchen! Since I love to cook, this fascinates me. When I grew up, famous chefs were men, Julia Child excepted. But the cooks at home were women. Now, many of the famous chefs are women and men have discovered food can be fun, so they don the apron at home. While my sister Sandra is amazingly creative in the kitchen, my brother Bill and his two sons are among the best cooks I know as well.

Today, the ERA is still in abeyance. The National Women's Party, flush with the hard-fought victory of the nineteenth amendment, focused on expanding women's rights. The Equal Rights Amendment, which began in essence in 1920 and was offered as an amendment in 1972 still is not law. While it passed Congress, it took until 2018 to get the thirty-eight states necessary to ratify the amendment, and it is no sure thing as of this writing that it will become law. Some argue too much time has passed to meet the constitution's requirements. Others say it is no longer relevant or needed.

What remains needed is flexibility and appreciation of everyday needs. For a working mother, there are never enough hours in the day.

Back in the 80s, Johnson & Johnson addressed the concerns of their employees with a radical redo of their New Jersey headquarters. I went to the plant and was amazed. They instituted a daycare center so mothers could look in on their children and also have the comfort of knowing they were in the same building. They wanted all their employees as healthy as possible and had a medical clinic on site, a stop smoking program, a track that ran around one of the upper floors, a gym, and a cafeteria which included stations based on ingredients and themes. J&J's turn-over rate was low, and the care they gave their employees resulted in a measurable increase in profit. I hoped other companies including Channel 5 would emulate them. It's always good to try.

Today, sex discrimination and abuse in the workplace have replaced the balancing debate. Harvey Weinstein is the poster boy for such discrimination, but his case and comments by his female attorney broaden the discussion. Weinstein sounds like every woman's nightmare. Have sex with me or you'll never work again. He was convicted and is serving time.

His attorney, asked by a reporter if she was ever assaulted, said no, she never puts herself in that position. That set off a storm. "Oh, so if you don't ask for it, nothing bad will happen?" "What about the altar boy and the priest, or the Olympian and the coach, or the unsuspecting woman in an elevator?" On the other hand, women ask, why would anyone go to a man's hotel room at 3 in the morning?

The last chapter on women will never be written. But every now and then perhaps it is enlightening to look at the broader picture, from where we have come, where we are, and where we hope to go. It is also good to realize how lucky we are to be women in America. Look what women go through in many other parts of the world.

Work and parenting will continue to evolve. More glass ceilings will be cracked. Yet, for those of us who opened closed doors, we smile as we see light continuing to filter through that glass.

CHAPTER 19

NewsCenter 5

On a daily basis in television news, time is the greatest pressure. There never is enough time to gather information, to shoot the story, to edit the story, to write the story, much less rewrite the story. Six o'clock, ready or not.

We didn't have Google back then, so I befriended a couple of wonderful librarians at the Boston Public Library who would take my calls late in the afternoon during the pressure-packed hour before airtime. Fact checking, of course, is crucial and it was a relief to have the confidence that a particular date or name or place was correct.

Time constraints can ask you to call upon your deepest reserves. I remember one day getting back from covering the anniversary of the game Monopoly made at the time by Parker Brothers in Beverly, Massachusetts. We were still working film then. One camera shot pictures and sound, another just pictures. I had a script in my head as my film editor Dick Molinari and I cut and hung the pieces for him to splice in an order I dictated to match the words in my mind. No time to write a script. I raced to the studio, again wind-blown, no make-up, and prayed my memory matched Molinari's, and my speed of speaking matched the number of frames we had designated. In other words, match pictures and stories to the second. Miraculously it worked. You have to be a little nuts to think afterward, "That was fun." It's the challenge. You have to love the challenge.

Time can play a defining role in decision making. I think you could say the basic definition of news is that which is new. Not everything new, however, is newsworthy. A television newscast is limited in time. 6 to 6:30 PM cannot be 6:02 to 6:34. There is a timed program that precedes and one that follows. So clearly judgments must be made about what is to be included and what cannot. Relevance, importance, accuracy—all play a role in the decision making. Logistics can play a part. Do we have enough time to cover this well? Will it hold until tomorrow? Back to the central question, what before us do the people need to know today? As you might imagine, arguments, often heated, were a critical part of the dialogue, as they should be.

Of course, just as important as to which topics to include, is the way they are treated. Most important is accuracy. Is it honest? Do we have the whole story? What's missing? Can we trust what we know or think we know?

A good example is a breaking news story in 1989 that shook the city of Boston to its core.

It was Monday, October 23. Shortly before the 11 PM news, we heard a call for help on the police radios. It came from outside Brigham and Women's Hospital in Boston.

911: "My wife has been shot. I've been shot."

Charles Stuart and his pregnant wife, Carol DiMaiti Stuart, were found in their Toyota near Mission Hill. Carol had been shot in the head. Chuck was shot in the abdomen. He told police a black man with a raspy voice wearing a black hoodie with red stripes had shot them.

Police combed the adjacent Mission Hill, home largely to the black community, looking for the man. It was an all-out search. It was a shocking crime. The woman had just attended a birthing class. That was all we knew as we went on the air that night and that is what we reported.

Carol died a few hours later in the same hospital where she had just attended birthing classes. Her baby was delivered by caesarian but did not survive. Charles was hospitalized and underwent two operations.

Meantime, police continued their hunt and in December, police arrested William Bennett, a black man whom they said fit Stuart's description. Considering how vague that description was, the arrest was suspect.

In January, Charles Stuart jumped off the Tobin Bridge to his death. The seventy-three-day story proved to be an extraordinary hoax perpetrated by Charles Stuart. He shot his wife and to avoid suspicion, shot himself, although more seriously than he likely intended.

His brother Matthew, complicit in the scheme, apparently felt guilty and confessed to police.

Now the city was in a greater uproar. White police against the black community again. How could police have believed his story? Why did they search Mission Hill? All the news media was taken to task for reporting the story, including us. I can understand the anger, but the charge against the media on the night this happened was not reasonable. Why wouldn't police believe Charles? He was shot. Who would have imagined at that moment that he killed his wife and shot himself?

He said a black man shot them. And it happened adjacent to Mission Hill. It seems logical for police to search that area. If he said it was an Asian man and it had happened in Chinatown outside Tufts Medical Center, I should think they would have searched Chinatown. Nevertheless, charges of a racist Boston Police Department were loud and long. Perhaps the police were too willing to believe the story and as time passed some said they should have been quicker to find the truth.

Perhaps Stuart did it for the insurance money. Whatever his motive, he took it with him beneath the cold water of the Mystic River. He left behind a devastated DiMaiti family, a shocked community, and another reason for blacks to believe the police were not on their side.

Covering news as it is happening is perhaps the ultimate challenge. Call it what you will. It tests your professional ability.

Reporting live! Breaking news! Alerts used so often they have lost their urgency. Everything is breaking news these days, breathlessly breaking. We didn't use the phrase breaking news in my earlier days. We came close with "this just in." In my first year at WCVB, I learned that covering news as it breaks can change on a dime, as it did during the Hotel Vendome fire in Boston.

I had been sent to cover the fire on Commonwealth Avenue. It was June 1972. The hotel, once the scene of elaborate weddings, now was undergoing renovations. A café was open for business during the construction work.

While I was there, midafternoon, firemen evacuated the building and around 4:30 indicated it was under control and allowed a nearby canteen to reopen. I went back to the station in Needham with the film. At that point it was a story with a good ending. I reported, "Thank goodness, no one was hurt." As we were broadcasting live, I got word the hotel had collapsed and firemen were hurt or killed. How could this be?

We quickly were back on the scene at the corner of Commonwealth and Dartmouth. A few hours earlier I had seen the building standing, intact. Now the building was gone, demolished, firefighters desperately trying to save their own. In the end, nine firemen lost their lives, while eight others were injured. It was the worst firefighting tragedy in the history of Boston.

I lived in Copley Square years later and walked my little bichon, Breezy, down Commonwealth Avenue every day. And every day we stopped at the haunting monument at the corner of Commonwealth Avenue and Dartmouth Street. It was erected on the twenty-fifth anniversary of the fire. It is a beautiful memorial to those brave men. Yet, in reading the reports from the fire department years later, it seemed this should not have happened. The building collapsed under the weight of water because of a new duct that had been cut beneath a steel column. As I stand before the tributes, I still remember my first report that June day so long ago, believing as did the chief, that all was good, reporting no lives lost. The day after that fire was Father's Day.

Years later, for me and likely most reporters, the most memorable days of reporting news as it is breaking began on September 11, 2001. I was playing golf in my first-ever competition at Brae Burn Country

Club. My cell phone rang and noticing it was my brother calling, I turned the sound off. Thinking it was a social call, I decided to call him back later and joined my partner in the golf cart. About fifteen minutes later, two carts carrying club personnel came shouting, "Natalie, get in the cart. The station is calling you."

Of course, none of us on the golf course knew anything at that moment. I got in my car and turned on the radio. A commercial plane had flown into the World Trade Center twin towers. An accident?

Oh, how I wished I had taken that call from my brother a few minutes earlier. I raced to the station in Needham, my insides churning. What followed was as frightening a time of reporting as I can ever remember. I was briefed quickly, moved to the anchor desk, no make-up, hat head. I didn't think about that. I was going on the air with little information and that was scary.

We reported what we knew, with pictures that were coming in while we were on the air. At 8:46 AM, AA Flight 11, a Boeing 767 with 20 thousand gallons of fuel, hit the north tower, near the top, killing hundreds, trapping thousands. The building was billowing smoke. At first it appeared it was an accident. But eighteen minutes later another Boeing 767, United 175, appeared and veered into the south tower. This was no accident. But what was it? Who would do this? Both planes originated at Boston's Logan Airport. This international story was also local.

At that point, another plane was reported heading to the Capitol. We knew nothing more. Who was flying these planes? How many more were there?

There was little time to reflect, as at 9:45, American Airlines Flight 77 crashed into the Pentagon. We later learned the target was the Capitol.

Fourteen minutes later, 9:59 AM, the south tower collapsed.

Meanwhile, we were getting word of a fourth plane, flying over Pennsylvania: United Flight 93 out of New Jersey. The passengers were hearing about the other planes on their phones and then saw armed men take over the cockpit. Some called their loved ones and then in act of extraordinary bravery, knowing they were going to die, decided not to allow this plane to crash into whatever its destination was. They overpowered the hijackers and crashed into the ground at five hundred miles per hour in Shanksville, Pennsylvania, 10:10 AM.

And then at 10:28 AM, the north tower came down.

We wondered if there was more to come. We had to report it as it was, we didn't know. Meantime, President George W. Bush was in Florida reading to a group of school children. We saw his chief of staff, Andrew Card, whisper in his ear and saw the president's shocked expression.

Without knowing if there were more attacks coming, or whether the president would be targeted, the secret service and military moved him around most of the day. He finally ended up at the White House that evening.

All civilian flights were grounded. Incoming flights were diverted to Canada and Mexico.

We were on the air all that day and night. The details were dribbling in. Take a deep breath. The United States was undergoing the greatest attack in its history and we had little information as to what was behind this.

For me and my colleagues, reporting a story of this magnitude as it was unfolding was a test of nerves. We didn't want to report rumors or speculation. Sticking to what we knew as fact was best. Watching our fellow Americans in NYC, trying desperately to save people, watching firefighters go into the burning towers, and not return, seeing two planes on route to the Capitol was all very bad news. Of course, we were as frightened as were our viewers.

There were so many unknowns we couldn't reassure people of anything. Yet, we didn't want to falsely alarm. Our instincts were to report what we knew and say, this is all we know as fact. Knowledge, information, however awful, is better than not knowing. We would learn together.

You really learn what great people you work with at a time like this. Everyone pitching in, digging for video, calling for information, collating what we could ascertain. Especially in a crisis, our team pulled together, maybe never more so than on this day. I was proud of us.

The next morning, I heard a commotion outside Trinity Place in Copley Square where I was living. Police were everywhere. I dressed quickly and ran outside. A police officer told me they thought they had several of the terrorists in the Westin Hotel. I called the station to send a crew. Whoever it was got away.

Meantime, since both planes that crashed into the World Trade Center were from Boston, we knew locals had to be on that flight. It turned out the captain of Flight 11 was John Ogonowski from Dracut, Massachusetts. Sometime after 9/11, producer Rosemary Lappin, photographers, and I drove to the Ogonowski farm where we met with his wife, Peg, and three daughters. Peg, gracious and welcoming, gave us a tour of the peach orchard, the cornfields now in their autumn descent. The pumpkins were strewn across the ground. The stretch of 150 acres somehow seemed haunting. John Ogonowski was just fifty years of age.

In the weeks that followed, our days were filled identifying the victims, hearing the heartbreak from their families, piecing together the events, the timeline, learning that American Airlines had let the hijackers on at the last minute. This was before the security we have today. Every time I stand in a long line at the airport, I think of how easy air travel was before 9/11.

Later we were told 2,996 people died that day. Perhaps as many more died as time passed as a result of that day.

The planes were all California bound, so they would be loaded with the most fuel. We would learn the hijackers were all members of al Qaeda from Saudi Arabia. We also learned later that they had taken flying lessons in the United States. They had no trouble smuggling box cutters and knives onto the planes. Osama Bin Laden at first denied involvement, but in 2004 admitted it. In 2011, the US finally found and killed him.

The country had never been through anything like this. Somehow you knew this wasn't the end. One week after the attacks, anthrax was found in envelopes addressed to several congressmen and to media offices in New York and Florida. The fear was that more was coming. Five people died, seventeen were sickened in the worst biological attack in US history.

The fact that all the terrorists were Muslims created a fear among many Americans, fear of people who looked like they might be from the Mideast. Of course, not all Muslims are terrorists or jihadists, so we thought it important to shed light on this. I asked our management if we could conduct a town meeting including Muslims, Jews, and Christians. Some thought it too touchy, but they agreed to allow me to host this forum. It was enlightening. The Quran actually uses language that can be interpreted as a call to jihad and I asked our Muslim guests to explain that. Christians were challenged on passages of the Bible. The participants challenged each other. Most importantly, everyone in the room was willing to listen to others. Some would comment, "I didn't know that," or "But you could also interpret that as…" People expressed anger, frustration, doubt, but it was just what I had hoped—a civilized, honest exchange of ideas and opinions. I think we all learned something during that program. All in all, I felt we did our job as journalists to do our best to separate fact from fiction and to offer a public forum for people to hear each other. As I recall, this was well received.

We would employ this "town meeting" type format again, when a topic of major concern needed a clarification of facts. Gay marriage in 2004 comes to mind, also universal health care in 2006 with then-Governor Mitt Romney. During that program, a leader from the legislature and Governor Romney were present and both said, as they often had, they support a Massachusetts Health Plan that covered the uninsured. But it never became law. Using the rare opportunity of the public moment, I asked them to commit to a date if they really thought the bill was the answer. They did. They missed the date by a few months, but their promise became law. Not everyone agreed with that new law of course, and that gave us more to cover on the subject.

I have always believed that honest information is key to our democracy and further believe that the public exchange of opinions leads to understanding and eventually to good policy. I believe we should never be afraid to hear why someone who has an opinion different from our own, believes what he does. We might learn something.

Time, lack of time, too often can limit the depth of coverage of important topics. A newspaper can print more pages. A newscast cannot add seconds.

Also, there is only so much time any single individual can devote to a story in a single day. Producer Dick Amaral came up with an idea that answered that dilemma, "Checkpoint." Three of us were assigned a single aspect of the lead story to air at the end of the newscast. Each piece was a minute and a half, combined with two others; we devoted almost five additional minutes to a single story. And by dividing the research among three of us, it was doable. For example, if the lead was a surge in COVID-19 cases, one person might cover the geography, another the age and severity of the cases, and another an interview with the medical expert. Amaral would pull it all together, so it flowed as a single story. It was an innovative way to maximize our resources.

Thinking back on these various efforts to bring our viewers information, I am reminded again of the teamwork within our news department that was critical. In a well-run newsroom, everyone has a voice: the reporters, the writers, the editors, the photographers, the management, and the producers.

Show producers are in charge of the content, the pace, the placement of stories. I think under the pressure it is easy for producers to get caught up in the logistics of getting on and off the air on time, but the good ones have an innate sense of the importance of what we are telling people.

Field producers sometimes accompany reporters in the field, more often when the story takes us out of town. I was lucky to work with

Linda Polach and Rosemary Lappin when out in the field covering various stories, such as political conventions. Not only is there not enough time for one person to get everything done, from making appointments with people to interview, to coordinating cameras, but also, a good producer brings another intelligent mind to the process. "Did you consider this?" "Shouldn't we include so and so?" "Maybe if we shoot the video here rather than there, the story will have more relevance."

There certainly were times when we were not in agreement. Tempers could flare. But I think in the toughest of circumstances, what saved us was knowing we all wanted the same thing, an honest story presented in the best possible way, and to that end we could find agreement.

Sometimes the producers from the programming side of the station teamed up with a news reporter. I had the privilege of working with one of our most talented producers, Jerry Kirshenbaum. He came up with an idea to trace the lineage of a Boston family with an idea to reinforce the fact that we are all immigrants or descendants of immigrants. We looked for a family of multiple generations and found an Italian family in the North End. Our story, "A House on Salem Street," took us to Molito, Italy, a city divided. Half remained torn apart from WWII. The other half was a thriving community. It was from here that our family on Salem Street came. For me, Jerry was a dream to work with, as he liked adlibbing the story rather than working from a script. We would talk about the information we wanted to impart and then he'd turn on the camera and I would just talk to you. It made for a more natural conversation with the viewers.

We had a good diversity of abilities on our reporting staff. Everyone could be classified as a general assignment reporter, and we didn't have assigned "beats," as was often the case at newspapers. Yet, it didn't take long to see the individual strengths begin to emerge. Ron Gollobin led the way in investigative journalism. Ron wrote the book on mob coverage, including mob boss Jerry Anguilo's indictments, which involved an attack on Ron in the North End. Jack Cryan recorded it all which made for a fascinating eleven-minute "A Section" story, another example of news director Jim Thistle giving airtime when he knew the story was worthy.

After Ron retired, David Boeri continued the investigative beat.

Susan Wornick moved into consumer reporting and became a trusted source for our viewers. After Bill Harrington, Janet Wu became our go-to person for political news. Dr. Tim Johnson continued to lead our medical coverage, Brian Leary, legal issues. We turned to Chet Curtis for aviation stories.

The day-to-day reporting fell to our general assignment reporters, who, like emergency-room doctors, have to make decisions quickly based on their skills and experience. We were blessed to have a great team.

It is dangerous to name people as someone will wrongly be missed. Yet, how can I write this book without mentioning Jack Harper, Kelley Tuthill, Don Gillis, Bob Copeland, Bob Clinkscale, Mary Richardson, Martha Bradley, Kirby Perkins, Brian Leary, Jim Boyd, Paula Lyons, Rhondella Richardson, Jorge Quiroga, Gail Huff, Pam Cross, Liz Brunner, Anne McGrath, Janet Wu, among so many others already mentioned. And Donna Hennessey remains in her "Director's Chair" at WCVB since the beginning, March of 1972. My apologies to anyone I inadvertently omitted from the reporters list above. I am lucky and grateful to have worked with each of you.

Bill Wheatley went to NBC to produce their evening news. Bill O'Reilly went on to Fox; Mike Taibbi to NBC; Martha Bradley, now Martha Raddatz, to ABC; David Muir is now the evening anchor of *World News Tonight* on ABC. David joined us as a young man and from the beginning, I saw in him the promise of an honest journalist, smart, curious, dogged, and caring.

Our BBI president, Leo Beranek added another group to our news family, interns. He created the Beranek Fellowship inviting smart African-American young people to join our team and learn to be reporters. They brought another dimension of thought to the newsroom, and some went on to be snapped up by the networks, including

Ron Allen and Bertha Coombs. Rhondella Richardson stayed with WCVB and continues to prove her mettle and versatility.

The photographers have a tough assignment. They need to adapt to a different reporter on each assignment and understand the reporter's vision. "Talking heads" are easy enough, but so many of the stories we covered involved creativity and nuance. A good photographer can make a story live.

So too the editors. The edit room is where the story comes together. Choosing just the right sound bite, the right "cutaway" (picture of someone listening or reacting to what is being said) is critical to the integrity of the piece. Marrying what is shot to the reporter's script or vice versa defines the story itself.

How many times did I drive my producers and directors crazy when I had to make just one more edit before flying down the hall to the anchor desk just in time to say "Good Evening"?

From the anchor seat, interviews can take many forms and offer opportunities to cover the news, break news, and report it.

For example, during a live newscast at say 6 or 11 PM, we might ask the "newsmaker" or an expert to join us live. I remember one day an issue before Congress was in abeyance and we asked Speaker of the House Tip O'Neill to join us during our broadcast. He did, and when I asked him how he would lead the vote in the House, he answered and that was "breaking" news.

Live interviews can also favor the interviewee, especially the experienced politician who knows you only have, say, two minutes, so he can "filibuster" the time away. I remember Senator Ted Kennedy doing just that as I tried to get him to answer a specific question. He rambled. I asked again. He rambled. Exasperated as my time was running out, I said, "You obviously don't intend to answer the question." The Senator smiled, even chuckled.

Well at least our viewers had the satisfaction that I called him on it.

One of the most famous live interviews didn't involve me or NewsCenter 5 at all but took place on the *Good Day* show. Host Janet

Langhart was interviewing the then-famous hot model Lauren Hutton. Janet asked Lauren how she managed to climb the ladder of fashion modeling so quickly. Hutton with a straight face and no emotion answered, "I f**** around." No one moved. This was live TV. You didn't say things like that on live TV! After that embarrassing moment, the station added a time delay to the broadcast.

As an anchor, I always felt I wore two hats, one representing WCVB and one representing the viewers. For example, in a car accident, I was concerned about the victims' loved ones and was careful our copy was sensitive to them. On the other hand, when encountering a viewer who was critical of a report they had seen on our news, I did my best to explain the circumstances. I wanted viewers to know we had a smart, caring group of people at WCVB.

In pre-internet days, we used to get a lot of mail from our viewers, which showed just how engaged they were in what they watched. That mail kept us in check, a constant reminder that what we reported had meaning and consequences. We had a responsibility to justify what we were reporting. So, with considerable difficulty, we convinced our camera-shy news director Jim Thistle to answer some of our mail live once a week during the 6 PM news. Chet and I culled through our mail and presented our viewers' comments and questions to Jim, who was great at answering. He just told it as it was. Sometimes he explained circumstances the viewer might not know about or difficulties getting certain information, etc. Sometimes he agreed we messed up. Whatever it was, he just told the truth of the matter. This was yet another way to allow our viewers to be part of this thing called news. We were all in this together.

Interacting with our field reporters during a live broadcast gave viewers a chance to participate in the process. For example, at the conclusion of a reporter's piece, I might have the opportunity to ask for further clarification or whatever thought was in my mind. And judging from my mail from viewers, my questions often mirrored theirs. Those moments also gave the reporter an opportunity to add information or an interesting tidbit that might round out the story. At times, it brought unexpected humor.

For example, Ron Gollobin was sent to NYC to cover the auction of Jackie O's pearls. After he concluded his report, I asked if he bought any of them. With a straight face, Gollobin replied, "Nat, I don't wear pearls."

Another opportunity to learn more about our viewers and allow them to share their views was to take the story to them. For example, during the primary I thought it would be interesting to learn more about New Hampshire voters and what leads them to their vote. This is back in the day when such an undertaking was not considered too time consuming. A photographer and I met with families from Manchester to the rural communities of the White Mountains. We would sit around a fireplace or a dinner table and I would learn about their lives—how they earned their money and educated their children. You began to see what mattered most to them. These were honest, hard-working people who were less motivated by political ideology and more interested in the character of the candidate and his or her ideas for the country. What is more interesting than learning the who and why of things? Getting to know people seems to me critical to reporting almost any story.

The flip side of learning about voters' thoughts is learning what the candidates offer.

Political interviews in our back yard made national news every four years. The first in the nation New Hampshire primary allowed us reporters from neighboring Massachusetts our only good opportunity to interview the people running for president. While the Granite State can be a make-or-break election, the blue Bay State got little attention from the candidates.

Again, true to its mission, NewsCenter 5 set out to allow viewers to better know the candidates. The station allowed me half-hour interviews with the candidates. Sometimes they were live and other times live on tape, meaning recorded and aired without editing.

Like most stories worth telling, these took a lot of preparation. My friends and producers Linda Polach and Rosemary Lappin were critical to our mission. You need to know someone pretty well to talk intelligently and elicit pertinent information in a half-hour interview. Sometimes these meetings brought surprises, other times, they brought a laugh.

The interview with Barack Obama was interesting in that he was not a leading contender at that point but was making news. I asked him about his ethnicity in the sense that he was dark skinned but not African American. He father was from Kenya, his mother, a white woman from Kansas. He calmly answered he identified as a black man and went on to talk about the advantages of his mixed-racial background. His handlers went bonkers after the show, screaming at me for bringing up race. I thought they were off their mark. Their candidate didn't mind at all. And what reporter wouldn't ask.

Another day, I arrived at our Manchester studio at 6:30 in the morning to find Hillary Clinton being interviewed by Charlie Gibson of ABC. I thought, oh dear, she won't be fresh for me after an hour with Charlie, especially so early in the morning.

So, I dared to begin by telling a story I had read.

"Senator, perhaps this is apocryphal. You tell me." Her antennas went up.

"You and your husband stopped at a gas station in Park Ridge, Illinois, near Maine Township High where you went to school. The gas station attendant told Bill that he had dated you in high school. When you left the gas station, Bill said, 'You know Hillary, if you had married that guy you would be the wife of a gas station attendant.' 'No, Bill,' you answered, 'he would be president of the United States.'"

Well, she howled and loved it and I got a relaxed interview.

Obama became the president and eight years later when Hillary ran again, she went on to be the nominee of her party. The media focus had moved from race to gender. The feminist movement of the 60s was knocking on the highest of the glass ceilings.

I realize as I write this that I keep coming back to our viewers. Well, what is news for? Most Americans are hardworking people, giving and kind. I saw the poorest of people find a dollar or two to contribute to the Muscular Dystrophy Association and so many other causes we championed. And when called upon to put on a uniform to protect our country, our men and women do not hesitate.

New England lost 205 soldiers in the Afghanistan and Iraqi wars. New England Cable News created a documentary, *Remember Us,* honoring our fallen citizens. Iris Adler, a brilliant documentary producer and NECN Station Manager, Charlie Kravetz, an honest, compassionate newsman, asked me to narrate the documentary. I was honored.

NECN invited all of the families of our fallen heroes to a screening of the documentary. Senator Kennedy and his wife Vickie attended. Before the film they spoke with every single person, and there were more than a hundred.

The documentary was gripping. We all cried. And when it was over, no one moved. Maybe we wanted to hold on and never let go. At some point someone spoke. And then, these aggrieved mothers and fathers and sisters and brothers, husbands and wives, stood in line to speak with me, one at a time. We hugged and cried. This likely went on for an hour. Toward the end, one woman warmly embraced me and said, "Natalie, when you get the news you most dread, somehow it is a little easier to take when it comes from you."

I've thought about that moment many times since and am always humbled and reminded that the most important connection among people is caring. We need to let each other know we care.

I loved interviewing people. People fascinate me in general and being able to learn from an expert or understand why someone did what they did is a privilege a reporter has.

Outside Channel 5, various organizations asked me to conduct an interview with a famous person to attract an audience for a fundraiser or to be part of a speakers' series. I relished the format. The idea of these conversations was for me to interview someone on stage before a live audience in a way that made those in attendance feel included. The "speakers" liked the format because it precluded them from having to prepare a speech. I liked it because it allowed me to just go with the flow of the conversation. I think the audience liked it because it was real, unscripted, natural.

Among the people I interviewed were Meg Whitman, perhaps best known for making eBay what it is today; US Speaker Nancy Pelosi, on the occasion of her becoming the first woman speaker of the US House of Representatives; and Walter Cronkite. Of course, Walter Cronkite was someone I looked up to. I found him to be comfortable, full of humor, and just delightful. What a thrill.

Walter was among the stars of Salem State College's long-running and highly regarded speaker's series. I was honored they asked me, as I was again when they asked me to interview former President George H.W. Bush.

On that night in 2007, there happened to be a traffic jam for some reason in Salem preceding our interview, so we were escorted to a small office to wait for people to arrive. We were together, just us, for about forty minutes. Not accustomed to chatting with presidents, I was a little ill at ease but quickly realized this was a great chance to ask at least a few of those questions local reporters never get to ask a president.

We talked about Operation Desert Storm following Iraq's invasion of Kuwait. There was that now famous moment when General Norman Schwarzkopf had Saddam Hussein in his sights and called the president to ask permission to take him out. Mr. Bush said "No." I asked why.

The president explained he had given his word to the Saudis and other Arab countries that his mission was to expel Iraqi forces restoring Kuwait's independence. Period.

"Can you imagine, Natalie, if I went back on my word? The Arab nations would never trust us again."

Well, we talked more about that and when we finally were on stage, I did not bring it up again. I had just spent twenty minutes listening to

President Bush explain that historic moment and I guess in my head there was nothing more to ask.

Oh my. I got letters from people asking why I hadn't asked him the one question probably at the top of most people's minds. It still haunts me.

Major issues tend to be cyclical, coming in waves from a bubble to a boil and retreating to simmer only to repeat the cycle a few years later. Among such major issues we continue to debate: education, race, abortion, gun control, immigration.

In 1990, the topic of immigration was rising to a boil again. That year Congress revised the Immigration Act of 1965 by implementing the H-1B visa program for skilled temporary workers and a lottery system which helped those unable to enter through the preference system. Applicants from Africa received 40% of the "diversity" visas. Overall, the Immigration Act of 1990 helped permit the entry of 20 million people over the next two decades, the largest number recorded in any twenty-year period since the nation's founding. The sheer numbers seemed to scare people.

A second-generation American, I was tuned in on this topic. America promised equality of opportunity. Equality of results was never guaranteed, but freedom was and is: freedom to speak and write and pray or not, freedom to choose—Liberty. The damsel on the Hudson still beckons.

There often was competition for jobs among immigrants who had established themselves and those just arriving. In Boston, the love/hate relationship between the Irish and the Italians who followed is legend. Eventually, both groups made their way up the social and economic ladders. The tensions have eased to the point that each can laugh at each other's disparaging jokes, most of the time.

The overarching belief among immigrants was that their children would have a better life because of their sacrifice. And those children, in my case, my parents, were appreciative, even when they were scared and starving in the Great Depression of the 1930s. From childhood,

I listened to stories of the hardships of life in the "old country." One needed no more incentive to be grateful to be born here.

My one and only trip to Serbia, then part of Yugoslavia, with my father and siblings in 1994 reinforced my gratitude. We drove for miles to Bilece, home of my father's family. I saw an older-looking woman working the fields, her head covered with a babushka. She turned out to be a relative. It was a shock to learn she was only in her 50s. My siblings and I could see first-hand that the opportunities we had in the United States were foreign to our contemporaries in Serbia.

My father's cousins put out a feast for us. Two people our age drove all the way down from Belgrade to meet us, six hours. The family killed two of their six lambs to roast and harvested a basket of vegetables from their gardens. I felt terrible that they had lessened their herd for us. We talked for hours as the lambs turned on the spits. My Serbian is basic, a child's vocabulary, so I missed much of what was said and often had to ask for translation. I did understand the compliments to my late mother. These women adored her and said she was the kindest and sweetest of Serbian women. How I wished she were with us. Everyone loved my mother. She had a gift of bringing out the best in everyone. I think it was because she saw people from their point of view. She often counseled us to realize there is more than one side to a story.

That trip became a history lesson as the older men talked of the past and what they feared was coming. The Serbs and Croatians were on the verge of war again. Serbs are of the Eastern Orthodox Faith; Croatians, Roman Catholic. Yet it was more than religion that divided them. WWII wasn't so long ago. Some who fought were still living and talked firsthand of the genocide of Serbs by the hands of the Croatian Ustashi. Their brutality against women and children as well as men had earned the respect of Hitler and Nazi Germany.

Now, years later, the Serbs would be accused of murdering Croatians. Serbs would say the Croatians again were trying to purge the country of Serbians. The fighting was vicious. President Clinton joined NATO in the bombing of Serbian areas of Yugoslavia in 1999.

Coincidently just before the NATO attack, I was sent to the White House to cover marathoners Billy Rogers and Joan Benoit Samuelson. The Clinton administration invited them to run with the president. It was an honor, of course, for them and an opportunity for Channel 5 to promote our Boston Marathon coverage.

While the three were out running, my crew and I were in the waiting area of the president's office having a fun time checking out the place, the office itself, the tiny secretary's desk just outside his door, and a narrow hallway connecting to the waiting room.

Turning to speak with someone in that hallway, I ran smack into, of course, President Clinton. I was embarrassed and eager to escape to more space. But Mr. Clinton calmly complimented me on the morning interview in the Rose Garden. I thanked him and added I would have liked to have asked him about more than running a marathon. He quickly asked, about what? I told him I was of Serbian descent and said Serbs in America were worried he was only getting one side of the story of what was happening in Kosovo. So, he said, "Bring me a group of Serbians. I'd like to hear what they have to say."

I called my father as soon as we left the White House to tell him of this unexpected opportunity to brief the president. He said he would call three men he knew who had just returned from Yugoslavia and had first-hand knowledge of what was going on. I had been introduced to one of Mr. Clinton's aides who said he would call with the details in a day or two. He never called and I was never able to reach him. I realized the president had already made his decision.

As it happened when the immigration issue was building again in 1990, I was headed to Athens, Michigan, for the one-hundredth-birthday party of my beloved Teta Rista, who had emigrated from Serbia as a young girl. I knew there would be perhaps a hundred Serbs from around the country in attendance and thought the Serbian gathering would be one good example giving immigration a personal perspective over a hundred-year period. My management agreed, and we hired a photographer in Michigan where I set the stage for the issues being argued. Once back at the station in Needham, we set up interviews and gathered what video we needed to tell the story that was seething all across the country. We talked with people who were angry, believing immigrants were taking jobs from American citizens. Others were upset their European relatives were being passed over in favor of people from another continent. I asked Senator Kennedy, a sponsor of the bill, about the uproar. He admitted that he and the senate had not done a good job of preparing Americans for the changes the new immigration laws would allow, specifically more people from countries outside Europe.

That period pales in comparison to what is happening on our southern border today. How is it our government can't get this right?

In discussing policy, its effects, people's concerns, suggestions for solutions, I think we did a good job of again separating fact from fiction, giving people on all sides a voice and hopefully furthering an understanding of how to move forward. Again, WCVB believed the money and time involved in a half hour prime time special was important.

CHAPTER 20

Nat and Chet/Chet and Nat

Speaking of teamwork, for the better part of twenty-five years, Chet and I were a team. What began as a chance pairing in 1976 to co-anchor the eight-hour live coverage of the Queen's visit to Boston became Chet and Nat, Nat and Chet.

People sometimes referred to Chet and me as though we were one person and I suppose in some ways we were. Chet and I had a rare partnership. We worked together anchoring our nightly newscasts Monday through Friday. We co-anchored our live coverage of special events, breaking news and fundraisers. We hosted numerous charitable and community events together. We were married and parents together, including Lindsay and also Dana and Dawn, two daughters from Chet's previous marriage.

Of course, we didn't do everything together. Chet might go off flying with friends. I might chase a little white ball around a golf course.

And clearly we had different personalities. Chet was laid back. I was a doer. Chet often was content with what is. I looked for ways to make what is, better. Chet loved all things about flying and we often argued over who got to sit in the left seat. He usually won. I loved cooking. We both appreciated good food. I like my home neat and organized. Messy didn't bother Chet. I was dedicated to fitness and exercise. Chet moved in and out on that one. Chet was a good storyteller. I can tell a story, but I think he was more entertaining, as I might be more likely to find the serious nature of a subject. I like to get things done, sooner rather than later. Mañana worked OK for Chet. So, on good days, we complemented one another; other times, we probably made each other nuts. Fortunately, most days the former was true.

We co-anchored our evening newscasts Monday through Friday but also covered stories individually, sometimes assigned, other times of our own initiative. And sometimes, it was just the luck of the draw.

As it was in 1974. Chet was covering a story for our news magazine, *Chronicle*, which sent him to the Poconos for several days. I was covering a fire in Boston when I got a call from the station asking, "How fast can you get to Logan to catch a flight to Florida?"

I was to meet up with the Concorde and fly back to Boston the next day. The Concorde was a British-French supersonic jet that flew at twice the speed of sound. This was to be her inaugural United States flight. What a story and what a great opportunity. I raced home, packed a bag and flew to Florida.

The next day I was strapped to a seat. The interior was rudimentary as the plane had not yet been fitted for commercial traffic. Take off was exhilarating. Flying at Mach II—1,350 mph, 800 miles faster than a 737—I could feel the pull setting me back in my chair. I was hoping I wouldn't get sick to my stomach. How embarrassing would that be? If memory serves, the flight was one hour and twenty minutes, half the time of a conventional jet. It was a celebrated landing in Boston and a history-making story to share with our viewers.

Chet was beside himself when he realized the trip he had missed. I felt sorry for him, for at least ten seconds.

On a professional level, Chet and I had something intangible going for us when co-anchoring non-scripted, special events, which we did for over two decades. In TV talk, we clicked. As often as we were asked about it, it is still a little difficult to define. I can say, we had complete confidence in one another. We knew our material. Neither of us was afraid of the unknown, whether it be a technical issue or a surprising comment from someone. We had a good sense of what was happening, what was unusual, what had been said, what needed repeating or amplifying. There is a perspective that is critical for an anchor to maintain when you are collating hours of action into a cohesive story.

Ours was not a nine-to-five job, and being married, we talked a lot at home about what was going on. We shared a "common sense," if you will, which guided our personal opinions of good and bad, right and wrong, important and not.

Thanks to the philosophy of WCVB, which encouraged coverage of any and all we considered important to our viewers, Chet and I had many opportunities to lead our team coverage of live events. Under the direction of our "we can handle anything" news director, Jim Thistle, we found avenues outside the daily newscast to inform our viewers.

For example, when Rose Fitzgerald Kennedy, matriarch of the Kennedy family, died in 1995, we broadcast her funeral, using the coverage as a history lesson of this famous Boston family. Presidential historian Doris Kearns Goodwin joined us. Maybe no one knew the Kennedy family better. She told me she spent nine years researching for her book, *The Kennedys and Fitzgeralds*, including years in Rose's attic, where she uncovered a treasure of family history. Our colleague Clark Booth shared the anchor desk as well on this occasion, adding a perspective only Clark, a sharp student of history, could provide. We were on the air some four hours. A lot of preparation goes into this kind of coverage, and Chet and I were appreciative of the challenge.

And what a challenge it was in 1985 when we learned Archbishop Bernard Law was to be elevated to cardinal. Thistle said we were going to Rome. Thistle, a Catholic boy himself, knew how much the church meant to most of our audience. For Chet, this was a dream come true. He went to Catholic schools through twelfth grade in Amsterdam, New York. The nuns, the priests, and the teachings were intrinsic to his very identity.

I am a Christian of the Eastern Orthodox Faith, not a Roman Catholic. But I know from my upbringing the role God plays in my life and in the lives of many. Believing in something bigger than life itself is based on faith, not science, and people can argue about it to the end of time, but the truth is, faith can bring peace and comfort and there are times when that is as important as putting food on your table.

Our colleague Clark Booth probably knew more about religion and especially the Catholic Church than most priests, Jesuits excepted. Both Clark and Chet added to the depth of our coverage as only smart reporters of the Catholic faith could have.

Our coverage was a mix of live audio mixed in Needham with pictures sent separately and reports we put together in Rome for inclusion in our newscasts. We did not have the technical ability to broadcast pictures and sound live from Rome. This went on for close to a week, and for this local Boston team, it was a rare opportunity to venture outside New England. Many of us had never been to Rome before. What a gift.

The trip to Rome was another example of the extent to which Channel 5 would go to connect with our viewers. I often say attitude is 90 percent of life. The attitude, if you will, of WCVB was the belief that we were but one part of the greater community of New England. Our job was to tell you what was going on and to give you information you needed to make intelligent decisions. When it came to events such as the elevation of your priest, we brought the pageantry to you. The celebration was yours.

In celebrations closer to home, Chet and I, together with our sports anchor, Mike Lynch, co-anchored the annual running of the Boston Marathon.

For Bostonians, the running of the Boston Marathon, the world's oldest continuing foot race, is a day of multiple celebrations. Patriot's Day is a Bay State holiday commemorating the 1775 battles against the British in Lexington and Concord. When we first began in 1972, WCVB aired a reenactment of those battles. We reporters and our cameramen spent the cold, rainy night at the battle scenes shooting actors dressed as British and American soldiers. It was quite an undertaking for this fledgling station. It sent a message that those promises made to the FCC were not just words. Boston Broadcasters, in fighting to gain the license to operate Channel 5, had promised a depth of innovative broadcasting that few believed could be done. We would deliver and then some.

Marathon Day is also a celebration of giving, ordinary people running to raise money to help others. My assignment each year was to begin the day around 6:30 in the morning in Hopkinton, where the runners gathered to begin the race. People raised thousands of dollars running for causes. For the elite runners, this was the big race to win. For the rest of the 20 thousand or so, it was personal. The 26-mile, 385-yard route takes runners through eight cities and towns from Hopkinton to Boston. The outpouring of spectators cheering them on along the entire route offering water strikes me as another example of the "hometown" sense of Boston.

From Hopkinton, I was driven to Boston to the Lenox Hotel at the finish line. Three-time Boston winner and Olympian Billy "Boston Billy" Rogers and Joan Benoit Samuelson, Olympic Gold medalist and two-time Boston winner, joined Chet, Mike Lynch, and me at the anchor desk. We had to crawl through a bathroom window of the hotel to get to the roof from where we broadcast. It was a perfect venue, as we could see the runners turning the corner onto Boylston Street and stretch for the finish line just below us. Rogers was amiable and glib and of course all knowing about the marathon and its history, an anchor person's dream. Joan was shy, and the first year it was difficult to get her to share her treasure trove of stories. As the years went by, she opened up more, and I think she actually enjoyed it.

While some complained that covering the marathon was like watching grass grow, I loved it, because it was another opportunity to feel part of our Boston community and experience it with our neighbors. Chet and Mike, as great as they were covering this event, didn't love it quite as much as I did. But Jack Harper, in the lead car covering the women, did, especially when the energetic Uta Pippig was in the race. In 1996, Pippig was clearly hurting. We later learned she suffered a bout of ischemic colitis, inflammatory bowel disease. Despite cramps and diarrhea, she stayed the course and became the first woman to win three consecutive Boston Marathons.

1980. "She didn't run the race!" "What?" "She didn't win." "Who?" "Rose Ruiz. She didn't win the marathon." People were shouting at me in the cavernous Hynes Auditorium in Boston where the runners gathered. "She cheated." "She jumped in." "She didn't run the whole race."

The runners of the 84th Boston Marathon were laid out on the floor trying to recuperate. I was wearing an earpiece, which allowed producers in Needham to talk to me. I heard a director say, "60 seconds Natalie." I was clear across the auditorium from where our live camera was set up. I had no way to talk to anyone at the station, so I asked a man in an official Boston Athletic Association, BAA, green jacket, "Do you know what these people are talking about?" "Yes." "Run with me."

With that we raced across the auditorium floor. "Natalie ten seconds."

We got to the camera just in time for the tech to throw me the microphone and we were on the air live. I explained to the viewers what had just happened and turned to the BAA official and asked what he knew. He said no one had seen Ruiz along the route. The front two women runners were given their positions at the 18-mile mark and they definitely would have seen her if she had passed them. He said that in retrospect, her post race interview was probably the first tip-off, as she didn't know her intervals or splits (measured times). And most notably, she wasn't really sweating, nor was she out of breath as she crossed the finish line.

After that newscast, Jim Thistle asked why I hadn't alerted him to this big news. I don't think he realized I was learning about it the same time our viewers were.

I figured Ruiz was likely at the Sheraton, where most of the runners were staying. I managed to get her room number and knocked on the door telling my cameraman to please roll. Who knew what would happen?

A short, dark-haired woman opened the door. I identified myself and asked to talk with Rose, the winner of the marathon. I didn't want to give it away too early, fearing she might shut the door and not let us in. But I glanced at the TV and saw it was tuned to Channel 5 so, well, she knew that we knew her run was in question.

Rose was on a couch with her legs up. To me, they didn't look like runner's legs. They were too muscular; she wasn't lean enough. And she did not appear exhausted; rather, she appeared nervous.

Rose insisted she had run the race and no amount of coaching would persuade her to tell the truth.

Her mother, who had answered the door, looked very uncomfortable. Eventually I had to give up, but we did have her denial on film, which no one else did at that point. We interviewed BAA officials and runners and filed a report for the 11 o'clock news.

The story dominated news about the marathon, and eight days later, officials declared Jacqueline Gareau of Canada the official winner.

To the best of my knowledge, Ruiz never publicly confessed to having cheated; however, a friend of hers told reporters years later that she had confided to him, saying she didn't realize the front runners had not gone by yet. Perhaps she was as surprised as anyone that she had come in first.

Rose Ruiz died of cancer at the age of sixty-six.

Many years later, in 2013, I was at Chicago O'Hare airport returning to Boston. I looked up at the TV screen and saw the coverage of the marathon. As I did every year since Channel 5 stopped covering the race live, I felt a pit in my stomach. After thirty years of covering this Marathon, it was painful to be a spectator. But suddenly I could see something was wrong. People were dropping to the ground. Ambulance sirens were wailing. I had to board my flight before I could find out what happened.

When we got to Boston I learned that two bombs had exploded about two hundred yards apart just before the finish line on Boylston Street. It was pandemonium. Three people had died and over 264 were injured.

Like everyone else, I was glued to my television set as the story continued. Two brothers, Tamerlan and Dzhokhar Tsarnaev were identified as possible suspects. We watched as police released a bar-rage of bullets at the two in Cambridge following the murder of a MIT officer. The older brother, twenty-six, was killed. The younger, nineteen, got away and an all-out search continued through the night. Residents of Watertown and Cambridge were told to stay inside, with doors locked, as the manhunt went on. In the morning, one resident noticed the cover of his boat in his backyard was askew. Beneath the cover, he discovered a man covered in blood. It was Dzhokhar.

The FBI investigated this as an act of terror and later the two were determined to have acted on their own, not representing any specific terrorist group. Dzhokhar was convicted and sentenced to death. As of this writing, he remains at a federal prison in Colorado.

This was the first big story in Boston since I had left Channel 5 in 2007. I struggled emotionally and walked the city for miles and hours trying to understand my own feelings. First and foremost, like so many others, I struggled to believe someone would actually do this! The same frightening feeling of vulnerability which we all experienced on 9/11 returned.

As I walked the marathon route on Commonwealth Avenue and stood before the spontaneous memorial in Copley Square, I thought about the deaths of innocent people, the lifetime of pain to come for those hurt. I looked at the flowers and candles and handwritten notes and felt we had all been robbed. This was the Boston Marathon! Who would ever have thought anyone was ever in danger? Terrorists. They can and do and will strike. The innocence of trust was taken from us, again.

I thought about the spontaneous burst of song at the Boston Gar-den that Tuesday night, and again at Fenway Park on Saturday. Funds were set up to help the victims and their families. Two jihadists scarred our city, but they could never destroy the strength that is Boston.

Chet and I often were asked to headline a fundraiser and serve as hosts of the luncheon or dinner. It was always a challenge to schedule considering our work obligations, but we did as many as we could, sometimes several a week. We both felt it a rare opportunity to help raise money for worthy efforts. Just because we were Chet and Nat, people would attend and donate. And it had the added benefit of allowing us to meet more of the people for whom we reported every night.

Chet and I were asked to join the board of the Genesis Fund. Begun by Dr. Murray Feingold, a pediatrician and geneticist, the Genesis Fund was created to raise money for children who were born with birth defects and mental disorders. Often when children are born with a problem, the pediatrician can struggle with a diagnosis. And often, one genetic issue results in other needs. Murray and his team coordinated that care among specialists. Murray was a gifted diagnostician. And he had an amazing way with the kids and their parents who trusted him and loved him.

The makeup of the board was unusual in that essentially there were three types of people: those who ran companies, media heads, and people like us who might help draw a crowd. So, all the decisions were made right there at the board meeting and if we were short, someone at the table would write a check.

Chet and I, together with our colleagues, hosted an annual telethon to benefit the Genesis Fund. Our annual John Havlicek Fishing tournament was our biggest event, involving several days on Martha's Vineyard or Nantucket, fishing, golfing, and enjoying great entertainment. We raised a lot of money. John brought in many of his friends from the world of sports, who were a draw for the paying customers. In addition to Murray, Brian McLaughlin was the driving force of the Genesis Fund, and without him, we could not have done what we did. He is smart and generous, a man with a giant heart.

Much has changed in the world of medicine over the past forty years, and the Genesis Fund, now Foundation, has tried to adapt and still honor our commitment to helping as many children as we can with the Feingold method of coordinated care. We lost Murray in 2015, but the mission is as strong as ever thanks in large part to Matthew Hoffman, our current president; an energetic, young board; and our talented and caring Dr. Catharine Nowak and her medical team.

Among the many charitable causes WCVB supported was the Jerry Lewis Labor Day Telethon. This Muscular Dystrophy Association (MDA) effort stands out as the annual event that brought all of New England together to help kids.

I actually began working for MDA when I worked at WBZ-TV. Together with Rex Trailer, a popular kids' entertainer at the time, we encouraged children to hold backyard carnivals to raise money for kids who needed help. It was heartwarming.

Every Labor Day, WCVB joined the national telethon for almost twenty-four hours of live television to raise money for research and care of children with muscular dystrophy. Chet and I hosted the telethon, together with our colleagues, which introduced us to some of the most extraordinary people, who became part of our family. These included little Jennifer Haskins.

She had curly red hair, freckles, a nonstop smile, and at just five years of age was in a wheelchair with muscular dystrophy. She is the most courageous person I have ever known. As the years went by, she lost more and more of her muscular ability. One night when our two families were out to dinner, I noticed she no longer could hold a fork. But never mind, it didn't bother Jennifer. Later as a teen, she traveled to Europe with a group of friends who took all her needs in stride, as she did, never losing sight of Jennifer and her insatiable appetite for life.

Jennifer went on to UMass, where she earned a degree in education and interned in her hometown of Foxboro. I asked how she managed to control a class of rambunctious kids. She said it wasn't an issue. They saw her, strapped to a wheelchair, and somehow were inspired to do the right thing.

While in her senior year, she called to say she had to share something. I remember where I was standing when I took the call and can still hear her voice.

"Natalie, I know you will be upset." I held my breath. "I have cancer and the doctors are going to remove my legs to keep me alive. The bad part is I will miss a few classes but I have completed my thesis so I should be able to graduate."

I couldn't believe it.

"It's OK," she consoled, "I couldn't walk on those legs anyway."

But later her father called to say the university was going to deny her graduation and degree because she would have missed four classes. Are you kidding me? So, she was going to have to forfeit the teaching opportunity she had in Foxboro. Dear God. Is there a God?

In the end, the school allowed her to graduate but denied her the degree she needed to teach. So, she had to give up the offer to be a full-time teacher.

Shawn McDuff had Duchenne, which is more common with boys. Every year Shawn's father would say this would be his son's last year on the telethon, as he likely wouldn't live much longer. My optimism wouldn't accept that, and neither would Shawn, who said to his dad on the air, "No ,I'll graduate, Dad. I will."

So, when Shawn did graduate from high school, Chet and I were there to cheer him on. And again, when he graduated from college. And yet again, when he married. It was a miracle. His parents' lives were consumed with caring for him. They, like the Haskins, dedicated their lives to their child.

The Haskins and McDuffs came to be very much a part of our lives. These families faced uncertainty, daily struggles, and fear with compassion, humor, and gratitude for what they did have. One would be challenged to match such strength and courage.

They and hundreds of other people with muscular dystrophy participated every year in our telethon, our boot drives led by the fire departments, and fundraisers throughout New England. It was a picture of a giving community, compassionate, generous, and together.

It is easy to get caught up in your life and forget the bigger picture of your neighbors. The telethon was a welcome reminder of the beauty of humanity.

And how about this? Jennifer and Shawn said they wanted to throw a party to thank Chet and me for our work with MDA. We said no. We needed no formal thanks, but we would be happy to go out to dinner with them and their families. So, one evening, after the 6 PM news, we drove to the nearby Sheraton hotel to meet the Haskins and McDuffs. We were led to a room and when the doors opened, the ballroom filled with our MDA kids greeted us, maybe a hundred people, most in wheelchairs, and there, on a makeshift stage, were Shawn and Jennifer.

We were guided to seats next to them. They introduced themselves as Chet and Nat. And there began one of the most extraordinary newscasts we were ever privileged to be part of. MDA kids played reporters in the field and in the style of a "roast" had fun with Chet and Nat. They filled the room with wit and laughter. One group made a book of candy wrappers cleverly designed to tell a story of MDA. Another made an album of pictures capturing years of telethons.

These kids could not have given Chet and me a greater gift. I have never been so moved in all my life and I cry as I write this. We were grateful that we had taken Lindsay with us. I hope she will also treasure the memory of challenged kids with big hearts and a great sense of humor.

One of the best self-promotions of Channel 5 was a series of spots based on the theme "Five is Family," created and produced by the highly talented Dan Driscoll and his company, September Productions. Not only was it a first-rate production, it was true. We did feel we were "family." Dan understood that.

Chet and I used to throw a Christmas party every year and included friends from our various walks of life: news, politics, flying, neighbors. I and a couple of my girlfriends would take a day off from work and prepare the food. That was almost more fun than the party. People would ask what to bring and I suggested their best dessert. My mother and I made little flags for each dessert to give each chef her due, and while we were out caroling, Mom would switch the dining room table from dinner food to dessert.

Chet said no one would want to go out caroling. "Who wants to leave a warm house for the freezing cold?" As it turned out, our guests loved it and the neighbors loved it. They would call to ask the date of the party so they would be sure and be home! And Chet, with the best voice in the crowd, had as much fun as anybody.

Neighbors would meet us at their doors with hot chocolate and cookies. Our Santa would give them candy canes.

I bought a Santa suit and each year we asked a different person to play Santa, primarily to get people into their coats and out into that freezing snow to sing carols throughout the neighborhood. As the years went on, Jim Thistle brought his guitar to lead this band of carolers. Bob Crane, Massachusetts State Treasurer, in later years brought his "Treasury Notes" to the party. Bob would call me every fall to ask the date. He said he and Mary didn't want to go to Florida and miss what he said was the best party of Christmas.

Over the years, the party grew from a dozen folks to a hundred, including many of our colleagues. Unfortunately, our house was not in any way big enough for that many, much less all the people we worked with. Chet and I highly respected our technical staff and the producers and writers and editors who made our jobs possible, so we decided to host a Thanksgiving Party at Tecce's Restaurant in the North End for them and their spouses.

We had come to be very close with the Tecce family, ate at their North End restaurant often. Papa Joe used to regale us with his stories of standing up to the mob. He told us when he refused the mob's insistence he use their laundry company, they drove by his place, then on Salem Street, and sprayed it with bullets.

No bullets flew on the night of our gatherings, but plenty of wine and good cheer. The station holiday party did not include spouses. We invited spouses and significant others, but no management. No offense intended, we just wanted everyone to be able to relax and know this party was for them. The fact that everyone who was invited came meant the world to us.

There is something special when you can say, I spend most of my waking hours at work, or getting to work, or getting home from work. And I like where I work, most of the time. And I like the people I work with most of the time. And now at Thanksgiving, Chet and Nat are saying we value you. Together, we reinforced our belief that Channel 5 was family.

That camaraderie played a significant role in a decision to stay at WCVB. Shortly before CNN was launched in 1980, two of the officers of the station flew to Boston to ask Chet and me to join their team as co-anchors of their Monday through Friday evening newscasts. It was certainly tantalizing, as CNN was creating a new effort to compete with the big three broadcast networks. Chet and I decided to stay in Boston, in part at least persuaded by our allegiance to Channel 5 and our colleagues.

CHAPTER 21
Michael Dukakis

Every four years, Chet and I were assigned to anchor our coverage of the political conventions from the various sites throughout the country. One of us would cover the Democrats; the other, the Republicans. In 1988, with the nominee from our home state, we were assigned to cover the Atlanta convention together. Bay State Governor Michael Dukakis was the Democratic nominee for president.

After covering the parade of candidates who trooped through New Hampshire every four years for the nation's first primary, to have the nominee from Massachusetts was big time. Immediately, news was anything and everything Dukakis.

Boston reporters had a leg up on the national guys. After all, we had been covering Governor Dukakis for twelve years. So, we had knowledge and access. In retrospect, we were babes in the woods, much as the nominee himself. Running for president is nothing like running for governor. And running against George Bush and the Reagan Republican team was nothing like running against Frank Sargent or Ed King.

But then, who could have anticipated a brutal Republican attack campaign, the likes of which we had not seen before.

The image of Michael Dukakis as an Eagle Scout seems to fit. His father-in-law, the lovable Harry Ellis Dickson, associate conductor of the Boston Pops Orchestra, told me a story he repeated often which speaks volumes. Dickson and Dukakis drive to Logan Airport in Michael's car to pick up his wife Kitty. Dickson urges Dukakis to park outside and leave the car with the state police. After all he is the governor.

"Nope."

Dickson says, "Dukakis insists on driving into the garage, paying the fee, and walking to the terminal."

He was thrifty, though his wife would use a stronger adjective. He bought his clothes at Filene's Basement, did the grocery shopping because, as Kitty told me, he thought she spent too much, and he famously took the subway to work, Brookline to Beacon Hill.

To Dukakis, right and wrong was black and white. Time-honored Boston patronage took a hit under Dukakis. He didn't do favors or hire friends. And they paid him back big time when he ran for re-election. His own party turned against him and chose Ed King as their candidate. Dukakis was dumfounded.

At his core, Dukakis believes in competence, honesty, and hard work. He is a first-generation American of Greek descent. He is very proud of his Greek heritage and of his immigrant father who went to medical school at Harvard.

People called him a technocrat. Many saw him as arrogant, stubborn and stuffy. He didn't see himself that way, so the criticism didn't faze him. Besides, he got things done, such as bringing unemployment down from 12 to 3 percent in his first term.

I got to know Kitty Dukakis by a chance seating on a dais at a charity event for breast cancer. We learned we each lost our mothers at a young age to breast cancer and talked of ways to raise money to combat the disease. Outwardly, Kitty is the opposite personality of her husband. She is vibrant, talkative, and energetic. While he talks in a near monotone, her speech is up and down the scale. Her father, Harry Ellis Dickson, adored her, and through Kitty I got to know this musical giant as a lovable teddy bear, warm, humorous, and affectionate.

While out of office, Dukakis taught at the Kennedy School of Government and, as I remember, there met John Sasso. Sasso was full of life and ideas, robust in his speech, a barrelful of energy. He would become Dukakis's team captain as Dukakis made a comeback to regain the corner office. He beat King and was reelected for a second term.

Sasso would engineer Dukakis's run for president. But Dukakis's strict adherence to correctness would lose him his kingpin. Sasso created a video of Joe Biden, also running for president, juxtaposing a speech Biden had given with one of British Labor Party leader, Neil Kinnock. Biden had plagiarized. He apologized and withdrew. Sasso knew Dukakis would never approve, as he was against attack ads, so Sasso hid the fact that he was the author of the video.

When the truth was known, Dukakis asked Sasso and Paul Tully to step aside. In retrospect, many might rightfully ask if Sasso had stayed on, might he have handled differently the onslaught of negative campaigning that was yet to come from the Bush team? Sasso did rejoin the campaign in September of 1987, but it was too late.

During the presidential campaign, Kitty revealed she had been addicted to amphetamines for twenty-six years. When I interviewed her, she said Michael didn't know until she was in therapy. It was a jolt to his campaign as people asked how a husband wouldn't have been aware. She painted a picture of the softer side of Dukakis as only she would know.

During a presidential debate, it was a question from a reporter about Kitty that may have hurt Dukakis as much as any of what was to follow. Dukakis was morally opposed to the death penalty. Bernard Shaw of CNN, asked if Kitty had been raped and murdered, would Dukakis be in favor of the death penalty for the killer.

Dukakis very calmly replied, "No, Bernard. I think you know I've always been opposed to the death penalty."

Those of us watching were thinking he surely would follow that with something about how much he loved his wife or how he felt when his father was mugged. Nothing. This lack of emotion reinforced an image of a cold, unfeeling man. He was not cold and unfeeling at all, but somehow he had trouble expressing himself in ways that would let people get to know him. It wasn't in his nature to talk about his inner feelings in public.

After the Atlanta convention, Dukakis had a 54-to-37 percent lead in the polls. It would evaporate quickly as the Bush team, led by attack dog Lee Atwater, launched one blast after another.

A rumor circulated that Dukakis had fought depression and that was why he refused to release his medical records. A reporter asked President Reagan if he thought Dukakis should release them. With his perfect Hollywood timing, Reagan quipped, "I wouldn't want to take advantage of an invalid."

Instead of blowing that off with a few jokes himself, Dukakis spent a whole week showing off his fitness, running and wearing muscle shirts. It was a waste of precious time and to many, he looked silly.

Dukakis signed on to a federal furlough program allowing prisoners, even murderers, to be given repeat weekend passes. One of them, Willie Horton, while out on furlough, attacked a Maryland couple in their suburban home. He beat and tied up the man and raped his fiancée multiple times. The Dukakis team defended the furlough program, as Dukakis believed it would inspire prisoners, even lifers, to better behavior in the prison. The Bush campaign was quick to air a scary ad painting Dukakis as too liberal and soft on crime.

Bush held a campaign stop in Boston with the Boston Harbor as a backdrop. The Boston Harbor was one of the dirtiest in the country at the time, and the video insinuated it was the governor's fault. Their ad portrayed Dukakis as anti-environment.

And maybe the one image that no one forgets was Dukakis riding in a tank wearing a helmet. Someone on his team thought that would be a good visual to show he would be a strong commander-in-chief. The national press in attendance in Sterling Heights, Michigan, howled, and the Bush team had a field day. The consensus was that Dukakis didn't look presidential. People thought he looked ridiculous.

Throughout all of this, Michael Dukakis would not fight back until it was way too late. He wanted to run a positive campaign and refused to believe the dirt being shoveled his way was burying him.

He lost. Bush won forty out of the fifty states.

A few years later, Lee Atwater, sick and near death, admitted he had made up the whole story about Dukakis fighting depression. He apologized. Atwater died at the age of forty-one of a brain tumor.

When the election was over, I couldn't help but recall the final night of the Democratic convention in Atlanta. It had been a rousing party for their candidate. He and Kitty were on top of the world.

Near midnight, Chet and I were leaving the convention hall when we spotted the motorcade in the distance. As they came closer, we decided to wait; maybe we would get a close-up of them on their way. Instead, the motorcade stopped, Dukakis rolled down the window and he and Kitty shouted for us to get in. With the four of us sandwiched in the back seat, I turned to look at him. I can still see him. He laid his head back, took a deep breath, and said, "It's over, we won."

Chet and I talked about it later and I asked him, "Did you hear him say 'it's over'? Does he not realize he has the fight of his life coming up?" Maybe he was just exhausted. We went back to Boston and the Dukakises went on vacation for two weeks.

Some years later, I had occasion to ask him about that vacation. He insisted it wasn't a vacation, that he continued working on gubernatorial matters as well as the campaign. Perhaps, but he was absent as the grenades continued to explode.

CHAPTER 22

The Respites

Beyond our life at Channel 5, Chet and I enjoyed our getaways. Every year for most of our married life, we spent a heavenly week or so on a tiny island called PSV, Petit St. Vincent.

A mile long, a quarter-mile wide, the island sits in the calm waters between the Caribbean and the Atlantic Ocean. Hazen Richardson and two of his friends built the resort of lava stone, twenty-three cottages, simple, all open to the sky. The water was clean and warm. The snorkeling offered an undersea world of color and an endless variety of fish. The food was simple. The rum drinks fantastic, although one needed to learn patience, as everything is on island time.

Patience begins with getting there. An early morning five-hour flight from Boston to San Juan, then a flight to Barbados, then another small plane and hair-raising landing at Union Island, where the pilot had to power up to the top of a hill and then kill the engines for a landing on a short strip that ended at the sea. Finally, twelve hours later, a relaxing thirty-minute boat ride to PSV where Haze and his wife Jennifer greeted you with a Mai Tai.

When Lindsay was a baby, the island workers made her a crib out of bamboo. Just precious. I vividly remember unpacking and wondering why we had so many boxes. Chet and our friend Jack Crowley had inadvertently packed a month's supply of baby products, formula, diapers—you name it. It turned out we had a great gift to give to the families who had babies throughout the nearby islands.

Lindsay got very sick. We were panicked: 104+ temp, no medical help nearby. We managed to get a call to her pediatrician in Needham who suggested alternating aspirin and Tylenol and bathing her in the sea, which was around eighty degrees as I remember it. I have never been so scared. The memory of my near death on that island a few years before didn't help. Eventually the fever subsided. Prayers answered.

The Richardsons owned six golden labs and for Lindsay, as a child, the dogs were the magic of PSV. She figured if we brought treats for the dogs, they would follow her and not sleep in someone else's cottage. My little towhead looked like a miniature shepherd as she roamed the island, six big labs dutifully behind her.

Nantucket, the "far away island," continued to be our sanctuary. It was a wonderful respite from the Mach 10 pace we lived on the mainland.

It was actually a news story that introduced us to Nantucket. It was the mid 70s, and in the newsroom, we got word that someone had spotted the *Andrea Doria*, an Italian transatlantic ocean liner that had sunk off the coast of Nantucket in 1956. The Italian vessel and a Swedish liner, the *Stockholm*, were traveling in opposite directions when a crewman misread his radar, putting the two ships on a collision course. Over fifty people died but over a thousand survived in one of the biggest rescue operations at sea. Chet was assigned to find himself a way out to the ship. Looking through the Nantucket phone book, he saw *The K Bird*, a Nantucket boat belonging to Pete Guild. He called and arranged for the transportation from the island.

Sometime later, Chet and I were eating dinner at the Jared Coffin House when we ran into Pete. He asked where we were staying and then handed us the keys to his cottage out at Surfside on the south side of the island. He said he rented it in July and August, but we could use it the other ten months. We were incredulous. That began an extraordinary friendship and our love of Nantucket.

Pete's cottage was heaven on earth. No heat but it did have indoor plumbing. What we loved was where it was, on the beach overlooking the Atlantic Ocean. We repaid Pete's generosity by caulking the bathroom, painting his shutters, and paying rent one of those summer weeks.

Chet and I would rent single-engine planes from Wiggins Airways in Norwood and often flew to Nantucket for the weekend. We packed a duffle bag with a pair of shorts, tee shirt, and bathing suit. No dress-up clothes, hair dryers, or make-up were needed here. Life was the Angler's Club and fishing with Pete, a true gem of a man, kind, giving, and sweet. Life was reading on the beach in the dunes, body surfing the waves at Surfside, building a fire in the sand, and cooking a hot dog. It was sing-along at the Muse and fried clams at Sy's. It was biking from town to Pete's cottage at Surfside, no lights, dirt roads, all part of the magic of the island. Nantucket is only sixty miles off the mainland, but the contrast between life there and in the city felt like another planet. And yes, you can see the planets there. No bright lights or industry to pollute the senses.

In the early 80s, Pete told us he had an offer to buy his Surfside cottage and wanted to give us first refusal. The offer was around $120,000. We were devastated, as we did not have the money to buy it and never dreamed someday we might make more money, but for now it was paycheck to paycheck. Some years later we did make enough money to buy a plot of land and after saving for a few years built a modest house well back from the beach. And a dozen or so years later, we had the money to buy a lot on the ocean not far from Pete's and built our dream beach house.

The allure of the island has changed for some people from beaches and fishing to hot tubs and pools. As one local put it, "So many people come here and want to change everything you think they would have come here for." If you could have but one photo to distinguish then and now it would be the airport. Private jets have replaced the single-engine planes.

Yet, there remains some of the small-town togetherness. Laws are decided in town meeting. Charities ask you leave a check taped to your door where someone will come and collect it. My hairdresser, born on island, works in a salon her husband created for her in their garage.

COVID-19 has limited our socializing and the population of the island has expanded dramatically, leaving many to wonder if such a small island and its fragile infrastructure can handle so many.

At Surfside, however, my neighbors and I live life pretty much as we always have. We still have a summer-long fishing contest. With the leadership of our longtime Surfside Association president, Tom Quigley, we met at a youth hostel twice a summer. That hostel now was sold, and we have a new association president. Yet life still centers on the beach, where come 5 o'clock, someone asks, "What's for dinner?" "I can make a salad." "I have scallops in the freezer."

And when my neighbor, Tom Quigley, decided his wife JByrd's culinary talents deserved a better kitchen, we all knew when the gas on the new stove would be turned on. Spontaneously, some twenty-five people gathered, drink and food in hand, and descended on their little cottage to celebrate. That's Surfside, where we can still enjoy Nantucket, as we think it was meant to be lived.

CHAPTER 23
Tip O'Neill

1991. We pulled up to the East Gate of the White House, House Speaker Thomas P. "Tip" O'Neill Jr. and I. The speaker seemed to bounce out of the limo and race to the car behind us carrying former President and Mrs. Gerald Ford. "Mr. President, how are you? Mrs. Ford. You know Natalie Jacobson."

Well, of course the Fords did not know me, but they were gracious.

We were at the White House to witness the 1991 Medal of Freedom ceremony. The Speaker was among the recipients, as was Red Sox legend Ted Williams. Tip, a die-hard Red Sox fan, told me he had never met his hero and was excited to finally shake his hand.

As we made our way up the steps to the East Room, Tip suddenly turned to me and asked, "Who shall I say you are?" His wife Millie, at the last minute, didn't join us as she wasn't feeling well. The devil in me chirped something like, "Tell them I'm your mistress." I thought he would laugh—and he normally would have—but he was clearly stressed. "Just say I'm a friend filling in for Millie."

It was puzzling to see him so nervous. "Mr. Speaker, you've been to the White House a million times. I'm the one who should be nervous."

We arrived to find the door to the East Room where the ceremony would take place guarded by a young man in formal military dress. I saw one lonely figure at the other side of the room. It was Number 9. I pleaded with the guard to let the speaker in to meet Williams, but he refused.

I had to think fast. There was no way I wasn't getting this shot, Tip meeting his hero, Ted, for the first time. So, I asked the guard if he would ask Williams to walk to us. He asked, Ted obliged, and I got my moment on tape. It was sweet actually, these two old Boston guys finally getting together later in life.

The angels continued to ride my shoulder as a member of President Bush's staff asked me if I would like to sit in Millie's seat for the ceremony and also take her seat at the luncheon which was to follow.

I had the speaker miked with hopes the president might whisper something in his ear when awarding him the Medal of Freedom. He did, and while it was just an off-handed comment, I had something the other networks didn't.

After the ceremony a young fellow told me someone else had been given Millie's seat at the luncheon. Oh well, at least I had her seat for the ceremony. Tip sent word to meet him at his office at 4 o'clock. My cameraman, producer Linda Polach, and I wasted a few hours and then met the speaker at the appointed time. As we walked into his office, he leapt from his desk chair and shouted, "I have a bone to pick with you young lady!"

I was shocked and at first thought he was kidding. He wasn't.

"I was seated next to first lady Barbara Bush at the luncheon. She leaned over to speak to me and noticed I had a microphone on my lapel. She said in a loud Barbara voice, 'Why Tip, you're wired.' I pulled the mike off and ended up knocking over her glass of water. It was a mess. I was so embarrassed. How could you have left a microphone on me?"

Well, I pictured the scene and wanted to laugh but of course didn't. I said I was sorry and explained that I never got to see him again after the ceremony to remove it, and besides, our microphone was so limited it couldn't have transmitted the sound past that table.

He didn't care. He really was angry. He eventually calmed down and granted us the interview. I needed him to tell us about his day, especially meeting Ted! Recounting that happy moment, brought back the Tip we knew.

We raced back to Boston and had the lead story no one else had.

Tip O'Neill was one of a kind. He was big in every way. Tall, heavy, with a booming voice, an eager hug or handshake, a big smile—he enveloped you. He was an Irish Catholic old-school liberal politician and proud of it.

Born in Cambridge, Massachusetts, home of Harvard and MIT, he and Millie did not move to Washington until O'Neill was elected speaker, twenty-five years after being elected to fill the seat vacated by John F. Kennedy, who had moved on to the Senate. That kept him close to the blue-collar voters as well as the elite.

You didn't have to like his politics to like him. He was that kind of a guy. Although, I'm sure his fellow congressmen had their moments. O'Neill was shrewd, powerful, and knew how to get his way. He also was not a fan of the two presidents during his speakership tenure, Jimmy Carter and Ronald Reagan, whom he always called Ree-gan. But he was a smart politician. Despite their differences, President Reagan and the speaker reportedly had a genuine friendship. Their relationship was based on their "6 o'clock rule," that all partisan fighting stops at 6. It was not uncommon for the Reagans to entertain the O'Neills for drinks and dinner at the White House. Ah, the Irish.

I had so much good material over many years involving O'Neill, from Boston College, to Capitol Hill, the White House ceremony, and interviews at his home on the Cape, I decided to put together a documentary. One piece that to me seemed important to his story was the Barry's Corner Gang from Cambridge. O'Neill kept in touch with his longtime friends from the North Cambridge area and they gathered regularly. The club itself, Barry's Corner, was just a room on the second floor of an old building. When the building was torn down, they met at the VFW Hall on Mass. Ave.

I badgered him to let me join him and film it. He said no female had ever attended, nor anyone from the media. He finally relented but was really worried his friends wouldn't like it. They must have agreed, as I found everyone to be very friendly.

I knew in a minute that I was right about wanting to know more about this aspect of his life. There was a familiarity and warmth among the men that spoke to years of friendship which we were able to capture on film. Here, O'Neill was just Tip, not the speaker. There were about fifty men in attendance as I recall. O'Neill engaged with each man.

"Hey, how's your son Mike doing? I remember he broke his arm in that football game. Twenty years? That long ago?"

His memory was incredible. I asked him later about that. He said he had always had a phenomenal memory for people, names, and their history. What a gift for a politician.

O'Neill believed government was all about helping the poor, the underprivileged, the unemployed, the sick. He loved his family, his country, his party. And, he loved the power the speakership allowed him. Unlike Mike Dukakis, O'Neill believed in patronage, giving friends a job.

He often worried about his wife Millie, who had been his high school sweetheart. Yet he preceded her in death, at the age of eighty-one due to coronary issues. Channel 5 covered his funeral live, on a cold winter morning in January of 1994 at St. John the Evangelist Church in Cambridge.

O'Neill had been christened here, married here, and now for the last time was here for his funeral, which drew people from the district and from Washington. Vice President Al Gore represented the Clinton administration, former presidents Carter and Ford attended, as did the leadership of both parties in Congress. Along with the rest of the press corps, I was assigned to stand outside the church and interview people as they entered.

His son, Thomas O'Neill III, eulogizing his father, captured Tip's Irish sense of humor. "When speaking of Republicans, especially President Reagan, Tip would say, 'Hate the sin, love the sinner.'

"To my dad all politics was local, but all politics was personal. And he loved everybody."

CHAPTER 24

The End of a Marriage

There was no one more surprised than I to finally accept my marriage was over. While it was clear to me for some time that Chet's feelings toward me had changed, I had been hopeful we could work through this.

It was very hard to work on television together and to work with our long-time colleagues. For three years, we kept it to ourselves. No one knew.

During those agonizing years leading up to our divorce, I was very worried about Lindsay, but my guardian angels pitched in. My niece Nicole, my sister Jean's daughter, came to live with us initially for a few months while she went to school. She stayed about two years. My cousin, Don Salatich's daughter Molly, came for a few days and stayed for about six months. They helped fill my life and, more importantly, came to be like sisters to Lindsay, who was in high school.

The three of them built a beautiful friendship. Nicole and Molly are about as different as two people can be. To see them develop a closeness warmed my heart. I remember one night when I couldn't sleep, I heard giggles and laughter from the other side of the house. I found the girls and the dogs sitting on the floor in the hallway at one in the morning having a great time. "Hey, I want in." *I need in.* So, I made popcorn and joined the party. They thanked me often over the years, and each time I told them, "You helped save me."

Finally, it was clear that Chet and I, after twenty-five years, could no longer continue as husband and wife. That day in 1999 in a lawyer's office was surreal. The meeting with the probate judge was a blur. We left the courthouse and in separate cars drove to work, meeting again on the anchor desk for the 6 o'clock news, as we had done a thousand times before.

No one knows what goes on in a marriage. Yet when the news became public, it seemed everyone had an opinion. It was topic A on radio talk shows. People have told me they were saddened by our divorce; some said they felt a loss and wondered what happened. I'm sensitive to their feelings, but I have never shared our private story and I will not now. It just isn't right.

I will only say I was devastated and still wonder how I survived it. I felt as though someone had cut me in two. Half of me had disappeared. Chet was my best friend and confidant, but he was no longer on my team.

Lindsay was about to go to college. I remember during orientation at Vanderbilt University in Nashville, the speaker advised parents not to change a thing between now and Thanksgiving. "Don't move a chair. Your kids are going to want to return to what they knew." I held my breath.

Lindsay would come home to a condo in Boston. The Needham homestead was no more. Dad had moved on. I was very afraid for her.

After Chet had taken his things and moved out, it took me three months to completely clear out our home. I would return from work at midnight and work a few hours on the basement or the attics or the closets. I filled at least three trucks with household furniture and appliances to give to those who needed these things. I had been supporting an organization which helped battered women get into apartments on their own. It was good to be able to help them. Dana and Dawn took what they wanted. Morgan Memorial and Goodwill took the rest.

The final night at 8 Old Greendale lives with me still. It was perhaps two in the morning. We had lived there twenty-five years, our entire married life. Lindsay knew no other home.

I walked through every room of our recently renovated home and allowed myself a happy memory of a time in each place. In Dana and

Dawn's room, a long chat from years past with Dawn came to mind. I smiled, remembering Dana helping with baby Lindsay. The guest room, where Molly and Nicole learned to help each other. Lindsay's room, where a crib once stood with a happy baby reaching to be hugged. The laundry room, where I lay on a tile floor with a new puppy. The kitchen where great smells, cooking adventures, and countless friends filled the space with joy. The dining table filled with holiday cheers, family, food. In the family room, looking at the dark TV screen, I remembered watching a recording of the Boston Symphony Orchestra fundraiser we hosted every year.

"Who is that big woman walking across the stage at the BSO, Chet?"

"That's you, Nat."

I was very pregnant with Lindsay.

I looked outside, my mind filling with pictures of the gardens, vegetables coming ready for harvest, roses forever in bloom, friends Bill Harrington and Jack Crowley planting new flowers, the pool where I swam laps every morning from April to November even before we added heat, the play area, the swings now gone.

The moon was up, I opened the garage door and swept out the last of the debris. I walked to our bedroom, for too long empty. Good night, Chet.

CHAPTER 25

Going It Alone

Following our divorce, Chet went to New England Cable News and I stayed at Channel 5. The whole awful experience was made even more difficult because it was all played out in public. I refused to listen to the radio talk shows. I was raw and couldn't handle it. I warned Lindsay not to listen also, but one day she got in the car and a station just happened to be on. I guess she got an earful of negative comments and came home in tears. I was worried about her. I had read enough about divorce and how it affects children. I did my best to try and stay in touch with her feelings and thoughts. Every weekend, I flew to Florida to be with her as she was competing in her final horse show season.

Anthony Everett and I were paired as anchors of our evening newscasts. He is a pro and easy to work with. As nice a guy as you will ever know, Anthony made the anchor transition easier.

Thank goodness for my little bichon, Breezy. Tramp had passed and I didn't have the heart to leave Breezy alone in an empty house, so I brought her to work with me for the next seven years. She was such a good little pup. I could trust her enough to sit under the anchor desk while I anchored the news. She never made a sound until Anthony ran over her tail with his chair. I don't think the mikes picked it up. The cameramen were wonderful and didn't have a problem with it. And the 11 PM crew, being smaller, embraced her. She was our nighttime mascot. She was my savior. I was grateful for my colleagues' indulgence.

Aside from the changes in my personal life, news was changing too, and had been for a while. Channel 5 was not immune to the changes experienced across the country. Our new general manager, Bill Fine, informed me that I would no longer be doing those "At Home" interviews with the candidates unless I could deliver them in a two-minute piece. Well, that wouldn't work; what can you learn about the character of a person in two minutes? Also, we wouldn't be doing the live programming we had done for years—although, after I had left, they did cover Senator Edward Kennedy's funeral and invited me to make a brief guest appearance. Innovative news programming, such as traveling to New Hampshire to understand the voters, or documentaries as I did with Tip O'Neill, live interviews during the newscasts, town meetings—all off the table. They would do shorter, headline-type stories, cut back on sports, increase weather. Reporters would not be given days to work on a story.

It is true that local stations have more competition and therefore less income from advertising than they once did. Even so, local news is perhaps more needed than ever in this globalized world, as people can relate best to their locality, their schools, their government, their sports teams, their potholes, and their weather.

I believe the success of the local Boston stations from the early 70s through the 90s was due to people believing their local news people cared about them. It was a trust I like to think we earned. We tried to prove it day in and out by bringing people honest information they needed to make smart decisions.

The choices we made in story selection, time, and money were all in the interest of doing our jobs to the best of our ability for our viewers' benefit. Not every story was a blockbuster, and sure, we made mistakes, but we learned from them. We continually questioned ourselves, challenged ourselves: what could we be doing better? Our news director, Emily Rooney, would convene a meeting on occasion including the entire newsroom. We questioned ourselves, argued about priorities and came away recommitted to doing the right thing. We believed we, the people, all the people, were in this together, this thing called life. No one person, no group, was less or more important than any other.

I like to think when you turned on our newscast, you took a deep breath and relaxed, feeling you were among friends. You were home.

To the annoyance of probably a lot of people, I am not likely to say, "Well, nothing we can do. That's just the way it is." I realize change is constant and that we need to adapt, and I also believe there is always a way. You just have to figure it out.

While contemplating the changes in news, I put together a proposal for the Hearst Corporation, which owns WCVB. It included programming ideas that I thought better used Hearst's enormous resources. The company owns television stations across the country, as well as radio stations, newspapers, magazines, and internet sites. I thought, for example, if all the Hearst TV stations coordinated with each other on topics of mutual interest, we could have local news lead a more national scope.

For example, the Boston Red Sox had bids out for new owners and possibly a new stadium to replace or renovate Fenway Park. Baltimore had recently gone through something similar with the same people vying for the Red Sox—Larry Lucchino and company, including his architect. With each station contributing to the story, we broaden the scope and introduce each other's viewers to one another.

On important issues, such as school vouchers and charter schools, we could report back and forth on how one city's system was handling it, what was working, what wasn't, and what did parents think? We might all learn something about the issue and also get to know our fellow Americans in other parts of the country.

I also offered to find the sponsors for a half-hour early evening show on the hot topics of the day. I would not ask to be paid for my efforts unless after a year it became a success.

I hoped my ideas would make the company money while producing innovative and newsworthy programming. I shared my thoughts with my general manager at the time, Paul La Camera. Paul and I started working at WCVB at the beginning, March of 1972. He said he liked at least some of my ideas, and yes, he would go with me to New York to make a presentation to the president of Hearst Broadcasting at the time, David Barrett.

When the day came, Paul decided not to go with me. It didn't take a genius to realize this likely was a fool's mission, gratuitous at best. Nothing would come from this meeting. I had to make a quick decision: bag it or go anyway? I went.

Mr. Barrett was gracious and for three hours listened, questioned, and seemed intrigued. At the end he said, "You have some terrific ideas for our company."

I was excited. "Great, which one do we start with?"

"None of them."

"Excuse me?" I was flummoxed. "I appreciate your time, but you need to explain. You like my ideas but don't want to pursue any of them?"

"Natalie, it is a lot easier for me to write a check for a syndicated show than to deal with ideas and personnel and all that goes into the kind of programming you are talking about."

Paul had understood this was a dead end.

The ride back to LaGuardia was emotional for me. I was fighting anger and disappointment

We had so many talented and intelligent, energetic people at WCVB. I knew we could produce new, good programming and make money for the station as we always had. We could adapt to changes. It just takes good ideas and the will to carry them through.

By the time I got back to Boston, I had forced myself to accept that my time at WCVB was coming to an end. The days of innovation were over. The golden age of television was on its way to the morgue.

I told Paul about the meeting and shared my feelings. He's a good guy and he probably felt my pain. He couldn't run the station the way Bob Bennett did. While Bennett had the backing of the original board members, Paul had to answer to New York. I've come to understand risk takers are few. Get along, go along, is easy and safe. And New York would play it safe.

CHAPTER 26

The Church Sex Abuse Crisis

Had Hearst agreed to teaming up with the company's other stations, we would have had a broader look at a crisis that at first seemed local but in fact crossed state and country lines.

Bernard Law, the Archbishop of Boston, was an imposing man. Tall, overweight, with a ready smile, Law was measured when he spoke. When asked about controversial subjects such as birth control or priests being allowed to marry, his line was, "Catholicism is not a cafeteria style religion." In other words, you had to be all in.

Greater Boston is largely a Roman Catholic community. The Irish and the Italians dominated city politics for years, although, with the election of an Asian woman as mayor of Boston in 2021, a new era has begun. The pageantry that accompanied the ethnic traditions has been very much a part of city life. For example, in the North End, every August the parades and parties in honor of Saint Anthony bring out the whole community and at least as many tourists.

The more dominant ethnic group, Irish Americans, preceded the Italians in Boston. St. Patrick's Day with its bands and costumed parade is front-page news every year. And perhaps nothing can compare with the annual St. Patrick's Day breakfast when the politicians let loose as only the Irish can do, with humor and song.

Who could have known that Cardinal Law would be at the center of the worst scandal to rock the Catholic church in modern times? Priests in the greater Boston area were accused of sexually molesting boys. Law protected his priests at all cost. He would transfer them to another parish. We would learn the church even paid victims money to keep them quiet.

It was the discovery of a pedophile Fall River priest, the Reverend James R. Porter, that unearthed the almost unimaginable travesty perpetrated on thousands of young boys and girls and adults. In the 60s, Porter abused some one hundred children at parishes in North Attleborough, New Bedford, and Fall River. And in 1993, he was sentenced to eighteen-to-twenty years in prison. Cardinal Law portrayed Porter as an aberrant. We later learned Law was not truthful and was covering up so much more. It didn't take long for this to be more than a Boston story. Abuse by priests engulfed the United States, Europe, and beyond.

In 2002, the *Boston Globe* published a far-reaching investigation as their Spotlight Team detailed one nightmare after another of young boys and girls being molested by priests. The victims' stories would break your heart. Not only did these now-grown men and women continue to deal with the psychological horror of abuse, but also, in some cases, with a loss of faith. The priest represented God and for many it seemed God had deserted them.

For me, the church sex-abuse story moved from numbers to real people one day late in 2002, when I received a call from a young man who lived in Needham. He asked to meet with me. He said he had a horrific story to tell about what a priest did to his family, and he would only speak with me.

Jim Perry and I met, and he told me the family was prompted to come forward after seeing a story on our newscast on December 5, 2002, about two files being released by the archdiocese as ordered by the court. Both files were labeled Father James D. Foley. One of the files details Foley's record dating back to the 60s, when Richard Cardinal Cushing was informed by the diocese in Calgary of Foley's womanizing.

The contents of a second file upended the lives of four Needham children. Rich, Chris, Jim, and Emily Perry lived their whole lives to this point believing their mother had died of an overdose of barbiturates in

1973. Watching the Channel 5 report of the second file, they learned that Reverend Foley had been at the home of a Needham woman and walked away as the woman lay dying, her three-year-old toddler in a crib nearby. Jim said they started to put the pieces together and realized the woman was their mother, Rita. They now knew the real story and they wanted it public and decided to call me.

After fact-checking as best we could, WCVB agreed we would let them tell their story. I thought it important to give the family enough time to talk about their experience, and the station gave me the *Chronicle* half hour.

The four siblings and I sat in comfortable chairs in a studio in low light. They quietly, hesitantly, began to tell the story that changed their lives. They said they had been told an anonymous caller had dialed 911, bringing police to their house. But they always wondered who made that call. And how was it that a young child was left there alone.

They now learned their mother and the priest were spending the night in their family home. They had an argument and she reportedly threatened suicide and collapsed. He panicked and left, leaving the child in the crib. He told two different stories, one that he left and came back and called police, another that he called the police and left.

Emily: "It is hard to believe. He admits he fled in fear and self-preservation."

Rich: "At the time we lived 1.4 miles from Glover Hospital. We believe the response time would have been adequate to save her life from an overdose."

Natalie: "Emily, you were the little girl in the crib the night they found your mother."

Emily: "Yes. I've been in serious denial for the past month. I can't focus. There is this hole in my life as I wonder what life might have been like if my mother had lived."

Foley had met with the four Perry children.

Natalie: "When Father Foley told you how much he cared for your mother did that bring you any comfort?"

Jim: "Nothing about this gives me comfort."

The new information revealed a twelve-year affair between their mother and Foley. He knew she had serious depression, in fact underwent a lobotomy, and they believed he took advantage of her. They were afraid to have DNA testing because they didn't want to learn Foley may have fathered Emily and maybe Jim.

To sit and listen to these four young people unwrap a lifelong agonizing mystery, piecing together details about their mother, was painful. Too often news reports, in their brevity and reliance on numbers: "Four children learned their mother died," don't include the effect on individuals.

For me this story was important to air in a long form, as we did. The Perrys wanted to talk about this, they wanted the world to know what this priest did to their mother and to them. And from my perspective as a reporter, their story put this extraordinary church sex abuse crisis in personal terms.

For the Perry family and so many others, I can only hope that faith is greater than the aberration of a priest.

CHAPTER 27

The Boston Red Sox, 2004

I wanted to be a baseball player when I was a kid and was crushed when I found out only boys could play major league. In my defense, I'm hoping I was only two years old when I made this major discovery. It must run in the family, as my father had tried out as a pitcher to play with the Chicago Cubs. Sympathetic to my disappointment, Dad took me to a women's professional softball game in Chicago. Well, that just didn't seem as exciting; they threw underhand and the ball was the size of a grapefruit.

Every kid has a hero. I guess it is no surprise that mine was the Splendid Splinter. When we moved from a flat in Chicago to our first house in Needham, Massachusetts, I was entering the sixth grade and fell in love with Ted Williams. While my friends plastered their bedrooms with pictures of Eddie Fisher and Debbie Reynolds, my wall was all Number 9. I read everything I could find in the library about Ted. I could quote you any statistic you asked about him.

I attended the Harris School in Needham, which was just a block from our house. The Red Sox games were on the radio, and if it was a home game and if I ran home as fast as I could, I could get to the radio in time to hear Williams' first at-bat. Since the home team bats second, and Williams was third in the line-up, I had a chance. Maybe girls couldn't play major league baseball, but girls could have heroes. And Ted was mine. I learned he had a daughter about my age. How lucky was she?

Many years later when I was working for Channel 5, I was asked to help with an organization raising money for scleroderma and lupus. I learned somewhere that Ted Williams had a second daughter who had been diagnosed with lupus when she was younger. So, the idea came to me that maybe Ted would want to headline a fundraiser for lupus. My dad was good friends with Curt Gowdy, former voice of the Red Sox. I called Curt and asked if he would present the idea to Ted. He said he would.

Throughout my life I've been accused of having unrealistic ideas. One news director accused me of wanting to produce *Ben-Hur* when all they wanted was "Jack and Jill." I paid lip service to such criticism but always believe in aiming for the moon. As the saying goes, you might not reach it, but you will fly higher.

The people on the lupus board probably thought my chances were zero, but you don't know if you don't try. Besides, I wanted to meet Ted Williams. I tracked down Ted's daughter Claudia and learned that, fortunately for her, the lupus diagnosis proved to be incorrect. Did that mean Ted wouldn't have the incentive to come? No, Ted said he would participate, as he was grateful his daughter had been spared.

I filmed an interview with Claudia and her brother, John Henry, which we would present the night of the fundraiser. I called the Red Sox and suggested they would want to buy tickets and fill the room in support of The Splendid Splinter. They did.

Man, was I excited. That night, Ted and I—how fun is it to write that, "Ted and I"—greeted people as they came to a VIP reception preceding the event. I saw a few pictures of me standing next to him and had to smile. My expression was that of the little girl who ran home from school to hear his at-bat.

So now, the show. The room is packed. Cameras are in place. Lights set. I welcomed everyone, introduced the Sox et al., played the videos of Ted's kids, and then the big moment. "With us tonight, Number Nine, my number one, the great Ted Williams!" The place was a cacophony of cheers and shouts and music amid roaming spotlights.

So much for Jack and Jill.

I was a happy duck but was so absorbed in the drama of the moment, I walked off the stage after the introduction, deciding Ted

Williams should have the spotlight alone. From a producer's point of view, it was the right call. But I denied myself the picture of me on stage with my hero. Numb nuts.

My dear friend Dick Flavin, who knows more about baseball, especially the Red Sox, than anyone I know, has regaled me with stories about his trip from Boston to Florida to see Ted when Ted was near the end of his life. Dick, Dom DiMaggio, and Johnny Pesky drove together and spent hours with Ted recounting stories and games, later captured by David Halberstam in *The Teammates*. Flavin, as he is wont to refer to himself, is the Poet Laureate of the Red Sox and, until recently, the home-game announcer at Fenway Park.

Being a Red Sox fan goes part and parcel with living in Boston. You live and die with the team. And every September for eighty-six years you, with a gillion other fans, said, "Just wait 'til next year."

2004 proved to be Next Year.

I get goose bumps just thinking about that season. And when you think of how close we came to losing, well, I guess it just had to be that dramatic.

My favorite part of every newscast that season was sports, when our sportscaster Mike Lynch and I could have a few seconds to talk Sox. No matter where I went, every conversation started with, "How are the Sox doing? Can you believe that catch in the ninth!" People planned their schedules around the games. "Sure, I'll meet you for dinner, but we have to go where there is a TV."

Sox fans don't remember every game. They remember every pitch, every at bat. And the Yankees series is seared in a Sox fan's memory. There was something in the air. You just knew this year would be different. Maybe it was the crazy team. They seemed non-plussed, casual, so comfortable. They seemed relaxed! Are you kidding? No one was relaxed. Eighty-six years is a long drought.

I was on the treadmill at the condo where I was living in Boston. A neighbor on an adjacent treadmill and I got talking about, what else, the Sox/Yankees series. He said he shared a box at Fenway with

Doris Kearns Goodwin and her husband Dick Goodwin, both friends of mine. Then he said, the man who usually shared the box with him would not be able to come and would I like the ticket? Oh my God. So, for the home games of the greatest ALS series of my life, I had a ringside seat. And to share it with Doris and Dick made it extraordinary. This is one of those moments when you say, life just doesn't get any better.

The Sox lost game one and game two at Yankee Stadium.

Game 3. Boston, postponed due to rain on Friday. Saturday October 16. My first game to watch from the box. Bang, right off the bat, the Yankees score 3 in the first. The Sox answer with 4 in the second! Yes! We are not dead yet. For the first time in the series, the Sox have the lead. But in a heart-stopping nine innings, the bad boys from New York win, 19–8. If you're a Sox fan, you never give up. You could look at this as one game left and no team wins down three. Or if you are a member of Red Sox nation, you say, this is a seven-game series.

Game 4 was a cliffhanger. 9th inning. Yankees lead 4–3. It is midnight. Mariano Rivera on the mound. Kevin Millar at the plate. Millar walks. Dave Roberts is sent in to run. He keeps teasing Rivera who almost gets him, but Roberts steals second. Bill Mueller at the plate, rips one to center field. Roberts makes it home. Tie game! We can do this! We can do this! Fenway was pulsating.

And so, it went tied 4–4 in the tenth. 4–4 in the 11th. And then in the bottom of the 12th inning, Manny Ramirez singles. David Ortiz sails one into right field! 34,826 people went nuts. Bedlam! Crazy Joy! I can still feel it, see it, hear it!

Just sixteen hours later after the last out, Fenway comes alive again at 5 PM for Game 5. Again, we find ourselves behind, 4–2. Eighth inning. Ortiz leads off with a homer. Millar walks. Roberts again, sent in to run, and again lightening speeder Roberts makes his way to third on a Trot Nixon single and scores on a Jason Veritek sacrifice fly. Tie Game!! Tie Game! 11th, 12th, 13th, bottom of the 14th, Two Out! Damon and Ramirez walk, Ortiz is up. He takes nine pitches and then on the tenth, to borrow from Harry Caray, Holy Cow! Papi rips one to center, scoring Damon. Sox win. Sox win. Sox win. The fans are delirious… "Who's Your Papi?"

The Sox are off to NY for games 6 and 7. It was a killer to have to watch the must-win sixth game on television after the exhilaration of Fenway Park. But what a game. Game 6, Curt Schilling on the mound for the Sox, pitches seven innings with a bloody sock. Sox win 4–2.

Game 7. Doris, Dick, and I watched from a bar in Concord. Derek Lowe delivered. The whole team delivered. 10–3 final. The Red Sox became the only team in the history of major league baseball to come back from a 3–0 deficit to win a championship in seven games.

All of Boston was on fire. The Sox would go on to win the World Series that year, sweeping the Cardinals, ending the Curse of the Bambino and an eighty-six-year drought. The Sox would go on to win three more World Series, but for me, nothing can compare with that series against the Yankees. Nothing.

When I announced I was leaving Channel 5 in 2007, Larry Lucchino, president of the Red Sox, gave me the gift of gifts. "How would you like to throw out the ceremonial first pitch at Fenway Park?"

Wow. I bought a couple of baseball gloves and a half dozen balls and practiced throwing for weeks before my big day. I begged anyone who came to the house to help me throw more like a boy. I started at thirty feet, then made my way up to sixty feet, six inches. I could do it, sometimes, but I didn't have a whole lot of confidence.

The day arrived. Fenway Park. Fans were getting their dogs and beers and taking their seats. Pitchers were warming up. The hum that is Fenway filled my ears. I was nervous, very nervous. A young man approached me with a cell phone and said Mr. Lucchino was on the line. I said, "Tell him I can't talk now. They are about to announce me to go to the mound." The kid turned pale, "Please take the call."

"Jacobson, listen carefully. Three things. One, don't go to the top of the mound, go to the bottom. Two, try and throw over the catcher's head, you'll have a better shot of getting it there. And three, no matter what the **** happens, when you throw the ball, smile. That's when they take the picture." The line went dead.

Out to the mound I went. I heard the announcer: "From WCVB-TV, please welcome, Natalie Jacobson."

I heard a smattering of applause, walked to the bottom of the mound. The plate looked a mile away. I looked up at the scoreboard and for the first time saw we were playing the Yankees. I had been so preoccupied I hadn't noticed. So, I have no idea what got into me. I assumed the pitcher's position, peered down to the catcher beneath my Red Sox cap, and shook off the sign.

I heard the crowd giggle.

Again, I assumed the position, looked down again, shook it off. Now I heard a mild roar, well maybe a few more giggles. I figured, OK. If I blow this, the fans will forgive me. I made them laugh.

Once more, the sign, the pitch. The bloody ball made it to the catcher! Maybe he ran thirty feet toward me, I don't know. I did it! It was over and people were cheering. I don't recall being carried off on a stretcher, so I must have walked back to the sidelines. There was my pal Mike Lynch with a microphone. I don't know what either of us said, but later Mike told me, "Nat, I have never seen you so nervous." Thank you, Larry.

CHAPTER 28

Goodbye

Two thousand and seven marked thirty-five years of my life at WCVB-TV. I spent many a day struggling with the thought of departing my home, my colleagues, my beloved television station. I wrote my goodbye and read it to my colleagues, as I didn't trust myself to make any sense if I didn't.

Referring to our "Five is Family" promotion I said, "Like all families, we don't always agree on everything and in a newsroom that is not only healthy, but critical to our mission, that being to provide the best information to our family of viewers, so they might make intelligent decisions about their own lives and share those moments of life with one another."

It was way too emotional. I saw some of my colleagues crying as I tried to express my appreciation and affection for them. I fought tears as well.

As I conclude this book, I think of the people with whom I worked for so many years.

The show producers, always under the gun, always faced with conflict from too little time to logistics.

I think of the assignment desk, a twenty-four-hour migraine. I don't know how they do it. Dick Molinari, transferred from editing, ran that dispatch center better than anyone when I was there. He had one ear always tuned to the police radios, another to the phones and his reporters and camera people. Some days he just didn't have enough cameras to cover a breaking story and a planned shoot. Of course, every reporter thinks she or he has the one piece that cannot be canceled.

I think of our technicians, too often the ones we blame when something goes wrong. Ah, but maybe the management bought the wrong equipment in the first place.

I think of our editors, especially in my case, Ray Smith, a warm and caring man with whom I spent umpteen hours over the years. He should get a gold medal for hanging in there with me story after story. The best part about Ray for me, aside from the fact he knew his craft, was his understanding of my need to be fair. He too knew a misplaced shot, the wrong look on a person's face in a cut away, an abbreviated sound bite, might give the wrong impression. Above all, our piece had to be clear and it had to be fair. And he worked tirelessly with me to make it so.

I think of the writers who, working on scripts not done by the reporter, with limited resources, usually have no more time than anyone else to get it right. And then they have to deal with producers who toss the copy back at them or me, who in the heat of the moment, could be less than understanding.

I think of the cameramen who have to figure a way to be in sync with their ever-changing partners among the reporting staff. Their work can make a story sing, or not.

And of course, I think of my fellow reporters. We had a team of people who believed in news, its impact, its importance, a team that believed in each other. These are people who would give that extra 2 percent to get it right, no matter the obstacles. I'm honored and proud to have been part of this innovative, hard working group of men and women.

And then there is the anchor team. Chet, Dick Albert, Mike Lynch, and I were together for years anchoring the 6 and 11 o'clock newscasts. We definitely had a camaraderie you cannot create. We came to be best friends, sharing time with each other and our families. I think part of our success stemmed from our attitudes. We loved what we did. We genuinely liked each other. We respected our viewers. We wondered aloud what we would do if we had to get a real job. When we came together on the anchor set, I felt the comfort of togetherness.

My final broadcast finally came. Saying goodbye to all of this was like saying goodbye to a part of myself.

I was nervous and also relieved. I delivered my farewell to our viewers with a sense of gratitude and loss. When it was over, I walked into the newsroom and was shocked to see it jammed with my colleagues of over three decades. Our beloved news director, Jim Thistle, who was battling cancer, left his deathbed to be with us. I later learned that he told his family, "I cannot die today. I have to be part of Natalie's last day."

His words remain with me still. He said I could be a real pain in the ass. Everyone laughed, including me. But then he gave me the compliment of a lifetime. As I remember it:

She believed we could always do better, do more. And that could drive you nuts. But by doing so, she elevated us. She challenged us individually and as a team to be the best we could be. This news department is better because of Natalie.

In truth it was Jim, the captain of our ship, who allowed us to be the best we could be. As sick as he was, a few months earlier he consented to be my "date" at the National Academy of Arts and Science awards (NATAS), where I was to receive the Governor's Award, an extraordinary honor. For me though, the overriding honor was the chance to acknowledge my dear friend before about a thousand people most of whom had either worked for him or were his students.

"He prodded us, cajoled us, scolded us, corrected us, and cheered us when we got it right. He could change a tire on a news vehicle as easily as he could change the lead to the 6 o'clock news seconds before air. He was a newsman's newsman."

He likely was taken aback when I extolled his virtues, and the crowd rose in thunderous applause for him that continued and continued and continued. I felt blessed to be able to orchestrate that moment for him.

A chain smoker, our dear Jim died of cancer shortly after. He was sixty-six.

A few months after leaving WCVB, on November 4, 2007, I lost my best friend, Breezy. She was not herself the week leading up to that Saturday. On the advice of our vet, I took her to Angell Memorial Hospital in Boston Friday evening. I was persuaded to leave her at the hospital for the night in an oxygen-assisted crate. I was told to come the next morning. No tests other than a cardiac ultrasound would be done.

The next day Lindsay and I sat in the waiting room for two hours, constantly asking what is going on. We were told Breezy was waiting for the ultrasound.

What a shock when a doctor came out, led us to a meditation room and said they had aspirated her organs to draw out cells to test. What?! We had been promised nothing invasive would be done without speaking with us first.

We saw our puppy for a few minutes, but she was not present. Her eyes were glazed. She did not look at either of us. We petted and kissed her. She was scared and hurting badly. The vets assured us this was the anesthesia wearing off and sent us to CVS to buy an appetite enhancer to give her later when we took her home.

Before I got to CVS my cell rang with a doctor saying they had inadvertently perforated Breezy's lung, which was leaking air making it impossible for her to breathe on her own. They were administering oxygen. Would I agree to let her go? "Is there nothing you can do to save her?" "We can put shunts in, but she is so damaged it won't really prolong her life and she might not survive the procedure." Then suddenly the doctor said, "Wait, she's breathing." She hung up. Within a minute, another call. "She's in trouble. I advise you to let us euthanize her." "Wait, I need to get Lindsay on the phone!"

"Lindsay, the vet is on the line. She wants our permission to put Breezy down. She cannot breathe." It all seemed so fast. We clearly were not expecting this. So, within seconds, with each of us hysterical, we gave permission. They put someone on the line for legal purposes to take the approval. It was beyond awful.

The rest of Saturday was a blur. Disbelief. It was impossible to accept what had just happened. I had cleaned her towels and food dishes in preparation for her return home. Looking at the bowls now, I thought, *this isn't happening.*

Breezy, my savior, the most important person in my life, next to Lindsay of course, was gone. She brought so much joy, comfort, and meaning. She didn't deserve to die that way.

One week later, we buried her in the same space where our precious Tramp lay. Gathered around the grave, we lit candles, which at first wouldn't light, said prayers, and I read this letter to her:

Dear Breezy, We miss you so much it hurts, a big hurt, on the inside. They only thing that makes hurt go away is you. But you are away.

It has been the saddest week. I am lonely without you. I put the key in the door knowing your wiggly little body won't be on the other side and I am overwhelmed with grief.

I sit on the couch and reach out to you. I go to bed and my hand looks for you under the covers. I hear a sound and think it is your footsteps. I look out of the steaming shower down to the bathmat looking for you. I filled your water bowl last Saturday thinking you were coming home. The water is all but gone now. Evaporated.

Yet even as I write this, I feel your kisses. Suddenly you are all around me.

Everywhere I look I almost hear you say, Look for me here. Look for my happy body when you turn the key. Look for me on the green couch, beneath the desk, outside the shower. Look for me begging to go with you every time you leave. Look for me in the seat next to you in the car. Look for me as we run the beach together in Nantucket. Look for me on the plane to our island. Look for me on the planes to everywhere.

I am loved. You are loved. No one and nothing, not even death, can take love away.

We said the Lord's Prayer and tried to blow out our candles. Despite the wind, we could not, and had to use our fingers to extinguish the flames.

When I got home, I lit a church candle and said a prayer. When I opened my eyes, I saw smoke from the candle encircling me. The circle grew taller and tighter until I was fully wrapped. I imagined my mother carrying little Breezy up to heaven.

Sometime later, I came across Breezy's birth certificate. It lists the sire as Wicked Willie. The Dam as White Dawn.

My mother's name was Dawn. She called my dad, Willie.

CHAPTER **29**

My Next Big Thing

I was in my early sixties at this point and started thinking, what's next? It was clear to me that the standard retirement at sixty-five no longer fits. People are living longer, and many, like me, are not ready to sit on the porch.

My generation was inventing a new way of living the next season of life. David Corbett created a Boston company, New Directions, to help people discern what they wanted to do with their time after the big career. They had a good formula, testing your likes and dislikes, your strengths and weaknesses, etc. They set up meetings with other men and women who had been successful in their respective careers and who were also trying to figure out their next steps.

While still working at WCVB, I did a report for air on several people who had been guided by New Directions. One was a woman who had run a major editing company of the time, Avid. In her sixties, a mother of six grown children, she realized her company needed a reorganization, which in her opinion, included writing herself out of her job. Uncertain of what to do next, she joined New Directions, where someone asked her what she had dreamed of doing as a child. She said she had wanted to be a sculptor. She decided to give it a try now. She learned she indeed had a talent for sculpting, and, being business oriented, she created a business selling her work. I asked her what connection sculpting had with running an editing company. She said she had the mind of an engineer, which is inventive and mathematical, the same mind of a sculptor.

I thought it might be possible to create a website where successful people could find the same guidance online as people did in person at New Directions. David Corbett had written a book, *Portfolio Life*, a guide to changing course and finding meaning and happiness. Dave was supportive and helpful. I would call my site "My Next Big Thing," and I worked with a local software company to produce a sample which I could beta test to show to prospective financial backers. The company produced "architecture" and nothing I could use. It was my lack of understanding of the underpinnings of software creation that led me to waste a lot of time and money.

I spent two years, while still working in news, meeting with people, studying and reading everything I could find about baby boomers. My dear friend Robert Popeo—of Mintz, Levin, Glovsky, and Popeo—liked my idea and offered to help raise the money. I also met with two major private equity companies, one of which had just poured millions into a California startup, LinkedIn. I spent hours over many months with angel investors Jean Hammond and Rose Saia, who were very interested and did yeoman's work to help me pull this together. Tom "Red" Martin, head of Cramer Productions, offered to invest. He put together a conference table of smart people who knew about testing, a key component of my site. Red allowed one of his top people, Darren Ross, to work with me.

My nephew, Bob Salatich, with a gifted imagination and keen mind, now with CBS, tried to help me by gathering his friends to help create the website. It didn't help that I understood so little about the medium. My cousin, Molly Salatich, another smart head, tried to help with marketing and trademark ideas.

Lyman Bullard—of Choate, Hall, & Stewart—convened some of his best and brightest to find me a CEO. I figured I needed two people on board before I would be comfortable accepting anyone's money: a CEO and a technology wizard.

We found a woman who had just sold her startup and was looking for a new challenge. I would let her find the right tech. She asked for a couple of months to think about her life and in the end decided she wanted to run a more technical company.

I began to realize this idea was too big for one person, so I went to New York and had an opportunity to pitch it to Quincy Smith, the brilliant entrepreneur running CBS Interactive. He thought my idea had "legs," but I guess those legs didn't walk fast or far enough.

I met an attorney who put me in touch with the ad agency in New York that created Match.com, one of the first of the popular dating sites. We spent months trying to create the right online format. It was fun and fascinating.

I met with people from AARP and thought tying in with this established business might be the ticket.

When the wonderful Darren Ross of Cramer Productions suggested I have a man in India he knew create the website, I realized I couldn't do this. I needed to work in the same room with someone, not a guy halfway around the world. You have to remember this was before Facebook, Google, Amazon, Twitter, Instagram, and pretty much everything people take for granted today.

I never did find the right people. And my idea languished in that all too crowded library of great ideas never executed. I blame myself. I should have made it my only priority. I should have educated myself to better understand the Internet and software. Just as I had asked the techs at WBZ to teach me the tools of television, I needed to learn the tools of online technology. In truth, I was out of my league in trying to create an Internet business. I had a great idea. I think it still has "legs," but I knew what I didn't know. How did I not find that person? What did I miss? To this day, I am troubled.

I was not and am not ready to retire from life, and honestly, I wasn't ready to leave television news either. Somehow I felt it left me.

But I am not one to sulk. Life is what you make it. I have much for which to be grateful. I believe you have to be a little lucky in life, but I also think in anyone's life there is a confluence of circumstances which we ignore or pursue. Those opportunities and decisions essentially write our life story. It is my nature to concentrate on the positive, including my upbringing, which was lacking in money but filled with love, family, and faith. I see my gender as having kept me from being a professional baseball player but having allowed me to be part of a generation which would shape a new way of life for women and best of all allowed me to become a mother. I look at being turned away from job interviews in television only to land one through a back door, complying with the government's requirement to ascertain the needs of the community, which was the perfect way to begin a career in broadcast journalism. I look at my forty years in television and feel lucky to have lived it as I did.

I remain filled with warm memories of my teammates. I hold dear our viewers and find comfort when they stop to talk with me. I smile when I think of 8 Old Greendale where family and friends gathered for twenty-five years.

So, as I look to the future, I take stock of the changed world in which we now live. We have been upended by COVID-19. Technology seems to rule to the point that I sometimes think of it as the tail that wags the dog. And the animosity among our citizens is unlike anything I have ever experienced. The anger and hatred is palpable. Can we bridge the divide, or will the chasm grow so deep we will destroy our unique country?

As you might expect, I believe the media plays a critical role in answering that question. The very definition of media has expanded from three broadcast networks that brought the country before their TV sets every night to hundreds of sources that both unite and separate us.

I remember television's strict adherence to the rules of the Federal Communications Commission (FCC), which demanded allegiance to honesty and fairness. In the 1980s, cable television argued it was exempt from those rules because cable did not use federal airwaves. Cable won its case in court. Importantly, by selling subscriptions rather than relying solely on advertising, cable proved it could survive with a narrower audience. As a result, cable was free to cater to a singular subject or ideology. Broadcast, by contrast, must cast a wide net to attract a big enough audience to garner the advertisers' dollars.

The Internet, including social media and apps and blogs, gives everyone a platform to post anything, accurate or not. So how do we know whom and what to trust? The consumer is forced to play editor. I find myself needing to watch both CNN and Fox, to read both *The Wall Street Journal* and the *New York Times* to get two sides of a story. Young people especially are slaves to their phones, where it can be difficult to separate fact from opinion and where a headline can be misleading.

Our founding fathers knew how critical an informed society is to a democracy.

The First Amendment:

Congress shall make no law respecting an establishment of religion, or prohibiting the free exercise thereof; or abridging the freedom of speech, or of the press; or the right of the people peaceably to assemble, and to petition the government for a redress of grievances.

The American Civil Liberties Union (ACLU), commenting on a free press, wrote:

The freedom of the press, protected by the First Amendment, is critical to a democracy in which the government is accountable to the people. A free media functions as a watchdog that can investigate and report on government wrongdoing. It is also a vibrant marketplace of ideas, a vehicle for ordinary citizens to express themselves and gain exposure to a wide range of information and opinions.

I honestly feel that we at WCVB-TV Boston, a local station in a six-state region, created that "vibrant marketplace." I feel lucky and proud to have been part of it.

So, what is next? What is MY next big thing? A few months before I left Channel 5, I was honored to receive the Lifetime Centennial Achievement Award from Suffolk University. I remember asking, only half kidding, could we rename this "Lifetime Achievement SO FAR"?

I am blessed as new life has found me. Lindsay married, and she and her husband Eric have two children, Olivia Dawn, now five, and James Chester, now three.

When Olivia was born, I was the "nanny" every Wednesday. I shuttled between Boston and Nantucket and every Tuesday night drove to their home and took care of her for a wonderful day. It was Baba Day!

Olivia opened up motherhood again. It was like reliving my precious Lindsay's baby time. And nothing in my life was better than my time with my daughter. Here I was enjoying the gift of a new life again. The biggest difference for me between being a mother and a grandmother is time. Without the responsibilities of a career, I have time, uninhibited, uninterrupted, uncompromising time. I can push the buggy, cuddle, read, roll the ball, laugh, pull the leaves off the clover, feed the birds, sing a lullaby. I don't need to be anywhere else.

When James was born, I happened to be at their home when, at midnight, Eric rushed down to my bedroom shouting, "The baby's coming! We're leaving now!"

I was able to be with Olivia in the morning. Lindsay stayed at the hospital for a couple of nights and when she and Eric and the new baby arrived, little Olivia looked at him and with the glow of a baby angel smiled and whispered, "ah." It was magic.

Until COVID-19 altered our schedules in 2020, I continued to care for the children once a week, and I never fail to feel lucky to have the energy to enjoy them.

Living with children as they grow is like watching a flower in slow motion open its petals to the sky. Have you ever heard a better sound than the uninhibited laughter of a child? What can surpass a child's bright eyes as she discovers something new? And is there any better feeling than the trust and loving hug of a little girl or boy?

As a mother, I could not be more proud of my daughter. She is smart, warm, dedicated and ever loving. I watch her and Eric juggle work and home and children and I am happy for them. I remember that time of life, exhausting as it is, as the best time of life.

And my next venture? Perhaps it is hiding in full view.

About the Author

Natalie Jacobson, born Natalie Salatich, was the first in her family to go to college. She earned a BA degree in English Literature from the University of New Hampshire in 1965 and lived the next two years in Bangkok, Thailand. Returning to a war-torn US, she entered the world of broadcast journalism working at two Boston stations on license renewal, interviewing hundreds of people to "ascertain the needs of the community." It was an unusual beginning which connected her with her viewers.

Following work as a producer at WBZ-TV, Natalie joined the fledgling Boston station, WCVB-TV, as a reporter in 1972. During her thirty-five years at Channel 5, as a reporter and anchor of their evening news, she enjoyed a unique relationship with the people of New England. She was honored over the years with several Emmys for her reporting and in 2007 received the Governor's Award, the highest award from the National Academy of Television Arts and Sciences (NATAS); the Lifetime Achievement Award from the Radio and Television News Directors Association (RTNDA); another from Suffolk University; the Yankee Quill Award from the Academy of New England Journalists; and the Sisterhood Award from the National Conference of Christians and Jews.

Natalie is a licensed pilot and enjoys golf, cooking, boating, and gardening. Most of all, she loves being a grandmother to Olivia and James. She resides on Nantucket, Massachusetts.

Endorsements

"It is impossible to overstate Natalie Jacobson's influence and stature during her days as anchorwoman. She was the voice of Boston, a face everyone trusted and in many ways was the conscience of an entire city."
   –Bruce A. Percelay, Chairman of Mount Vernon Company, publisher of *Nantucket Magazine*

"For a generation, more New Englanders looked to Natalie Jacobson for the news and the truth than from any other newscaster. She was the very best."
   –Jack Connors, Jr., Co-Founder Hill, Holiday Advertising

"There's a reason generations of New Englanders faithfully turned to Natalie Jacobson. She has a gift, and they sensed it. For Natalie, it was always about the audience. What do they want asked, what do they care most about, what worries them at night. Natalie knew this because she was one of them. On the news, 'Nat' was having a conversation with friends and neighbors every night. It might seem like a simple idea, but for those of us lucky enough to have witnessed her at work, it was magical."
   –David Muir, Anchor, ABC World News Tonight

"She is the sweetheart of Boston TV who became its grande dame. She brought us the news for all those years with grace and compassion. Now she brings us the details of her own life, the triumphs and the heartaches the same way. It's what made us all fall in love with her in the first place."
   –Dick Flavin, Writer/Commentator

"Nat Jacobson's book is a beautifully written love letter, to Boston, to the hardiness of the human spirit through the pain and loss and joy of the struggle. And most of all, it's a testament to the truth, trust and service that news should embody. Any Bostonian, any woman, any American, will relate to this personal journey, and her courage and tenacity as a newswoman will remind us of what we've lost and what news, and human, integrity ought to look like."
  –**Marcy Carsey**, co-founder Carsey Werner Company

"As a friend and colleague for 50 years, I can honestly say that no one has a better eye for the life and soul of Boston than Natalie Jacobson. I saw first-hand her devotion to accurate news and her ability to tell the human stories behind the headline. Now you too can share that 'eye on Boston' in the reading of this intimate and honest memoir."
  –**Dr. Tim Johnson**, Retired Medical Editor, WCVB and ABC News.

"Natalie Jacobson is a classic modern American story. The offspring of a Serbian-American family whose father became head of Gillette North America, Natalie herself rose to unprecedented heights as a pioneer woman journalist. She embodied the highest ideals as the face and voice of the best of what a local television station could be. Natalie's is an important and engaging story and one told by a gifted storyteller."
  –**Paul La Camera**, President and General Manager WCVB-TV
  1994–2005

"I'm delighted Natalie Jacobson has written this wonderful memoir. Every life is indeed a story—and Natalie's—full of warmth, wit and adventure—is a riveting account of her pioneering work as a highly trusted and much-loved journalist and television anchor. A role model for the ages, Natalie continues to inspire all of us to fearlessly seek the truth and to treat one another with compassion."
  –**Michelle Dillon**, Dean, College of Liberal Arts, University of New Hampshire